MYSTICAL ONE:
GEORGE HARRISON

AFTER THE BREAK-UP OF THE BEATLES

ELLIOT J. HUNTLEY

MYSTICAL ONE:

GEORGE HARRISON

AFTER THE BREAK-UP OF THE BEATLES

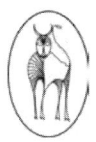

GUERNICA

TORONTO · BUFFALO · CHICAGO · LANCASTER (U.K.)

2004

Antonio D'Alfonso, editor
Guernica Editions Inc.
P.O. Box 117, Station P, Toronto (ON), Canada M5S 2S6
2250 Military Road, Tonawanda, N.Y. 14150-6000 U.S.A.
Gazelle, White Cross Mills, High Town, Lancaster LA1 1XS U.K.

Typeset by Selina.
Printed in Canada.
First edition.

Legal Deposit – Second Quarter
National Library of Canada
Library of Congress Catalog Card Number: 2004101874
National Library of Canada Cataloguing in Publication
Huntley, Elliot J
Mystical one : George Harrison : after the break-up of the
Beatles / Elliot J. Huntley.
ISBN 1-55071-197-0
1. Harrison, George.
2. Rock musicians – England – Biography.
I. Title.
ML420.H319H95 2004   782.42166'092   C2004-901103-0

CONTENTS

Introduction 9

Chapter One 17

Chapter Two 45

Chapter Three 71

Chapter Four 96

Chapter Five 105

Chapter Six 120

Chapter Seven 139

Chapter Eight 161

Chapter Nine 175

Chapter Ten 190

Chapter Eleven 202

Chapter Twelve 218

Chapter Thirteen 233

Chapter Fourteen 248

Chapter Fifteen 273

Chapter Sixteen 283

Chapter Seventeen 304

Chapter Eighteen 312

Chapter Nineteen 316

Postscript 324

George Harrison Songs .335

Dedicated to Laura and Charlie

INTRODUCTION

Bing Crosby once asked this rhetorical question – if a singer as good as Frank Sinatra came along only once in a lifetime, why did it have to be during *his* lifetime? George Harrison the songwriter could easily have asked the same thing about Lennon and McCartney.

The flap of the proverbial butterfly wing that decreed that Harrison be born in the same city within three years of the duo was both Harrison's blessing and his curse. Without doubt, he was one of the greatest songwriters of his generation, yet his genius would forever be overshadowed John and Paul.

The threesome had been together since 1958, and with Ringo Starr, they would conquer the known world, and achieve a level of fame and wealth that mere mortals could never hope to comprehend, yet there is a perception that Harrison grew to resent his own destiny.

Of the Fab Four, Harrison was always the one least interested in the trappings of stardom, the one who most detested the hysteria that came with Beatlemania and the one most in favour of their decision to quit touring. "It made me nervous, the whole magnitude of our fame," Harrison would confess many years later.

Cynical about the cult of celebrity, Harrison preferred to concentrate on the thing that mattered: the music. At the tender age of twenty-three, George declared, "I asked to be successful, I never asked to be famous. I've got more famous than I wanted to be." Later he would come to terms with it saying, "If you're going to be in a pop band, then it might as well be the Beatles."

Harrison's contributions were essential to the Beatles'

allure. He was the best looking of the four, the best dressed, the one with the best hair and his dry wit was easily the equal of Lennon's more caustic repartee. Their producer, George Martin considered him the best musician of the group, and it's true that Harrison was always a criminally underrated lead guitarist. The fact that he was never prone to pyrotechnic onanism was his appeal, never his failing. Harrison never resorted to free-form scatting, his solos were always thoughtfully composed, tailored to the requirements of the song, always melodic and original, and always invested with feeling.

Harrison's guitar work was essential to the spine and fabric of the band: his jangly twelve-string Rickenbacker work on *A Hard Day's Night* influenced a lineage of bands from The Byrds to R.E.M.

Indeed, George's contributions often guided the band's direction: introducing Dylan to the band's palette in the mid-1960s, flavouring *Rubber Soul* with a distinct country texture, and, most famously, adding the Indian influence from 1966 onwards, his sitar adding an extra dimension to the Beatles' golden years.

Furthermore it was George who was most instrumental in replacing Pete Best with Ringo Starr, and it was he who was also often responsible for bringing in outside help to Beatles' recording dates, whether it be Eric Clapton, Billy Preston, or a variety of Indian musicians.

"George had something stronger than power: he had influence," George Martin once stated. "Witness the fact that all of the boys followed him to India to sit at the feet of the Maharishi."

The significance of George's fascination with the East is difficult to determine, but there is no doubt that it was Harrison who was responsible for bringing Indian musical influences to the attention of the western world.

Yet, in the eyes of the public, Lennon and McCartney overshadowed him and Harrison was always seen as the lesser genius. It was clear that Lennon and McCartney felt the same way when it came to song-writing, restricting Harrison to a mere twenty-two Beatles songs. George's main error was temporarily retiring from composing after "Don't Bother Me" (in 1963) until 1965 after which he was playing catch-up. Though Harrison did not match the output of Lennon and McCartney until the group started to implode, each Beatles album from *Help!* onwards saw George take a giant leap forward in terms of song-writing.

Lennon would claim that Harrison had been lucky to be around such skilled songsmiths as himself and McCartney. That Harrison refused to be intimidated by their success and reputation is to his eternal credit. Harrison learned fast and his development is there for all to hear on the *Rubber Soul* and *Revolver* albums with his songs, "Think for Yourself," "If I Needed Someone," "I Want to Tell You," "Love You To" and "Taxman."

Within two years of his "Lennon-McCartney-esque" songs on *Help!* Harrison would create the epic, philosophical "Within You, Without You," "The Inner Light" and the "Wonderwall Music" film score that he wrote to "turn people on to Indian music." A staggering achievement for a young man in his early twenties!

After forming his own publishing outlet, Harrisongs, in 1968, Harrison's attitude to writing changed. As he became more prolific he began to blossom and find his own voice. Nonetheless, he would forever find himself restricted to two songs per Beatles album by Lennon and McCartney, whose enthusiasm for his tunes can charitably be described as lethargic. "The usual thing was that we'd do fourteen of their tunes, and then they'd condescend to listen to one of mine," Harrison would say many years later.

While Harrison seemed embittered about this treatment long after the break-up, he did acknowledge his debt to Lennon and McCartney in becoming songwriter in the first place. "To get it straight," he was quoted as saying, "if I hadn't been with John and Paul I probably wouldn't have thought about writing a song, at least not until much later. They were writing all these songs, many of which I thought were great. Some were just average, but, obviously, a high percentage were quality material. I thought to myself, if they can do it, I'm going to have a go. But it's true, it wasn't easy in those days getting up enthusiasm for my songs. We'd be in a recording situation, churning through all this Lennon/McCartney! Then I'd say, [meekly] 'can we do one of these?'"

While McCartney would later apologise for this behaviour, it's still a shame that such limitations were imposed, because it was clear that Harrison had a tremendous amount to offer the Beatles artistically. His compositions were invariably built on the firm architecture of interesting chord progressions, while his study of Indian music had enhanced his ability to devise more complex melodies than those usually found within the average three-minute pop song. Furthermore, Harrison was a consummate lyricist, the depth and consciousness inherent in *his* songs were invariably more thought provoking than those of either Lennon or McCartney.

That's not to say George was solely preoccupied with weighty spiritual subject matters, "Harrisongs" could equally be defined by their understated humour, "Taxman" being the first example of a sub-genre that would later include "Piggies," "Savoy Truffle" and "Only a Northern Song."

On songs like "Something," "While My Guitar Gently Weeps" and "Here Comes the Sun," Harrison also demonstrated that very elusive facility to find a perfect, matching bridge for the verse. Let's not forget he did so without the help of a song-writing partner.

However, even with songs of this quality, it was clear that he was never going to be allowed to override the two songs per album stipulation imposed by Lennon and McCartney's dominance. During the last years of the group, this became a source of rancour and deep-seated resentment.

As a result, with insufficient opportunity to display his emerging talents, Harrison was the one who had the most to gain from break-up of the Beatles. For a while, George was easily the most successful ex-Beatle, releasing the gargantuan *All Things Must Pass* that would rightly be acknowledged as one of the greatest albums of all time.

For an encore Harrison would organize and stage the Concert for Bangladesh, becoming the first rock star philanthropist, long before it was fashionable. With this concert, Harrison set the template for every rock 'n' roll altruist who followed in his wake.

Within a few years, however, his solo career began to falter as critics and casual listeners gradually began to tire of his spiritually preoccupied lyrics, that were described as preachy by less appreciative members of the rock press. A high-profile lawsuit with Bright Tunes over the unconscious plagiarism in "My Sweet Lord" further undermined his confidence as a song writer, and after a while George simply no longer wanted to play the shallow fame game, often indulging in long periods of wilful career inactivity.

Harrison did continue to make records, albeit sporadically, and those records continued to sell, mainly because Harrison continued to match the eloquence and quality of his *All Things Must Pass* masterpiece, most notably on *George Harrison* and *Cloud Nine*.

Unlike McCartney, who worked hard, pursuing his solo career with zeal and always making himself available to the press, waging what one journalist once described as an almost Napoleonic campaign against the threat of his own irrelevance, George preferred to take it easy. A modest, private man, Harrison could often barely be bothered to promote his own records, seeming disinterested in whether people bought them or not.

Talking about the absence of promotion of one album, Harrison would say, "It's one thing writing a song, taping it and then making a record, but I wasn't interested in promoting it myself after all that had happened with the Beatles . . . I'm not about to jump up and down shouting, 'Hi folks, look at me, I'm cool and groovy!' That's not what George Harrison is all about."

For choosing the quieter life, Harrison was often been branded a recluse, but he was quick to point out that he was like that before he was famous. "When I lived on the outskirts of Liverpool," he would explain, "I used to walk miles along the mud cliffs of the Mersey to be on my own."

The senseless assassination of John Lennon in 1980 prompted Harrison to withdraw further from the public eye. In 1990, when Harrison discussed Lennon's death, he would describe how the prospect of being accosted by a crazed fan petrified him. It would be hard to put into words how much his world must have rocked after he was stabbed in 1999 by a deranged fan in the Friar Park home that he had always considered his fortress.

This ostensible invisibility led many people to perceive that his solo career had been a failure, a view that is not borne out by the facts, particularly in America where Harrison was hugely successful: enjoying three number one singles (one more than Lennon), while only one of his ten studio albums, *Gone Troppo*, failed to reach the top twenty on the Billboard charts. Furthermore, his solo career garnered an impressive total of six Grammy awards.

It was also a solo career that was defined by its consistency. Harrison was never one to simply toss off product;

instead he stuck to his guns and kept his music personal and full of his beliefs on peace and God realisation. Though many people were unwilling or unable to share George Harrison's spiritual vision, his sincerity was never in dispute, and the sound he created was both authentic and distinctly his own.

I never met the man, and I don't claim to understand him better than anyone else, because that's not what this book is about. This book is hopefully about giving an underrated idol due credit for the wonderful musical legacy he left behind. Credit that he didn't fully receive until after his death on November 29, 2001.

CHAPTER ONE

1969-1970

It's just that it wasn't as much fun for us in the end as it was for all of you.

George Harrison

The year was 1969, and as early as January 2nd, it was clear that the Beatles were breaking up. It was on this day that the Beatles began work at Twickenham Film studios on what would eventually become the album and film, *Let It Be*. It was bad enough that the best band on the planet was breaking up, but to make matters worse the Beatles also consented to documenting every step of the split on celluloid.

Originally titled *Get Back, Let It Be* was McCartney's baby. The plan was two-fold: firstly, he wanted the Beatles to rehearse new material for a live show to be staged at an unspecified venue. Secondly, by filming the proceedings, McCartney hoped to show the Beatles at work, reminding everyone, including themselves, that they could still cut it as "a great little band."

McCartney's reasoning was that since it was music that had brought them together, they should "get back" to the basics of playing live as a four piece band without studio effects and overdubs – naked for the world to see, just as they had been at The Cavern and in Hamburg. Although conceptually a great idea, the other Beatles weren't too keen.

The project's end product, however, was ill defined. Nobody could agree on where to stage the live show – suggestions included an ocean liner, in front of empty seats, a Roman amphitheatre, Ethiopia and even a stage at the foot of a volcano. Ringo flatly refused to do it outside of England; George (the most in favour of ending touring) didn't really want to do it, and Lennon just didn't seem to care, continually suggesting that maybe it was time for the Beatles to call it a day.

Only Paul appeared to still have any real enthusiasm for being in the band. Lennon had latterly swapped his *de facto* leadership of the Beatles and safe family life for heroin addiction and a relationship with Yoko Ono, and Ringo had just grown sick of all the bickering.

George, meanwhile, had tired of being treated as, in his words, "a second class Beatle" by John and Paul, and was beginning to even question his motivation for being a member of the by now not so "fab" four. This patronising junior status contrasted sharply with the respect he'd received from the other musicians such as The Band and Bob Dylan he'd hung out with in Los Angeles in late 1968.

"I spent a long time in the States," George would recall, "and I had such a good time working with all these different musicians and different people. Then I hung out at Woodstock for Thanksgiving and, you know, I felt really good at that time. I got back to England for Christmas and then on January 1st we were to start on the thing which turned into *Let It Be*. And straight away, again, it was just weird vibes. You know I found I was starting to be able to enjoy being a musician, but the moment I got back with the Beatles it was just too difficult. There were just too many limitations based upon our being together for so long. Everybody was sort of pigeon-holed. It was frustrating."

For George to have to go back to the Beatles, where his songs were either routinely ignored, not taken seriously, cursorily rehearsed or simply rejected by the almighty Lennon and McCartney, must have been an almighty chore.

To George's credit he soldiered on and took the brickbats, contributing heavily to the *Get Back* project in terms of songs. Though they would ultimately be rejected, "Isn't It a

Pity," "Hear Me Lord," "All Things Must Pass," "Let It Down" and the pleasant though unreleased "Window, Window" were all rehearsed during the Twickenham sessions, alongside "For You Blue," "I Me Mine" and "Old Brown Shoe."

"Something" was also written around this time, showing just how far George had progressed as a songwriter. Fast catching up with McCartney (even in the ballad stakes), Harrison had even overtaken Lennon in terms of both quantity and quality. However his status within the band meant that George would be restricted to a mere two songs per album right to the very end.

George would explain his predicament thus: "The problem was that John and Paul had written songs for so long it was difficult. First of all, because they had such a lot of tunes and they automatically thought that theirs should take priority. So for me, I'd always have to wait through ten of their songs before they'd even listen to one of mine. I had a little encouragement from time to time, but it was very little. It was like they were doing me a favour. I didn't have much confidence in writing songs because of that. Because they never said, "Yeah, that's a good song." When we got into things like "While My Guitar Gently Weeps," we recorded it one night and there was such a lack of enthusiasm. So I went home really disappointed because I knew the song was good."

Ensconced at Twickenham, it wasn't long before all the old tensions and rivalries resurfaced. It is well-documented that the seeds of discord had been sown on *The White Album* a year before, with the band increasingly pulling in different directions musically, often working autonomously and without all four Beatles present on several of the tracks. Ringo had even left during the sessions, feeling unappreciated and unable to "get through" to the rest of the group, though he returned after two days.

The cold and cheerless surroundings that January can't have helped the mood either. The Beatles were used to recording in the dead of night at Abbey Road; instead, to accommodate the film crew, they were forced to rehearse at the unfamiliar Twickenham Film Studios, in daytime to boot. Similarly, George Martin was not present at Twickenham all the time (the sessions were taped by Glyn Johns), an absence that added to the disorganisation. Michael Lindsay-Hogg, meanwhile, was shooting the film footage.

These factors almost certainly contributed to the substandard performances found on some of the bootlegs of the early rehearsals. It had been such a long time since they'd actually played together as a four-piece; these tapes reveal a band woefully out of shape.

The first days of rehearsal were shabby to the point of ineptitude. Frustrated by their lack of progress, they would habitually drift away from working on their new material, turning instead to playing rock 'n' roll chestnuts.

Dissatisfaction with the quality of the songs seemed to be at the heart of the discontent. The reality of the situation was that it had not been too long since the completion of *The Beatles* double album and the *Yellow Submarine* soundtrack, and quality *new* material was thin on the ground.

Many of the songs rehearsed at Twickenham were plainly unfinished (notably Lennon's "Gimme Some Truth" and McCartney's "Teddy Boy"), and it seemed that the group simply didn't seem to have the motivation to help finish each other's songs. As a result, John's "Child of Nature," later to metamorphose into "Jealous Guy," never made it to Beatle vinyl.

In fact, Lennon's song-writing powers had temporarily diminished – three of his contributions to the *Let It Be* album and the B-sides of its two singles were resurrections from the past: "Across the Universe" from 1968, "You Know My

Name (Look Up My Number)" from 1967, and "One After 909" from 1963.

Yet even with John scraping the barrel of Abbey Road's archive, Harrison's "Let It Down," "Hear Me Lord," "Isn't It a Pity" and "All Things Must Pass" would all still be rejected. (Only "All Things Must Pass" would be included on the McCartney instigated *Let It Be . . . Naked* album released in 2003.) Even though this would benefit Harrison in the long run, it seems perverse that Lennon, McCartney and George Martin would cursorily reject these four songs, especially when the two ballads could have become standards of "Something" proportions, had they been released by the Beatles.

George Martin would later say, "I am sorry to say that I did not help George much with his song-writing, either. His early attempts didn't show enormous promise. Being a very pragmatic person, therefore, I tended to go with the blokes who were delivering the goods. I never cold-shouldered George. I did, though, look at his new material with a slightly jaundiced eye."

John was heard during the sessions complaining about the lack of up-tempo numbers, bemoaning the amount of ballads, which explains the lack of attention shown to the aforementioned George songs.

Contrary to popular myth, it was Lennon who seemed to be the most opposed to George's songs. Lennon did not even play on "I Me Mine," on either the released version or in rehearsal, allegedly deeming the song not good enough for the Beatles. Instead the *Let It Be* film would see him patronisingly waltzing with Yoko while the others put the song through its paces.

McCartney, meanwhile, would always contribute manfully to Harrison's songs. "When it came time to do the occasional song of mine," George would later recall, "Paul would always be really creative with what he'd contribute. For instance, that galloping piano part on "While My Guitar Gently Weeps" was Paul's, and it's brilliant right to this day . . . And you just have to listen to that bass line on "Something" to know that, when he wanted to, Paul could give a lot."

George's grievances with Paul seemed to be based more on their contrasting working practices. Harrison preferred to rehearse songs all the way through and get comfortable with each song as a whole, while Paul liked to perfect each part of a song before attempting complete run-throughs.

Paul's constant nagging in his search for perfectionism was also misplaced. His idea to record a "warts and all" album became nebulous when the Beatles found themselves doing take after take to obtain one without flaws or, under Paul's direction, making multiple attempts at getting certain guitar parts right.

The bottom line was that each composer was getting more precious and less collaborative when it came to his own songs. The tapes of the *Get Back* sessions, as transcribed in Doug Sulphy and Ray Schweighardt's excellent book *Get Back – The Beatles' Let It Be Disaster* eavesdrops, that January, on Neil Aspinall and George Martin sympathising with the problems that George faced within the group. Their feeling is that Lennon and McCartney consistently team up against George, and didn't offer him enough freedom within their songs. Indeed, Paul would often tell Harrison how he wanted the guitar solo, which naturally angered George – after all; he knew how to play a guitar solo.

Harrison would later recall, "What Paul would do, if he'd written a song, he'd learn all the parts for Paul and then come in the studio and say, "Do this." He'd never give you the opportunity to come out with something." The others just didn't have the energy to match Paul's drive, or the patience to deal with his chivvying.

If tension was an uninvited guest at the sessions, so too was Yoko Ono. Lennon's virtually Siamese need to be with Yoko meant that she had to be present at all Beatle sessions. John felt Yoko was the woman he'd been seeking for years. Her conviction in her avant-garde monkey-shines both captivated him and provided him with the artistic nourishment that his first wife Cynthia and the Beatles could no longer provide.

Previously, Beatle wives had been seen and not heard and Yoko's ubiquity was much to the chagrin of the other three. As ever, McCartney was the most diplomatic. He shrewdly realised that if he pushed John on this issue and put his foot down it would probably send him home for good. If Paul had got on his high horse, Lennon probably would have got back on the narcotic horse.

According to McCartney, Yoko's presence "made it very difficult. He [John] wanted a very strong intimate life with her . . . You had to understand, he had to have time with her. But does he have to have that much time with her – was the sort of feeling in the group." Yoko would also attend band meetings, muscle in on photo shoots, and would invariably speak for John, who seemed unable to commit even his own opinions to the project.

When Lennon did speak, it was invariably to belittle one of Harrison's songs. This cattiness seemed to be motivated out of simple jealousy that George (whom he still viewed as the lap dog three years his junior from the Liverpool days) had caught up and overtaken him.

Nonetheless, it was McCartney with whom Harrison seemed to have the most issues. In an interview published in *Guitar World* magazine in January 2001, George would recount, "At that point in time, Paul couldn't see beyond himself. He was on a roll, but it was a roll encompassing his own self. And in his mind, everything that was going on around him was just there to accompany him. He wasn't sensitive to stepping on other people's egos or feelings." George did reveal in the same interview that Paul had long since apologised for his behaviour towards him during this period.

Still, it's amazing that George kept his cool. Whilst trying to attain spiritual fulfilment from the eastern philosophies in which he had immersed himself – here he was arguing with John and Paul over trivia, such as the stand-up row he'd had with Lennon after he'd seen Yoko take a biscuit off his amp.

The famous altercation that found its way into the *Let It Be* film came during a run through of "Two Of Us." The scene shows that Paul is unhappy with George's guitar playing and tells him so, though he stresses he's not getting at him personally. Harrison, nevertheless, takes it personally and the whole scene is very ugly. Harrison tells McCartney, "I'll play whatever you want me to play or I won't play at all if you don't want me to, whatever it is that will please you," while Paul keeps quiet, aware that the cameras are rolling. It's uncomfortable viewing.

John and George allegedly hated the film, which would explain why it has remained buried for so many years. Lennon described it as "a project set up by Paul, for Paul." Lennon would later sum up the feelings within the group on this issue by saying, "We got fed up with being sidemen for Paul." George, meanwhile, was probably equally fed up with being a sideman for Yoko Ono.

George was the most angry at "the Yoko factor." He and John had been as close as they'd ever been whilst living out in Weybridge and Esher, experimenting with LSD. Just as George thought he was edging Paul out of John's affections, someone else came along to push him down the pecking order.

George was the only one to voice his objections over Yoko and her presumptuous contributions to band meetings on John's behalf. Paul was trying not to upset John, and

Ringo was being polite. At least George tried to make a stand and, on January 10, he quit the Beatles and stayed away for nearly two weeks, a departure that coincided with the January 17 release of the *Yellow Submarine* soundtrack that included Harrison's "Only a Northern Song" and his organ-driven "summer of love" anthem, "It's All Too Much."

Nonetheless, Harrison vowed never to return and to underline his seriousness, he suggested the others advertise for a replacement in the NME.

The popular misconception is that George left because of a disagreement with Paul, but all available evidence points to the fact that it was John with whom he had fallen out. Harrison had been infuriated by Lennon's public statement in January 1969 that if Apple kept losing money at the current rate, the Beatles would be broke within six months. Further contributing factors were John's inability to communicate, and his derogatory comments towards George's songs.

Lennon didn't seem too bothered about Harrison's departure and quickly suggested they draft in Eric Clapton, though this may have been disingenuous machismo. Maybe Yoko wanted to join the group as George has jokingly intimated at various times.

Maybe Yoko could have played a conceptual air guitar or contributed some of her virtuoso avant-garde caterwauling, as indeed she did in George's absence, screeching John's name at the top of her lungs as the other three accompanied her with noise and feedback.

A summit meeting was soon arranged to persuade Harrison to return.

Since Yoko's presence was a non-negotiable area as far as Lennon was concerned, George's terms for returning boiled down to four caveats. Firstly, there would be no more talk about a live show at some ludicrous venue, and secondly, the songs already rehearsed would be recorded to make a new album. George was happy for filming to continue as long as it was for a film about the Beatles, making an album. And lastly, the band would relocate to their own brand-new Apple Studios.

This, however, posed problems. The construction of Apple Studios had been entrusted to their resident electronics wizard, "Magic" Alex Mardas, who had promised to provide 72-track equipment and an invisible sonic force-field to isolate Ringo's drum kit. Unfortunately, his inventions were basically useless and rented equipment had to be brought in.

That the other Beatles did so readily accede to Harrison's demands was testament to his power within the group. Notwithstanding the fact that they were getting nowhere without him, they certainly didn't want George to actually leave the group. George Martin would describe George's role as "something stronger than power, he had influence. Witness the fact that all of the boys followed him to India to sit at the feet of the Maharishi."

George would further assert this influence by bringing in organist Billy Preston for the remainder of the *Let It Be* sessions. Reflecting on how this came about Preston would recall, "I was with Ray Charles in London and George was in the audience and he recognised me and called me the next day and invited me over to see the guys. When I went over, they were in the studio, you know recording and filming and they asked me to sit in with them. You know I wasn't expecting anything. It was a thrill enough just being there and playing with them."

As with Eric Clapton on "While My Guitar Gently Weeps," Preston had been brought in by Harrison to serve as an emollient to buffer the friction between the Beatles. "'While My Guitar Gently Weeps' worked out well," George would endorse, "I liked the idea of other musicians contributing."

Since all the Beatles' had known Preston since 1962 (when he had been a member of Little Richard's backing group) he was someone they *all* liked and respected, in direct contrast to their feelings about Yoko Ono. The aim was that Preston would put the boys on best behaviour and bolster the musicianship.

George would later comment on Preston's arrival: "It's interesting to see how people behave nicely when you bring a guest in because they don't really want anybody to know that they are so bitchy . . . Straight away it just became 100 percent improvement in the vibe in the room."

You can see from the finished *Let It Be* film that the playing did improve upon Preston's arrival. Lennon was so impressed with Preston he wanted him to join the group permanently. McCartney demurred and instead suggested they pay him £500 for his troubles.

Even though he was now back within the fold, it would appear that during his absence, Harrison decided to withdraw his compositions from the live show, feeling that justice would not be done justice to them.

As a result George seemed content to let the *Get Back* sessions be complete with only "For You Blue" recorded. Had George hatched the idea for *All Things Must Pass* during his two-week hiatus? If so, that would have necessitated the need for quality songs such as "Let It Down" and "Isn't It a Pity." "For You Blue" meanwhile was no more than a harmless twelve-bar, the sort of thing George could knock off in his sleep.

George seemed to be reserving his enthusiasm for his extra-curricular activities: producing singles for his Apple protégés, Jackie Lomax (who recorded Harrison's excellent "Sour Milk Sea"), and the Radha Krishna Temple. Two of his productions for the Krishna devotees ("Hare Krishna Mantra" and "Govinda") even became British top thirty hits.

Due to Harrison's steadfast refusal to perform before an audience, the Beatles and Billy Preston finally decided on January 30 as the date to stage their concert on the roof of the Apple offices in Saville Row, London. With no fanfare or publicity, this move was almost certainly the opposite of Paul's original intentions. At least he got his concert: all forty-two minutes of it that saw the band play "Get Back" three times, "Don't Let Me Down" twice, "One After 909," "Dig A Pony" and "I've Got a Feeling" twice, George staying true to his promise of removing his songs.

George and Ringo didn't look at all happy, probably due to the grey, cold weather, but despite that the Beatles played great! The eight hours a day rehearsal had paid dividend, or was it that they just decided to raise their game for the sake of history. A sense of history completely lost on all the bankers and insurance men who phoned the police to have the disturbance stopped.

Word was put through to Paul, who sensing a suitable dénouement for the *Let It Be* film, urged the band to carry on until the police found their way upstairs with their handcuffs. Unfortunately the coppers *didn't* arrest them, and the Beatles kind of limped away. Was it all over?

Wedding bells were breaking up the gang. On March 12, Paul married Linda Eastman at Marlyebone Registry Office, the very day that George and his wife Pattie were busted for possessing 120 joints by notorious super-sleuth Sgt. Norman Pilcher, head of one of the biggest police drug squads of the late 1960s. Pilcher's stated aim was to wipe out drugs from Britain, by terrorising the rock stars he believed were promoting drug use via a copycat effect.

After high-profile busts of Donovan and The Stones, Pilcher was working his way up to "The Fabs." Pilcher first set his sights on Lennon. When he found out that Pilcher was coming after him, John painstakingly cleaned the premises of all the drugs left over from previous resident, Jimi Hendrix. When he arrested Lennon in October 1968, for possession of cannabis, the suspicion was raised that Pilcher and his men had planted the resin.

Next on the hit list was George. Sgt. Pilcher and his Lonely Hearts Club ransacked the Harrisons' home in Esher looking for illegal substances which they duly "found." George and Pattie were taken to jail and charged with possession of marijuana and released on bail.

Talking about his drug bust years later, Harrison would say: "They chose Paul's wedding day to come and raid on me, and to this day, I'm still having difficulty with my visa to America because of this fella. They took us off, fingerprinted us, and we were busted. It was written in the papers like a fashion show: 'George was wearing a yellow suit and his wife Pattie had on . . .'"

George would also later reveal that he did have a stash of pot, but not where the cops claimed to have found it. Unfortunately this defense did not stand up in court and a week later George and Pattie were both charged with possession of cannabis and fined £250 each.

Protesting his conviction, George would say, "I'm a tidy sort of bloke, I don't like chaos. I kept records in the record stack, tea in the tea caddy and pot in the pot box. This was the biggest stick of hash I have ever seen and obviously I'd have known about it if I'd seen it before."

The implication being that once again, the dope had been planted. Luckily for everyone concerned, Pilcher's reign of terror was short-lived when it was discovered that he himself had committed perjury in court. For this he was sentenced in 1972 to four years in prison, which meant that Sgt. Norman Pilcher wound up spending considerably more time at Her Majesty's Pleasure than all his rock star victims combined.

Eight days after Harrison's arrest, Lennon married Yoko Ono in Gibraltar. Whilst honeymooning in Paris, the couple staged one of their peace-promoting bed-ins, acting as though they had copyrighted peace for themselves and it was their will to grant it to a grateful planet.

John and Yoko further alienated their public with their trilogy of atonal rubbish (*Two Virgins, Life With The Lyons* and *The Wedding Album*). Lennon however was not the only Beatle trying to establish his avant-garde credentials. May 1969 would see the release of George's *Electronic Sound*, a truly apt title if ever there was. The album consisted of two sides of noise from George's new toy – a prototype moog synthesiser. George had recorded side one ("Under the Mersey Wall") in Esher and side two ("No Time Or Space") in California with the help of moog guru Bernie Krause, who would later attempt to take credit for this particular *waste* of time and space. Krause claimed that side two of the album, "No Time Or Space," was merely an edited tape of the lesson he'd given George in turning the contraption on.

Released on the Zapple label (the Apple Records sub-sidiary created specifically for such experimental music), George sounds as though he made no effort to actually com-pose anything for this release, and soundscapes would be too grand a description for what sounds like George twiddling with every knob on the switchboard. Though the album had a shorter shelf-life than milk, the record reached number 191 in the American charts, which suggesting that even a record-ing of George literally flogging a dead horse would have sold in 1969.

Electronic Sound should only really be judged as an his-torical musical document and a necessary purchase only for serious Harrison collectors. George himself would sum up the release in the sleeve notes of the 1996 CD re-issue: "It could be called avant-garde, but a more apt description would be (in the words of my old friend Alvin [Lee]) *'Avant Garde Clue'*!"

Electronic Sound was Harrison's second taste of freedom away from the Beatles mainframe. Between the end of 1967 (at Abbey Road) and January 1968 (in Bombay), he had recorded the soundtrack to an obscure film named *Wonderwall,* starring 1960s pin-up Jane Birkin.

George had accepted the job because it gave him an opportunity to promote Indian music, and due to the fact the director Joe Massot gave him complete control over the content. The 19-track instrumental soundtrack that followed was a coherent mixture of experimental western pop and Indian-style improvisations, mostly performed by The Remo Four and Indian studio musicians alongside contributions from Eric Clapton. As a result, *Wonderwall Music* was a more atmospheric and much more entertaining album than *Electronic Sound.*

Wonderwall Music was the first Beatle solo album and without doubt whetted Harrison's appetite for further solo projects. Like Harrison, Lennon too couldn't wait to get out and pursue his and Yoko's various vanity projects such as planting acorns to further the cause of peace.

Lennon desperately wanted to divorce himself from his former life, and felt that he needed to consolidate his emotional and creative needs into one person. But the blame for the break-up can't be solely put down to Yoko Ono. The others didn't like her but that was hardly a reason to break up the band; the real nail in the coffin was Allen Klein.

John, George and Ringo wanted Allen Klein to be the Beatles' new business manager, a position that had desperately needed filling since Brian Epstein's death in 1967. McCartney, who was later accused by Lennon of trying to take over the group after Epstein's death, was not enamoured by Klein, and instead wanted his new in-laws to fill the role.

The Eastmans did at least have the benefit of being established New York legal brains, with shrewd business acumen and clean criminal records.

The case for Klein was that he had done a good job renegotiating The Rolling Stones record contract. Nonetheless, Mick Jagger had told the Beatles that Klein was a man not to be trusted.

In reality, any fool could have renegotiated record deals for the Beatles. EMI had signed them when they were no more than kids and they knew they were milking the group. When they became more successful than they could ever have imagined, it was only Epstein's gentlemanly conduct that had prevented him from renegotiating a deal that was surely there for the taking. Klein would not be so pusillanimous.

Klein was born on December 18, 1931. He'd got his start in the music business as an accounting clerk, auditing the books of record companies. By 1960 he had moved into the field of business management for recording artists, negotiating contracts on their behalf, either with record companies, or music publishers. His ability to recoup thousands of dollars in royalties and back payments had made him a feared man in the industry.

Klein had read Lennon's "broke in 6 months" quote and quickly arranged to meet John and Yoko at the Dorchester Hotel, on January 27, 1969. Klein courted the *pair* of them and this was what attracted Klein to Lennon: he didn't patronise Yoko and treated her with respect. Ultimately, therefore, the fate of the Beatles lay in the fact that Klein didn't take an instant dislike to Yoko, when others preferred to save themselves the time.

Lennon was so impressed that he immediately asked Klein to make enquiries into his financial position and was so effusive that George and Ringo asked Klein to do the same for them.

Klein made it clear to them that the financial position of the Beatles was perilous and that the current liabilities of their Apple companies exceeded their current assets. To alleviate this situation Klein set about renegotiating the existing recording contract with EMI/Capitol for Canada, Mexico and the U.S.A., in which the Beatles' royalty increased from seventeen and a half percent to twenty-five percent, providing the Beatles recorded two albums per year as a group, or individually.

Paul was impressed, but not enough to accede to Klein's demands for a 20% cut of the deal. Paul said 15% maximum and managed to delay signing any agreement with Klein. (It would later emerge that Klein was charging 20% on the whole income coming to Apple, and not just the increase that he'd procured.)

Paul didn't trust Klein and rightly saw through him from the start. After seeing millions go into the hands of others, Paul was not willing to allow anyone else take control of his money. His father-in-law had also warned him about Klein's bad reputation and his history of shady business dealings. Unfortunately this wasn't enough to dissuade George and the others. George was over the moon with Klein, impressed with how much money he was making for him and how he was stopping the rot at Apple.

Brian Epstein had originally presented the Apple business concept to the Beatles in 1967 as a tax dodge. The Beatles were advised that they would lose £2 million if they didn't invest the money in a business. According to Beatles publicist Derek Taylor, "Apple was set up purely and simply as a tax saving project . . . Apple was never meant to try to save the world, despite popular myth."

The Beatles used Apple as the economic unit to spring their ideas on the world. It had five divisions: records, music publishing, films, electronics, and retailing. Lennon called it "a psychedelic Woolworths."

A headquarters in Saville Row was purchased and it cost a fortune to renovate and install the recording studio. According to former Beatles' assistant Alistair Taylor's recollections: "Luxurious furnishings were ordered and delivered. Drink cabinets were filled to overflowing. Every comfort was contained in that building, but the whole venture lacked a man such as Brian to take charge. It was like a ship without a captain and it sank lower and lower supporting the dead weight of numerous freeloaders. It became a Mecca for dropouts and out-of-work aspiring musicians. I could see us all being swallowed up in a quagmire of inefficiency. Big business was not their forte, and they had found themselves losing a game that they didn't know how to play."

Apple quickly got out of hand. John would state in an affidavit, "The staff came and went as they pleased and were lavish with money and hospitality . . . We also owned a house which no one can remember buying." The drink bill was £600 per month and the food bill was close to that, while the phone bill was £4,000 for a quarter. DJs, producers, journalists were going to night-clubs on Apple's accounts. Thousands of pounds were poured into Apple Electronics with nothing to show for it.

Allen Klein was put in charge of getting rid of the hangers-on, hustlers and spongers that Apple had attracted. Half the staff was fired and personal expenses were slashed. Even the budget for Apple Records (which had been declared the most successful new record company of 1968 with Mary Hopkin's *Those Were The Days* selling 4,000,000 in four months world-wide) was cut with contracts unrenewed and releases cancelled. The Zapple subsidiary was cut altogether, denying us the chance to hear more of George's moog synthesiser doodles.

On June 4 the Beatles would release *The Ballad of John and Yoko,* though only John and Paul appeared on the record due to Lennon's impatient rush to issue the record. The B-side was "Old Brown Shoe," perhaps the most ambitious Harrison song yet, certainly in terms of the vocal, recorded in a corner of the studio to obtain a natural echo. For those interested, this was Harrison's first vocal after having his tonsils removed.

The song was a sizzling rocker with a ferocious Harrison guitar solo. Even John was audibly excited by this tune, adding enthusiastic and energetic backing vocals throughout the record, and undoubtedly sounding as though he wished he'd written the song himself.

It's a shame that "Old Brown Shoe" was tucked away on a B-side, because it would have made an excellent addition to the Beatles last album as a group, *Abbey Road*. Even though *Let It Be* was meant to be rough and ready, it was still in no fit state to be released. Started in July 1969, *Abbey Road* would be its polar opposite.

Seemingly able to put aside their differences – you can almost taste the enthusiasm on *Abbey Road* – the Beatles once again sounded like young men with a point to prove rather than the tired, old lags of *Let It Be*. It was as though they made a conscious decision to create an album that was as polished and as slick as it was possible to make: an intentional and fitting swan-song and a sonic tour de force that underlined their mastery of the recording studio.

By all accounts the mood was brighter on *Abbey Road*, helped no doubt by the presence of George Martin and Geoff Emerick and the familiar surroundings of Abbey Road studios.

Abbey Road would see all Beatles contributing to each others' songs in the fullest sense for the first time since *Revolver*, each Beatle contributing to the shared vision of the album and all four at the top of their game on their respective instruments.

The album was most notable for two things: the extended song suite on side two and, as far as the critics were concerned, the final coming of age of George Harrison as a song writer, weighing in as he did with the album's two strongest cuts, "Something" and "Here Comes the Sun," must have knocked George Martin for six, as he had previously written off George's songs as "dreary." "Something" was the album's obvious A-side (released in October), although "Here Comes the Sun" could easily have been another.

"Something" had been an attempt to write a Ray Charles homage but George achieved something even greater than that. The marriage of lyrics and melody was truly heaven-made. The song also showed what a good singer George could be. Given that Harrison took the lead vocal on less than thirty Beatle songs, it wasn't hard for this particular skill to be relatively well-hidden. His softer vocal in the verse provides the perfect springboard for the middle eight on which George delivers almost certainly the most passionate, heart-felt vocal ever delivered on a Beatles record.

"Something" was George's "Yesterday." No less an authority than Frank Sinatra would describe it as the "finest love song of the past fifty years," and has garnered dozens and dozens of cover versions (none of which improved on the original) ensuring that George never needed to work again, a notion he would often take all too literally.

With a classic George Martin score, one of McCartney's best late-1960s bass-lines, not to mention arguably the most sensitive and exquisite guitar solo George ever played in his life, Harrison had every reason to be proud of the song. It's a masterpiece in every department.

As was "Here Comes the Sun," on which George delivered an appropriately vivacious vocal, ably backed by some great Beatle harmonies. The Beatles had never before put this amount of effort into George's songs and the difference shows. Like "Something," the structure of "Here Comes the Sun" is fascinating: the instrumental section in the middle is easily the most complex piece of playing on a Beatles track, perfectly building up the tension before the band return to the main body of the song.

These two songs show not only just how far George's song-writing had progressed in a short space of time, but how effortlessly he was able to produce perfect pop songs by 1969. Imagine if he'd kept them for *All Things Must Pass*. That would have made for one almighty critical eulogy. Instead they were Harrison's parting shots: his final contributions to Beatles immortality.

Abbey Road was the group's most ambitious album, on which the Beatles do things even they'd never done before: an extended song cycle, a three-way guitar duel, and even a drum solo! The harmonies on side two, of which George was an integral part, had also never sounded sweeter, particularly on "Because."

John, Paul, George and Ringo would never again find the musicians who shared the symbiotic chemistry to perform such musical derring-do. Popular music played by two guitars, bass and drums would never be bettered. The combination of their four personalities gave rise to a rare studio environment that none of them could later duplicate individually, nor has any succeeding group recaptured it. Still this was not enough to keep the Beatles together.

The August 20, 1969 session for "I Want You (She's So Heavy)" would mark the last time that all four Beatles would ever be in the same studio together. Soon after they would never again be in the same room.

In an Apple meeting on September 20 meeting, McCartney broached the subject of the band's future and it was at this point that John dropped his bombshell that he was leaving the Beatles.

As McCartney recalled the meeting, "John kept saying we were musically standing still. So I came into the idea of going to village halls which hold a couple of hundred people. Have someone book the hall . . . and we'd just turn up there in a van and people would arrive and we'd be there. I thought that was great. John said, "You're daft." At the time John's thing was playing for 200,000 people because he'd been at a big festival or something. So he wanted to do that . . . So then John said, "Anyway, I'm leaving the group." He literally said, "I want a divorce." And for the first time ever, he meant it."

But did the others believe him, or did they think Lennon was talking out of his scouse backside? Either way, everyone agreed to keep quiet, at least until the ink was dry on their new recording contract.

To cover their tracks John, George and Ringo would all mislead the press, as to the status of the group. John told Melody Maker that "after *Get Back* [sic] is released in January, we'll probably . . . do another one." In February 1970 Ringo told the NME, "Everything's fine. I've got things to do and George has things to do and Paul has his solo album and John has his peace thing. We can't do everything at once." In the same article George would add, "We've got unity through diversity, because that's what it is . . . we had to find ourselves, individually one day."

During this period of uncertainty, in December 1969, George went on the road with Delaney and Bonnie, the husband-and-wife-fronted blues ensemble, who were enjoying a mercifully brief fifteen minutes of fame. Touring with Delaney and Bonnie was a bizarre move for a man who had seemed pathologically disinterested in performing before an audience only months before.

George had gone to watch the band that included Eric Clapton and Dave Mason (ex-Traffic guitarist) at The Royal Albert Hall on December 5. Delaney Bramlett recalled,

"George met me backstage and said, 'Could I be in the band too?'"

"We drove to his house," Bramlett continued, "and saw all the equipment out front. He was ready. I knocked on the door, and he said, 'I got a couple more things and I'll be ready to go.' I didn't think Pattie liked that, George going off with a bunch of damn hillbillies."

During the short British tour that took in Bristol, Sheffield, Newcastle and The Liverpool Empire, not many audiences even realised Harrison was on the stage, as the quiet one underlined his image by hiding in the shadows at the back. "I was told not to make a deal out of this thing", remembered Delaney, and even credited George as "Mysterioso" on the "Delaney & Bonnie & Friends on Tour with Eric Clapton" live album.

When the tour went to Europe, George went too, in place of Dave Mason who usually played the slide guitar parts. One night in Copenhagen, George agreed to fill Mason's breach. "I kinda showed him how," self-genuflected Bramlett, without sounding convincing, "but he already knew . . . He had his own attitude from the off." Thus a trademark of thirty-plus years was born.

Even though Lennon had left the band, the Beatles still had unfinished business. Showing that relationships had yet to deteriorate beyond repair, the 1960s ended with Paul, George and Ringo and their respective partners enjoying a New Year's Eve party at Ringo's house in Highgate. Three days later the trio recorded George's "I Me Mine" with Phil Spector at the helm (John was in Denmark on vacation).

Surprisingly, Ringo was the first to make his solo move, recording his *Sentimental Journey* album of old standards. Lennon redoubled his efforts to bring about world peace and McCartney went into hibernation in Scotland where he would start work on his eponymous first solo album. George for his part would busy himself guesting on records by virtually anyone who cared to ask while preparing himself for his own solo onslaught.

Meanwhile, George and John authorised Allen Klein to hire Phil Spector to make some sense out of the shambolic *Get Back* tapes. Paul was not consulted and would no doubt have refused. It was strange for George and John to now be calling the shots on a project they had not cared to be part of. Perhaps if they'd have shown the same enthusiasm for *Let It Be* while it was being recorded Spector might have had a better palette to work from.

Originally the *Get Back* album had been slated for release with a mix by Glyn Johns and a cover photograph with the Beatles in exactly the same place and position as they'd been on their *Please Please Me* début, to symbolise how they'd come full circle. Both the cover and the Glyn Johns mix were rejected.

When *Let It Be* was finally released in May 1970 it was to mixed reviews, for which Phil Spector took the brunt of the blame. Although he should at least be credited with making a releasable album from the Glyn Johns tapes, it was Spector who decided to add the ill-fitting orchestral and choral scores to "Across the Universe," "I Me Mine," "Let It Be" and "The Long and Winding Road." By doing so, Spector not only destroyed the original feel of those particular songs, he also wounded the balance and flow of the whole album. He certainly decimated the original back-to-basics concept.

The stripped-down and ultimately more powerful versions of the latter three songs on *The Beatles Anthology 3* versions would show how much better these songs were without the unnecessary, and illustrated the stark contrast between Spector's and McCartney's *original* vision of how the material should have been presented.

Spector also made some rather debatable decisions concerning song selection. "Don't Let Me Down" was easily the best new song Lennon had offered to the sessions, yet Spector completely ignored it!

The Beatles themselves were not at fault for writing bad songs, but for choosing to work on the wrong songs. George was clearly saving his best songs for his solo album, while Lennon ignored finishing off "Child of Nature" and "Gimme Me Some Truth" and submitted "Dig a Pony," which is close to being the very worst song he ever wrote for the Beatles.

Had it been just a collection of the songs (including "Don't Let Me Down"), with a production closer in spirit to the original Glyn Johns' mix the album, would have at least sounded much more like a unified entity. This certainly would forever be Paul's view, if the fact that he was still moaning about over thirty years later is anything to go by.

Paul would be especially enraged over Phil Spector's changes to "The Long and Winding Road," particularly the overdubbing of an orchestra and a female choir, and one can imagine his apoplexy when Klein refused to allow him the permission to rework his own song.

What Spector did to the *Let It Be* album, which in many ways had been Paul's baby, was just one of many reasons that made McCartney feel more than slightly litigious.

Furthermore, the contract Paul had signed with the others meant basically that all money from solo records would go to Apple and be split four ways. Although McCartney no doubt predicted that he would have the bigger hits of the four, in the short term he would be wrong.

And there was yet more misery for Paul when Klein (with George and John as his deluded acolytes) attempted to put back the release date of his first solo album, *McCartney*, so *Let It Be* could be released without a clash. The fact that Paul was not consulted on such a major decision showed how low relationships had sunk. John and George sent him a letter asking him to consent to the postponement of his album and signed the letter saying, "Don't take this personally. Love John and George."

When Ringo was dispatched to Paul's house as mediator, it was clear that McCartney *had* taken it personally. Later, in a court affidavit, Ringo described the event: "To my dismay, he went completely out of control, shouting at me, prodding his finger toward my face, saying, "I'll finish you all now" and "you'll pay." He told me to put on my coat and get out. . . . While I thought he had behaved a bit like a spoiled child, I could see that the release date of his record had a gigantic emotional significance for him . . . and I felt . . . we should let him have his own way."

Eventually, Paul did get his own way when *McCartney* was released on April 7, 1970. For the press the album contained a self-interview Q&A sheet – in which Paul effectively announced to the world that the Beatles had split up. Although Paul did not say, "the Beatles have broken up permanently," the message was clear.

> Q: Do you foresee a time when Lennon-McCartney becomes an active song-writing partnership again?
> A: No.
> Q: What is your relationship with Klein?
> A: It isn't. I am not in contract with him and he doesn't represent me in any way.

After denying Paul's "announcement" of the demise for three days, Apple then confirmed everyone's worst fears in a statement on April 10 on behalf of the Beatles. Written by Derek Taylor, it signed off with a perfect Taylorism: "The world is spinning and so are we and so are you. When the spinning stops, that'll be the time to worry. Not before. The Beatles are alive and well and the beat goes on. The beat goes on."

Even *after* Paul's announcement, George and Ringo

dropped hints that this was not really the end. Ringo was quoted as saying, "I just feel it in my bones that we'll probably all be recording together again before very long." George also seemed to think that the situation as not terminal, saying, "Everyone this year is trying to do his individual album, but after that I am ready to go back and work together again." Or maybe George and Ringo were just sticking to their promise to keep quiet until the new record contract had been signed, sealed and delivered.

For Paul to break his silence was unforgivable as far as Lennon was concerned. John seemed bitter that Paul had made the announcement, saying in May 1970: "It's a simple fact that [Paul] can't have his own way, so he's causing chaos. I put out four albums last year, and I didn't say a f***ing word about quitting." It is almost certain that Lennon's ego would have preferred to have been the one to break the news.

Paul, however, realised that *his* continued silence entitled Klein and the others to cut him out of crucial business decisions and do with his songs and release dates as they saw fit. Paul realised that he was saddled with the contract he'd signed in 1967 that would bind him to the other three and Allen Klein until 1976.

In short, McCartney wanted this contract torn up. Paul would explain the obstacles thus, "The trouble is, the other three have been advised not to tear it up. They've been advised that if they tear it up, there will be serious, bad consequences for them."

Harrison would later retort, "[Paul] wanted . . . his in-laws to run it [Apple] and we didn't . . . That's the whole basis. But that's only a personal problem that he'll have to get over because . . . the reality is that he's out-voted and we're a partnership. We've got these companies which we all own 25 percent of each, and if there's a decision to be made, then, like in any other business or group you have a vote, you know. And he was out-voted three to one and if he doesn't like it, it's really a pity. You know, because we're trying to do what's best for the Beatles as a group, or best for Apple as a company. We're not trying to do what's best for Paul and his in-laws, you know."

Paul would nonetheless agonise for months over whether to take legal steps to dissolve the Beatles' legal partnership. Unfortunately this meant suing his former band-mates since Klein was not actually a party to the contract.

"All summer long in Scotland," Paul would reason, "I was fighting with myself as to whether I should do anything like that. It was murderous. I had a knot in my stomach all summer. I tried to think of a way to take Allen Klein to court, or take a businessman to court. But the action had to be brought against the other three. The build-up is the thing: all these things continuously happening, making me feel like I'm a junior with the record company, like Klein is the boss and I'm nothing. Well, I'm a senior. I figure my opinion is as good as anyone's, especially when it's my thing. And it's emotional: you feel like you don't have any freedom. I figured I'd have to stand up for myself eventually or get pushed under."

Paul chose the former.

CHAPTER TWO

1970-1971

*It looked like a great thing to be in the Beatles,
but it was also a great thing to get out of.*

George Harrison

With the Beatles over, Harrison was free to concentrate on his solo career, and curiously he seemed to be the least affected by the break-up. Indeed, the timing of the break-up could not have been more propitious for Harrison: the very fact that Lennon and McCartney had kept his blossoming songwriting talents from flowering would prove to be his secret weapon. "Something" and "Here Comes the Sun" had underlined how fast Harrison was approaching his peak as a writer during this time.

More importantly he had a backlog of readily available material with which to begin his solo career. Harrison would describe the chance to record his wealth of material as "like having diarrhoea and not being allowed to go to the toilet." Written within the fiercely competitive Beatles mainframe there was every reason to believe that these songs would be of the highest quality. Harrison would later claim, "Even before I started I knew I was gonna make a good album because I had so many songs and I had so much energy. For me to do my own album after all that – it was joyous. Dream of dreams."

Meanwhile, Lennon and McCartney were men on the verge. John was undergoing his primal scream therapy with Arthur Janov, while Paul had retreated to Scotland to stress himself into drink, while deciding whether or not to sue his former band-mates.

The only upheaval in George's life was buying a new

house. On January 14 George purchased Friar Park, an abandoned convent in the riverside town of Henley-on-Thames, for £135,000. The property had been designed and built in 1896 by eccentric nineteenth century lawyer and adviser to the Liberal Party, Sir Frankie Crisp. Its flamboyant Gothic style and idiosyncratic design features made Friar Park one of the most unique residences in England.

The place was ideal for its new owner, particularly the scope its thirty-three acres of parkland offered a keen gardener such as Harrison. "I'm not really into lots of little flowers though," George would muse. "I like gardening in a landscape way – like great artists painting pictures . . . I like what you can paint with trees and stuff."

Harrison fell in love with its thirty-three acres of grounds, its man-made lakes and the fact that Crisp had installed an underground river, as well as the visual jokes, such as light switches in the shape of monk's noses and the double-edged "Don't keep off the grass" signs in the garden.

While looking for a new home George had masqueraded as a chauffeur while Apple employee Alistair Taylor posed as the potential buyer to the estate agents, believing that the price would be artificially inflated if it was known that a Beatle was interested in the property. The house purchased, George and Pattie would move into Friar Park in March.

George spent a fortune renovating the dilapidated estate – installing an alpine rock garden and a 100-foot high replica of the Matterhorn, constructed with 20,000 tons of rock brought by train from Yorkshire. Harrison also half-filled the labyrinth of subterranean caverns with water and purchased rowing boats with which to navigate them.

The gardens of Friar Park were originally laid out as miniature Swiss Alps, complete with lakes and grottoes inhabited by carved spiders and monsters. Crisp had divided the lakes in such a way that anyone crossing the bridge over the lower lake would appear (to anyone watching from the house) to be walking on water. Harrison's first solo album would create a similar impression!

Not that Harrison seemed in any rush to begin recording his début and instead he would spend most of 1970, leading up to *All Things Must Pass*, guesting on other people's records.

Having recorded "I Me Mine" at the start of January 1970 with Paul and Ringo, the end of the month would see George working happily with John Lennon, contributing lead guitar and piano to Lennon's "Instant Karma" single. Harrison even felt charitable enough to add his guitar chops to Yoko Ono's B-side "Who Has Seen the Wind?"

After assisting John it was only fair that George should lend a hand to Ringo, producing and adding his distinctive guitar arpeggios to Starr's début 7-inch, "It Don't Come Easy." When the song was released it would be credited solely to Starkey, but legend has it that Harrison helped the drummer write the song, and a polished version with George on lead vocals does exist. Either way it was a world-wide top ten smash, which was a good sign for upcoming Harrison releases. George also produced Ringo's follow up single – "Back Off Boogaloo" which was, if anything, an even bigger hit in March 1972, certainly in Britain.

In late April Harrison traveled to New York City to check out Apple's new offices on Broadway and visit a few friends. While he was there George gave a frank interview to a New York City radio station, in which he discussed Paul's recent break-up announcement.

The compelling interview is confusing because on the one hand Harrison seems convinced that the Beatles will work together again, saying: "I'm sure that after we've all completed an album or even two albums each, then that novelty will have worn off."

Though Harrison stated he felt it would be "very selfish if the Beatles don't record together [again]," it was abundantly clear that Harrison was *relieved* to be an ex-Beatle, saying, "I got tired of being with the Beatles. Because musically it was like being in a bag and they wouldn't let me out the bag, which was mainly Paul at that time. The conflict musically for me was Paul. And yet I could play with any other band or musician and have a reasonably good time."

It was clear from the interview that Harrison had a number of issues with Paul McCartney that would take several years for the two of them to fully resolve. "I get on well with Ringo and John," Harrison would explain, "and I try my best to get on well with Paul . . . It's just a thing like, you know, he'd written all these songs for years and stuff, and Paul and I went to school together. I got the feeling that, you know, everybody changes and sometimes people don't want other people to change, or even if you do change they won't accept that you've changed. And they keep in their mind some other image of you, you know. Gandhi said, 'Create and preserve the image of your choice.' And so different people have different images of their friends or people they see."

"I got the impression," Harrison would vent, "he still acted as if he was the groovy Lennon/McCartney. Because there was a point in my life where I realised anybody can be Lennon/McCartney, you know. 'Cause being part of Lennon/McCartney really I could see . . . I could appreciate them – how good they actually are. And at the same time I could see the infatuation that the public had, or the praise that was put on them . . . But the point is nobody's special. There's not many special people around . . . If Lennon/McCartney are special, then Harrison and Starkey are special too . . . What I'm saying is that I can be Lennon/McCartney too, but I'd rather be Harrison, you know."

Indeed, George had every reason to "rather be Harrison,"

bragging during the interview that he had "lots of new songs . . . enough songs for about three or four albums, actually."

Not that he seemed in any rush, when, on May 1st he teamed up with Dylan at New York's Columbia Studios under the premise of coming up with one or two new songs for Dylan's next album *New Morning.*

Though the NME ejaculated, "Dylan and Harrison Wax LP together," all this historic summit really amounted to was a spot of informal jamming.

Harrison and Dylan ran through about twenty-five songs, including several Dylan classics, a few old rock 'n' roll numbers and even a Beatles tune or two.

Most of the songs would later see the light of day on bootlegs but for the most part the music they performed was not fit for public consumption. One recording, however, "If Not For You," was seriously considered for inclusion on *New Morning* but was replaced at the last minute by a superior version recorded at a later date, the Harrison version eventually finding its way onto Dylan's *The Bootleg Series* boxed-set released in March 1991.

George obviously liked the song and would record it himself for his first solo album. And perhaps it was this session with Dylan that was the catalyst in getting George to begin work on his début when he returned to London.

In late May, Harrison ran through potential material for Phil Spector on his acoustic guitar – "Everybody Nobody," the lyrically incomplete "Beautiful Girl," "Tell Me What Has Happened to You," "Nowhere to Go," "Mother Divine," the excellent "Cosmic Empire," Bob Dylan's "I Don't Want to Do It" and "Window, Window" (a pleasant folk tune premiered during the Beatles' ill-fated *Get Back* sessions at Twickenham).

It should be stressed that none of these recordings sound remotely finished, and were performed very much in embryonic form. Indeed, it's debatable whether any of these songs were ever *seriously* considered for inclusion on *All Things Must Pass* and of the self-penned demos only "Beautiful Girl" ever received the accolade of an official release, when it appeared six years later on *Thirty-Three and 1/3*. Nonetheless, the fact that none of these songs appeared on his debut album showed, once again, how extraordinarily fecund this song-writing period was for Harrison.

On July 7, George's mother, Louise, died from a brain tumour and was cremated three days later. George would later recall her illness: "She'd got a tumour on the brain but the doctor was an idiot and was saying, 'There's nothing wrong with her, she's having some psychological trouble.' When I went to see her she didn't even know who I was. I had to punch the doctor out because in England the family doctor has to be the one to get the specialist. So he got the guy to look at her and she ended up in the neurological hospital. The specialist said, 'She could end up being a vegetable, but if it was my wife or mother, I'd do the operation,' which was a horrendous thing where they drill a hole in her skull. She recovered a little bit for about seven months. And during that period my father, who'd taken care of her, exploded with ulcers and was in the same hospital. I was pretending to them that the other one was okay." As the Beatle parent who had most championed their talents, even keeping up correspondences with many fans world-wide, Louise Harrison's passing was an especially sad loss.

Luckily work on his début album was an ideal way to exorcise some of the sadness. George finally got around to commencing work on what would become *All Things Must Pass* shortly after returning from the United States. In his April interview on New York radio George had warned that his first album would be "a production album," and so it would prove to be.

George's first step was to enlist Phil Spector to co-produce. Alongside Spector's "Wall of Sound" and the engineering expertise of Ken Scott and Phil McDonald, the sessions would be further complemented by the arranging skills of fellow Ravi Shankar pupil, John Barham, with whom George had worked on *Wonderwall Music*.

While Lennon and McCartney, in their own different ways, had opted for pared down studio albums to mark their solo débuts (*Plastic Ono Band* and *McCartney*), Harrison would instead continue the gossamer production values of *Abbey Road*.

Whether making up for lost time or redeeming himself for the mess he'd made of *Let It Be,* Spector really pulled out all the stops on this album. *All Things Must Pass* would be Spector's real comeback, allowing him to utilise his full bag of tricks: the cast of thousands, the brass section, the massive orchestration, cavernous drums, and, above all, layer upon layer of acoustic guitars and a phalanx of backing vocals dubbed the "George O'Hara-Smith Singers."

The result? A majestic album that was simply breathtaking in its breadth and ambition, an indispensable classic for any self-respecting collector of modern music.

Harrison and Spector assembled an unparalleled orchestra of musicians, the album's credits reading like a who's who of the early 1970s rock scene. Since George had played guitar and added backing vocals to Derek and The Dominoes' "Roll It Over" in June, Clapton would return the favour, bringing not only his slow-hand but his rhythm section of keyboardist Bobby Whitlock, bassist Carl Radle and drummer Jim Gordon as well. Unlike the other Dominoes, Clapton's work would go uncredited on U.K. editions of the album for contractual reasons.

Likewise uncredited at the time was a nineteen year-old Phil Collins (soon to join Genesis) playing congas on "The

Art of Dying," according to Harrison's recollections thirty years later.

Among the other musicians in attendance were Apple protégés Badfinger on acoustic guitars; Traffic guitarist Dave Mason; Procol Harum organist Gary Brooker; pedal steel guitar ace Pete Drake, saxophonist Bobby Keys and trumpeter Jim Price (veteran sidemen better known for their long association with the Rolling Stones); Plastic Ono Band drummer Alan White and, soon to be Harrison mainstay, keyboardist Gary Wright (formerly of Spooky Tooth). It goes without saying that Jim Keltner and Ringo would also be there to pound the skins alongside the ever-present Billy Preston on piano.

All deposed to appear would be suitably impressed by George's compositions, in stark contrast to the attitudes George had endured within the Beatles. Harrison would say, "I'd play it to them and they'd say, "Wow, yeah! Great song!" And I'd say, "Really? Do you really like it?" I realised that it was okay . . . "

Though George initially only planned a single album, sessions went so well the album evolved into a double, and then, in an act of supreme chutzpah, a treble, a first for popular music by a single artist.

All Things Must Pass was described by the *Melody Maker* as "the rock equivalent of the shock felt by pre-war moviegoers when Garbo first opened her mouth in a talkie: Garbo talks! – Harrison is free!" Histrionic hyperbole aside, a triple album must have seemed like a lottery win for George fans.

The album kicks off with the haunting, dream-like lullaby – "I'd Have You Anytime" – co-written with Bob Dylan at his home in Woodstock, during Harrison's stay there in late 1968. "I'd Have You Anytime" was a perfect choice to open the album – the drifting quality of Harrison's vocal (reprised on the quieter parts of "Let It Down") is superb, and in many ways it is a pity that George didn't pursue this vocal approach throughout his solo career.

The song also marked a rare song-writing collaboration for Dylan after he gave George the words to set music to. "I was at Bob's house," George would recall, "and we were trying to write a tune. And I remember saying, 'How did you write all those amazing words?' And he shrugged and said, 'Well, how about all those chords you use?' So I started playing and said it was just all these funny chords people showed me when I was a kid. Then I played two major sevenths in a row to demonstrate, and I suddenly thought, 'Ah, this sounds like a tune here.' Then we finished the song together."

The song would mark the first major indication of George's close friendship with Dylan. The whole album is as strongly influenced by Dylan as it is by Spector's production, and oscillates between the two influences. Although the Dylan-esque numbers are outnumbered and somewhat over-shadowed by their Spector-esque counterparts, they provide the album with a change of pace it probably needed from the sometimes exhausting Spector "Wall of Sound."

"I'd Have You Anytime" finishes with a tastefully beautiful guitar solo and then it is straight into the transatlantic mega-hit single, "My Sweet Lord."

Of course everyone knows how Harrison was successfully sued for plagiarising the Chiffons' "He's So Fine." George was sadly the victim of his own success. The fact that it was such a huge hit was almost certainly the cause of the vulturine lawsuit. George had originally given the song to Billy Preston for inclusion on his *Encouraging Words* album, a recording that had met with a world-wide indifference. Strange that George should have given such an obvious hit away because when George recorded it the song became the biggest hit of the early 1970s, and was granted an amount of air-play usually reserved for Beatles songs.

The songs are very similar in sound but the comparisons should stop there. Had the song been such a direct rip-off of the Chiffons' hit – why hadn't their song captured the imagination as spectacularly as "My Sweet Lord"? Because "My Sweet Lord" was so much more hook-filled and catchy is why. But more of the court case later.

On "My Sweet Lord" Harrison crafted a richly instrumented anthem that gave every religion that I know of at least a passing mention. Maybe George felt that if he included every religion more people would buy it, though I doubt that was his motive. Harrison would later claim that "My Sweet Lord" is not a great song but a great record. Indeed, it seems strange that a simple tune invoking the Lord caught on the way it did.

On "Awaiting on You All" (on side three) Harrison sings that by chanting the name of the Lord one can be free of the temptations of the material world. Ironic then that by chanting the name of the Lord he would later make so many lawyers rich, and I'm not talking spiritually. Nonetheless, on "My Sweet Lord," Harrison chanted His name and was rewarded with a number one single all over the world.

Track three is "Wah-Wah," which builds and builds from its menacing opening guitar riff and just keeps going. Spector adds layer upon layer of sonic bombast, noticeably his trademark brass, percussion and backing vocals, until it reaches a virtual musical orgasm. Spector fans must have been in seventh heaven with this particular track. The song was allegedly written right after George had temporarily quit the Beatles during the *Let It Be* sessions in January 1969, and musically the song reflects the intense atmosphere of the Twickenham sessions. Lyrically the song expresses his feelings about his colleagues around this time, calling them "cheaper than a dime," and describes how they were giving him a "wah-wah." "Wah-wah" being scouse slang for headache, as well as the name of the effects pedal that the song makes liberal use of.

George would say: "I just got fed so up with the bad vibes – and that arguments with Paul were getting put in the film. I didn't care if it was the Beatles, I was getting out. Getting home in that pissed off mood, I wrote that song. "Wah-Wah" was saying, 'you're giving me a bloody headache.'"

"Wah-Wah" has always been one of the outstanding tracks of George's career, a definite to-be-played-at-maximum-volume song. It's a pity George would not write more out-and-out rock. In fact, he would not write another flat-out, kick-ass rocker for a long time.

If George had been angry on "Wah-Wah," the next song "Isn't It a Pity" would be an elegiac, plaintive song of reconciliation. The song starts off deceptively simply with George's voice singing along to the earnest strumming of acoustic guitars, and like "Wah-Wah," builds to an ecstatic climax. First, Ringo's unmistakable drums kick in, followed quickly by the soaring strings and then George's sublime slide guitar solo takes the song into the heavens, where it stays. The composition itself is a simple one built around a simple chord pattern which gives the repetitive fade-out a hypnotic mantra-like quality which is irresistible, even over the course of seven minutes.

Like the title track, it's mystifying that "Isn't It a Pity" didn't become a fully-fledged standard, indeed the song is often overlooked. If "Something" was Harrison's "Yesterday," then "Isn't It A Pity" is his "Hey Jude." Even the harshest critic would be hard-pressed to come up with a better opening sequence of four songs.

Side two kicks off with the galloping "What Is Life," a supreme slice of almost Beatle-esque pop that deservedly reached the top ten in America. It was hard to understand why George didn't release it in Britain, though this wouldn't be the last time Harrison would turn his back on the opportunity of a sure fire hit. Instead it would be left to Antipodean chanteuse Olivia Newton-John to capitalise on the song's obvious appeal by taking her version of the song into the British top twenty in March 1972.

Side two then settles down into a more relaxed groove with a cover of Dylan's reflective "If Not for You" and "Behind That Locked Door." Both songs came complete with Pete Drake's inimitable pedal steel guitar, complementing the country and western feel of the two songs with their honky-tonk piano and shuffle beat drums. The two tracks would not have been out of place on Bob Dylan's *Nashville Skyline* album.

While "If Not for You" was written *by* Dylan, "Behind That Locked Door" was written *about* Dylan, and is a love song to the great man.

Harrison expresses his tender feelings about his friend's reluctance to appear in public with lyrics like "why are you still crying, your pain is now through, please forget those teardrops, let me take them from you."

Showcasing George's melodic flair, "Behind That Locked Door" would, if anything, be more country and western than "If Not for You," which is one in the eye for critics who implied that *All Things Must Pass* lacked variety. It's interesting to speculate why George didn't pursue recording more songs in this genre when certainly he seems perfectly at home in these comfortable surroundings. There has always been a school of thought that George was never really a rocker but a more countrified gent in the Carl Perkins mould, and songs like 'Behind That Locked Door' underline that.

Harrison in this mood had clearly been influenced by Dylan and The Band's back-to-basics approach of *The Basement Tapes* that had been meant as statement against the excesses of late-1960s psychedelia. Unfortunately their explorations would not catch on for long as the 1970s drifted away on a wave of progressive, glam and heavy rock. Indeed, Harrison could have been in the vanguard of the new breed of singer-songwriter had he pursued these acoustic perambulations.

It might even have been interesting had the whole of side two been given over to ersatz country and western *à la* side two of The Rolling Stones' *Exile on Main Street,* but instead the album would revert back to the Spectorian mode – and with a vengeance.

I simply don't have enough hyperbole for "Let It Down." The drums are great, the bass playing wonderful, and the organ and piano mixture subtle and beautiful. Spector really earns his corn on this track, the song is so densely compact and yet each and every part is clearly audible.

Once again George showed that he was the master of building up the tension. "Let It Down" combines a soft/loud approach, the verses a dream like ballad, the chorus a thundering, echo-drenched crescendo. This soft/loud approach would of course be ripped off by every indie band in the world a generation later, albeit without the same subtlety.

I've never quite been able to decipher what George is singing about on "Let It Down" without the aid of a lyric sheet. I don't know whether this is an indictment of Harrison' scouse diction, or Spector's burying him in the mix, as he would do on several of the album's bigger production numbers.

After "Let It Down," George finished side two with a return to the more *au naturel*, acoustic feel with "Run of the Mill," an essay on the situation within the Beatles, and another of the songs on the album that screamed, "Cover me!"

Side three kicked off with the regal and mystical "Beware of Darkness" on which George yet again builds the musical tension to breaking point – this time with his majestic guitar solo. Lyrically the song was quite portentous, or pompous, depending how you look at it. But if anyone had earned the right to "give it some large," it was George Harrison.

The album would again change tack on the delightfully playful "Apple Scruffs," the most Zimmerman-inflected number on the album. Complete with Dylan-esque harmonica solo the song was an affectionate tribute to the groupies who loyally maintained a vigil on the doorsteps of the Apple Offices in London's Saville Row, hoping to catch a brief glimpse of their idols. George describes them in the fog and rain, watching the passersby all stare, which he pronounces "stir" – giving us a brief flash of his strong scouse brogue that was always so endearing. After the heavy lyrical content of several of the songs, it was nice to hear that George hadn't lost the sense of humour that defined some of his best known songs. Rumour has it that when George had finished the track he invited the Scruffs inside to hear it.

After a song dedicated to the Saville Row motley, "The Ballad of Sir Frankie Crisp (Let It Roll)" would be a tribute to the man who built his Friar Park mansion. George obviously felt a personal affinity with the eccentric Crisp, and the album cover would show George sitting happily in the Friar Park garden with a few of Sir Frank's Bavarian dwarfs worshiping at his feet. Or were the gnomes meant to symbolise John, Paul, George and Ringo?

Like "Let It Down," the next track, "Awaiting on You All," is another song I love so much I can barely express it. The song, which wittily sums up George's attitude to *organised* religion, encourages people to open their hearts and let in the Lord, explaining that you don't need a passport, a visa or even legal emigration paperwork before you can see Jesus.

For such spiritual subject matter the arrangement is very

much that of a rock song, book-ended by a great riff, rapid fire drums and lashings of slide guitar. Spector really gives it both barrels on this song with a gospel choir appropriately chanting in the background.

The title track would close side three and would be one of the most beautiful songs Harrison ever wrote, if not *the* very best. A haunting hymn about the mortality of everything, the song was made even more poignant in light of his mother's death, although it was probably written more as a reflection on the break-up of the Beatles. In its sentiments, the song would actually have been an equally fitting conclusion to *Abbey Road*.

As the centrepiece of the LP, the title track should possibly have been sequenced as the album's closing track – at least to give side four a little more "oomphpapa."

The first song on side four – the lubricious "I Dig Love" is probably the closest thing to filler on the entire album. But then things would be a bit boring if every song was classic. "I Dig Love" is a rather scantily clad four-chord throwaway, with a lyrical repetition of how George digs love in the morning and in the evening. Almost a novelty number, "I Dig Love" (alongside "Apple Scruffs") did, at least, provide a little light relief from the album's heavier numbers.

"I Dig Love" can best be described as audacious songwriting, believing that everything will work out in the studio. And the song succeeds almost despite itself.

From the simplest cut on the album George would again shift gears – this time with his foot to the floor on "The Art of Dying," certainly the most dramatic song on the LP. This song is one of the most scintillating rock songs in the Harrison canon, setting off at breakneck speed from its firecracker lead guitar intro. "The Art of Dying" deals with reincarnation, a subject close to George's heart, and one that he would often discuss at length in interviews.

After "The Art of Dying" came the second version of "Isn't It a Pity" which is shorter and pared down as compared with the magnum opus that closes side one. Rehearsed during the *Get Back* sessions, it simply beggars belief that the track was rejected by Martin, Lennon and McCartney – three men whose reputations rested on their ability to spot a good tune when they heard one.

The closing track is appropriately another soulful hymn, "Hear Me Lord," another number given the full gospel treatment by Spector. On this album, Harrison would be the first white man to combine gospel and rock without sounding ludicrous – far too often people use the gospel device as an appalling attempt to disguise fundamentally weak songs.

Eighteen songs and remarkably there were further tracks recorded during the making of the album. These included "I Live for You," (finally released when the album was re-issued in 2001), "When Every Song is Sung" (later to appear on Ringo's 1976 *Rotogravure* album, where it was renamed "I'll Still Love You" and re-arranged, without Harrison's assistance and much to Harrison's litigious chagrin) and the upbeat "Down to the River," a Basement Tapes-inspired 12-bar yodel about the joys of fishing (that was later drastically reworked as "Rocking Chair in Hawaii" on the posthumous 2003s *Brainwashed* LP).

And still there was another whole disc to go – although the music on record three was never intended to be as breathtaking as its two vinyl predecessors.

Disc three, entitled "Apple Jam," contained five tracks, four of which were improvised jam sessions, complete with obtuse titles like "I Remember Jeep" and "Thanks for the Pepperoni" (named after a snippet on a Lenny Bruce comedy album). Recorded at Friar Park during the course of the album sessions, the jams featured Harrison, Clapton and his Dominoes, plus Bobby Keys, Jim Price, Gary Wright, and visiting New York rock journalist Al Aronowitz. Allegedly, Ginger Baker plays drums on "I Remember Jeep."

The all-star jams had a heavy blues feel about them and revolved around the usual three or even two chords. That's not to say they're unlistenable and in some places they are quite enjoyable, and certainly the musicians seem to be having a good time. Without being a piece of vinyl that demanded repeated listening, they would be a lot higher up my play list than George's previous two experimental albums, Lennon's avant-garde rubbish, or *Bad Boy,* Ringo Starr's hit-free stinker of 1978.

The exception to the instrumentals on record three was "It's Johnny's Birthday," on which George added new lyrics to the Cliff Richard Eurovision entry "Congratulations" penned by Martin and Coulter. The song had actually been George's thirtieth birthday present to John Lennon.

Whilst critics felt that the final disc may have been dispensable, they also carped that it made the box set unusually expensive. Nonetheless, the jams should be regarded as a bonus rather than an integral part of the album.

The first four sides are one huge flash of brilliance, genius from start to end. Lyrically the album is exemplary – where humour and love songs sit equally alongside songs that deal with Harrison's religious and philosophical pre-occupations. At least these are philosophically sincere, and don't use religion as a money-spinning device like some artists I can think of. Several songs also dea with the break-up of the Beatles, which George was able to express more poignantly and more eloquently than the others. Ringo, for instance, would reduce it to comedy on his "Early 1970" B-side to "It Don't Come Easy."

And let's not forget Phil Spector, as we lavish praise on Harrison. On *All Things Must Pass* George found a talent equal to his own, someone who was able to bring out the best in his songs. Some critics implied that the horn, strings and choir attack was there to compensate for the thinness of George's voice, but this is patronising nonsense; Spector always employed these techniques. And since when did George Harrison have a thin voice? George's voice is in superb form throughout, particularly on the ballads.

Admittedly sometimes instruments *are* louder in the mix, particularly on "Awaiting on You All" and "Wah-Wah." Perhaps Spector wanted to showcase his wide-screen production chops in the *All Things Must Pass* shop-window. There can't be too many complaints because in disguising George's voice on these tracks the technical brilliance of Harrison's guitar playing comes to the fore far more than it had on the majority of the Beatles' albums.

When the album was released, critical reaction was one of astonishment, which is surprising given that this was the man who had written "Something," "Taxman" and "While My Guitar Gently Weeps." Of course critics were aware that George could deliver top quality within a two songs per album remit, but they asked: could he do it consistently over a double album? Their happy conclusion was, of course, yes. Epic, sweeping, even grandiose, *All Things Must Pass* remained George's best album, an album that rivals most if not all of the Beatles LPs.

Ben Gerson, who reviewed *All Things Must Pass* for *Rolling Stone* magazine, hailed the sheer sound as "Wagnerian, Brucknerian, the music of mountain tops and vast horizons," and summed the album up as an "extravaganza of piety and sacrifice and joy, whose sheer magnitude and ambition may dub it the *War and Peace* of rock 'n' roll."

Some reviewers have suggested that *All Things Must Pass* is the most "Beatley" of all the solo albums (because many of the songs had been written for the Beatles) but I don't know if this is so; the album is pure Harrison. The breadth and depth of the album was George's vision alone, overdubs on the scale of *All Things Must Pass* and the cast of thousands were never really on the Beatles agenda, and nor was this album's overt religiosity. Whilst many of the songs would not have been out of place on a Beatles album, Nicholas Schaffner rightly points out in his book *The Beatles Forever* that it would be "hard to picture John and Paul Hare Krishna-ing along with 'My Sweet Lord.'"

George had made a double album of songs to equal *The White Album, Blonde on Blonde* and *Exile on Main Street*, a certifiable every-home-should-have-one classic, and arguably the best-ever Beatles solo album.

Sales of *All Things Must Pass* were phenomenal and reached number one on both sides of the pond, a doubly impressive achievement, given its expensive retail price. To date, the album is certified double-platinum in the U.S.A. and has sold more than three million copies world-wide – more than *McCartney* and *John Lennon/Plastic Ono Band* put together. Far from being overshadowed in the Beatle solo stakes by Lennon and McCartney, Harrison had emerged in 1970 as the early pacesetter.

McCartney was charitable to his former colleague – quoted around the time of the album's release he would say, "I think George has shown recently that he was no dummy. I think we're really good, each one of us, individually."

Lennon, however, seemed less impressed saying in late 1970, "Every time I put the radio on it's 'oh my Lord' – I'm beginning to think there must be a God!", referring to the fact that the lead single "My Sweet Lord" had reached number one in both Britain and The States simultaneously.

Harrison was clearly upset by Lennon's comments, which he heard about from a third party. "I remember John was really negative at the time," George recalled, "but I was away and he came 'round to my house, and there was a friend of mine living there who was a friend of John's. He saw the album cover and said, 'He must be f***ing mad, putting three records out. And look at the picture on the front, he looks like an asthmatic Leon Russell.'"

Not that George would have lost too much sleep over Lennon's jealousy because, for the meanwhile, everything he touched turned to gold. *All Things Must Pass* was such a masterpiece that topping it would be a mountain to climb. The perception that he failed to do this would lead many critics and fans to dismiss the rest of his career, which is completely erroneous.

Despite its title, the album has stood up well to the passing of time. As fashions changed *All Things Must Pass* would be a forgotten album for a long time, though its time would deservedly come again.

After such a tsunami of songs Harrison still had more to give. Sitting contentedly on top of his pile of accolades, gold discs and number ones, George volunteered to try and resurrect Ronnie Spector's career. As part of her husband's deal with Apple, John and George had requested his wife's signature on an Apple record deal of her own.

In early February 1971, Ronnie was flown over to England to record some songs with George and Phil Spector overseeing a backing group that included Jim Gordon on drums, Klaus Voormann and Carl Radle on bass, and Leon Russell and Gary Wright on keyboards.

Ronnie had been excited at the prospect of singing a hit like "My Sweet Lord." What she got instead was "Try Some, Buy Some," which, from her own account of the sessions in her autobiography *Be My Baby,* the chanteuse unreservedly loathed – feeling it was in too high a key for her.

She also claimed not to understand the lyrics – "Exactly what it was he was trying to try and buy wasn't exactly clear," Ms. Spector grumbled. "Religion? Drugs? Sex? I was mystified . . . by the time he got to the second verse I was completely lost. I had absolutely no idea who or what he was talking about. All I knew for sure was that this was not 'something in the way she moves'."

Even though Ms. Spector would later describe the melody as "droning" and felt that the record "stunk" – "Try Some, Buy Some" *was* released as a single, peaking at number seventy-seven on the Billboard charts in America. Even though Ms. Spector's heart wasn't in it, her recording has allegedly always been an all-time favourite of one David Bowie, who released his own version of the song on his 2003 album *Reality*. Indeed, the slowed-down version that George would use (with his own vocals replacing Spector's) on his next album is superb.

There were plans to do an entire Ronnie Spector album, and to this end a backing track of "You" was also laid down, although Ronnie never recorded a vocal, leaving George free to superimpose his own vocal on the song for his 1975 *Extra Texture (Read All About It)* album. Even though John Lennon also offered his help, the Ronnie Spector project never got off the ground, because, according to Harrison, "Phil couldn't last in the studio for more than a few hours." Instead, Ronnie was flown back to the Spector compound.

While George celebrated the spectacular success of *All Things Must Pass* his mood must have been affected by the famous Beatles court case of 1971. Any speculation that the Beatles break-up was a trial separation and not a divorce was brought to an end on December 31, 1970. On this date, after a long year of deliberation, Paul instituted proceedings in the Chancery division of the High Court against the rest of the band to dissolve their partnership and place Apple in the hands of a receiver.

The suit was filed against John Lennon, Richard Starkey, George Harrison and Allen Klein on three grounds. Firstly,

ELLIOT J. HUNTLEY

the group no longer performed together; secondly, Allen Klein had been appointed as business manager by the other three Beatles, against Paul's wishes; and thirdly, McCartney never saw audited accounts of the bands revenue after Klein had been brought on board. In short, McCartney charged that Klein was incompetent, and that Apple was a vast bookkeeping mess.

The main bones of personal contention for McCartney were Phil Spector's production of "The Long And Winding Road," describing it as "intolerable interference with his work," and the delayed release of his first solo album which he called "a restraint of trade." Paul was also ticked off that ABCKO had transferred the film rights of *Let It Be* from Apple to United Artists without his authority.

When the eleven-day court case opened on January 19, 1971, Paul was the only Beatle to attend. The court case ultimately hung upon Klein's commercial integrity. McCartney and his lawyers tried to persuade the judge that Klein was fiddling the commission, that he was awarding himself on royalties, and to prove that Klein and his various companies had had a chequered business history. McCartney's case was helped immeasurably when it was revealed that a New York court, on January 29, 1971, had found Allen Klein guilty of ten U.S. tax offences in "unlawfully failing to make and file return of Federal income taxes." McCartney's QC, Mr. David Hurst, stated that this news had "obviously not enhanced Mr. McCartney's confidence in Mr. Klein."

In his own defence Klein would say that he had saved Beatles from "almost total bankruptcy," and claimed that the current Beatles partnership would benefit Paul in that he would get a quarter of the earnings from "My Sweet Lord."

With only Paul in court, the opinions of the others had to be heard in the form of written affidavits. Harrison's affidavit blabbed, "The only serious row was between Paul and me. In 1968 I went to the United States and had a very easy co-operation with many leading musicians. This contrasted sharply with the superior attitude which, for years past, Paul has shown towards me musically. In January 1969, we were making a film in a studio at Twickenham, which was dismal and cold, and we were all getting a bit fed up with our surroundings. In front of the cameras, as we were actually being filmed, Paul started to "get at" me about the way I was playing. I decided I had had enough and told the others I was leaving. This was because I was musically dissatisfied. After a few days, the others asked me to return and since I did not wish to leave them in the lurch in the middle of filming and recording, and since Paul agreed that he would not try to interfere or teach me how to play, I went back. Since the row, Paul has treated me more as a musical equal. I think this whole episode shows how a disagreement could be worked out so we all benefitted. I just could not believe it when, just before Christmas, I received a letter from Paul's lawyers. I still cannot understand why Paul acted as he did."

Ringo would be more optimistic saying, "The Beatles may yet stay together as a group," although his deposition would also describe to the court how Paul threw him out of his house. Ringo's affidavit would admit how he was "shocked and dismayed, after Mr. McCartney's promises about a meeting of all four Beatles in London in January, that a writ should have been issued on December 31. I trust Paul and I know he would not lightly disregard his promise . . . My own view is that all four of us could even yet work out everything satisfactorily."

Lennon meanwhile would be more disingenuous. In his own lengthy deposition, Lennon stated: "Paul's criticism of Mr. Klein was not fair. Klein is certainly forceful in the extreme, but he does get results. So far as I know, he has not taken any commission to which he was not entitled" – words that would come back to haunt him.

Since the case hinged upon Klein's integrity, Klein had to set out before the court a summary of his commercial history and of his dealings with and for the Beatles. In his affidavit Klein denied that having him as their manager had prejudiced the group. "On the contrary," he contended, "they have greatly benefitted." Klein would also boast that he had almost doubled the group's income in the first nine months of becoming their manager and that due to him the assets of the Beatles partnership were no longer in jeopardy.

In this regard Klein was correct, the Beatles' earnings had improved under his stewardship. Klein's records showed that the group had earned £7.8 million between June 1962 and December 1968, not including song-writing. During the nineteen months of Klein's involvement The Beatles earned £9 million, with £8 million coming from record royalties. Judge Stamp, in turn, rightly pointed out that ABKCO had charged 20% on the whole income coming to Apple, and not the increase that Klein procured.

Paul's argument for dissolving the Beatles business and financial partnership was that the group had split up, each had their own solo career, there were still no audited accounts and basically he did not accept Allen Klein as his manager. Four aspects were shown in support of McCartney's case: the jeopardy of the Beatles' assets from their association with Klein, exclusion of a partner, lack of good faith towards a partner by other partners and the likelihood of eventual dissolution.

In his summing up Judge Stamp stated, "I am satisfied that the financial situation is confused, uncertain, and inconclusive," and called Klein's book-keeping "lamentable." As a result, on March 12, 1971, judgement was given in McCartney's favour and a receiver was appointed to manage the Beatles' business interests until the case was settled. The Beatles' partnership would not be officially dissolved until January 9, 1975.

To "celebrate" the result, John (with George and Ringo in tow), allegedly drove round to Paul's St. John's Wood home, climbed over the wall and threw a brick through his front window!

Paul's victory meant that the Beatles partnership no longer existed and Klein no longer had the power to act on their behalf, although he would still act for John, George and Ringo, at least for the time being. Within a year of the judgement, the other Beatles would not renew Klein's management contract, a move that sparked off several more years of lawsuits between Klein and Apple.

John seemed to take Paul's victory the hardest, starting a spiteful and public war of words with his former partner which reached its zenith on "How Do You Sleep?" – a song that accused Paul of surrounding himself with "yes men" and having done nothing of note except "Yesterday."

The track would be included on Lennon's *Imagine* album and handling the lead guitar chores was one George Harrison. Lennon asking George for help? No doubt John was hoping some of George's gold dust would rub off on him.

Harrison appeared on four other tracks on *Imagine:* playing dobro on "Crippled Inside," slide guitar on "I Don't Wanna Be a Soldier Mamma, I Don't Wanna Die," guitar on "Oh My Love" and the astonishing lead guitar solo on "Gimme Some Truth."

Yet it was the swinging anti-Macca diatribe that elicited the most column inches. George's slide work on the song is nothing short of outstanding – its stinging tone adding to the appropriately acidic feeling of the whole track. Maybe this was George's way of getting some of his anti-Paul feelings out of his system too! "I enjoyed 'How Do You Sleep,'" Harrison later told *Musician* magazine. "I liked being on that side of it, rather than on the receiving end of it."

Lennon would say, "Did you know George wanted to redo his guitar solos on 'Gimme Some Truth' and 'How Do You Sleep?' That's the best he's ever f***ing played in his life! He'd never get that feeling again. He'd go on forever if you let him."

After helping John record a few songs, George now had more pressing matters to attend to – saving the world, though Lennon would not be on hand to repay the favour.

CHAPTER THREE

1971–1973

The Beatles had been trained to the view that if you're going to it, you might as well do it big and why not make a million dollars.

George Harrison, 1971.

After *All Things Must Pass* and "My Sweet Lord," and his distance from Lennon and McCartney's embarrassing public slanging match, George couldn't have got any more popular in the eyes of the public in 1971. But in many ways he was able to top the achievements of his first triple album on his second trial, *The Concert for Bangladesh*.

The Bangladesh concert was certainly the first ever rock extravaganza set up to aid a high profile global crisis, and Harrison became an overnight trailblazer for those who followed in his wake.

George's philanthropy, however, was purely altruistic, and in this way he was arguably the first rock star to show the world that musicians had the potential to be proactive and do something genuinely positive.

The backdrop to the Concert for Bangladesh story was the civil unrest in Pakistan. Eastern Pakistan wanted its independence from West Pakistan's domination and wanted to call itself Bangladesh.

The trouble brewed originally from a language issue. Bengali is the mother tongue in what is now Bangladesh, a predominantly Muslim country. In 1971 the Islamabad government in West Pakistan wanted to make Urdu the national language throughout both Pakistans. The Bengalis objected strongly to this and it led to a large-scale, internecine civil war between the Islamabad Government in West Pakistan and

Bengali-speaking East Pakistan. The situation was exacerbated further when the Indian Army stepped in as a liberator and established the Bangladeshi Government before leaving abruptly.

"Being Bengali-speaking myself," concert co-organiser Ravi Shankar would recall, "I felt sympathetic towards Bangladesh, but even more so for the refugees who had crossed the border into India and were suffering so much, especially the children."

Around this time George and Pattie had begun a six-month stay in America, renting a place in Los Angeles. It was there that George went to visit his Bengali friend Ravi Shankar, a meeting that precipitated the Concert for Bangladesh. Ravi asked George if he could provide some advice on how to raise awareness and money for his war torn native country. Thousands of starving refugees were dying every day and the Pakistan army was doing its level best to destroy the Bangladeshi people. Yet the plight of the Bengalis was invariably mentioned only as a footnote in the daily news.

As Ravi tells it, "My concern was that many of my relatives were there. They came as refugees, a lot of children. So all that was very painful to me and I was at that time planning to give a benefit show and maybe raise 20,000 . . . 25,000 . . . 30,000 dollars, and George happened to be in Los Angeles at that time and he saw how unhappy I was, and I told him. He said, 'That's nothing, let's do something big.'"

George and Ravi had met for the first time at the home of Peter Sellers in June 1966. When George and Pattie went to India in September of that year, Ravi oversaw the start of Harrison's serious study of the sitar, and a friendship and professional relationship that continued throughout Harrison's life was born. Harrison no doubt felt he owed Ravi a debt of gratitude and now it was time to pay him back. "The

Beatles had been trained to the view that if you're going to it," George would say, "you might as well do it big and why not make a million dollars."

George continues the story: "America was actually shipping armaments to Pakistan who were, you know, just massacring everybody, and the more I read about it and understood what was going on I thought well we've got to do something and it had to be quick. And what we did really was only to point it out."

Harrison hatched the plan of staging two benefit concerts with a line-up consisting of a variety of his celebrity friends, compered by comedy genius Peter Sellers (who did not appear). George set the ball rolling quickly: "For three months I was on the phone setting up what became 'The Concert for Bangladesh,' trying to talk people into doing it." Arrangements for the concert, to be staged at New York City's Madison Square Garden were finalised by the end of the month.

According to Ravi, George "immediately, like magic, phoned up, fixed Madison Square Garden and all his friends, Eric Clapton, Bob Dylan, and it was magic really. George called Ringo in Spain where he was working on a film, and talked to Leon Russell and contacted Mr. Klein who has taken care of the business and administration. To conceive a plan and execute such a large scale program and do it successfully in such a short time must be a setting a record in the history of world entertainment."

Harrison would later recall the recruitment process: "I said, 'If you want me to be involved, I think I'd better be really involved,' so I started recruiting all these people. It was difficult at first, but once it got closer to the show I had commitments from so many people that some had to be turned down. Everybody wanted to be in it."

Even more impressive than his networking was Harri-

ELLIOT J. HUNTLEY

son's instantaneous composition of the song "Bangla Desh" as an anthem for the charity project.

Naturally, given George's stature at the time, the straight-forward and genuinely heartfelt single was a huge smash and the Bangladeshi plight was known overnight all over the world, shining a light as it did on those oppressors who George termed the "Pakistani Hitlers."

The unjustly overlooked B-side of the "Bangla Desh" single was "Deep Blue," a plaintive acoustic guitar tune written after a visit to the hospital where his mother was dying.

"I wrote the song 'Deep Blue' at home one exhausted morning with those major and minor chords," Harrison recalled. "It's filled with the frustration and gloom of going to these hospitals, and the feeling of disease that permeated the atmosphere. Not being able to do anything for suffering family or loved ones is an awful experience."

Not being able to do anything may have influenced Harrison's decision to take on the "Bangladesh" mantle, a situation his fame and commercial cache *could* do something to alleviate.

Harrison's commitment to the cause was absolute – calling on favours from the guests who would ultimately appear on the shows, writing, recording and promoting the single; calling finance men, lawyers, and even contacting John and Paul.

McCartney (the tireless campaigner for the pipes of world peace) refused point blank to be part of the equation – citing the Beatles continued business differences as his excuse.

Paul would explain, "George came up to me and asked me if I wanted to play 'Bangladesh' and I thought, 'Blimey, what's the point? We've just broken up and we're joining up again?' It just seemed crazy."

It goes without saying that the "point" was to save starving

Bangladeshi children, but in the end George simply gave up on Paul. Although mystifying in light of the cause, Paul's refusal can be excused when you consider how the other three had treated him and how isolated he must have felt. Nonetheless, as the Beatles main cheerleader he must have been aware of the fund-raising possibilities of a Beatles reunion.

Lennon's non-appearance is more complex. George had made it clear from the get-go that Yoko was not on the embossed invitation list. John hadn't seemed to mind at first, but somewhere along the line something or someone changed his mind and he refused to perform at the concert, unless Yoko was allowed to perform too.

George quite rightly stuck to his guns: Yoko's musicianship was not on par with the other stars he had lined up, and her drawing power was basically nil. Besides, why on earth would George let Ono perform? The show was his baby, and the sight of Yoko would surely have put many a ticket buyer off. The aim was to feed the staving Bengalis; not to deride them with caterwauling. As a result, John unsurprisingly pulled out at the last minute.

It's a deep shame that John and Yoko, two wannabe political crusaders, couldn't even swallow a little bit of pride to help a nation. I have sympathy with Paul, the others had stuck together against him and now they wanted him! Yoko's selfishness and John's pusillanimity are harder to defend.

Humbly, George would nonetheless credit Lennon as an inspiration behind his desire to do something to help Bangladesh: "One of the things that I developed, just by being in the Beatles, was being bold. And I think John had a lot to do with that, because if he felt something strongly he just did it. And you know I picked up a lot of that by being a friend of John's. Just that attitude of, well, we'll just go for it, just do it."

However, the Bangladesh episode can be added to a whole series of "what ifs" that plague the Beatles story. If they'd got back together to do this worthwhile gig maybe, just maybe, they would all have enjoyed the experience enough to get back together for good. We shall never know!

Lennon and McCartney were not the only problems George encountered when it came to personnel. There was also uncertainty surrounding the appearance of the other two main scalps, Bob Dylan and Eric Clapton. Neither had played live for a while and both were rarely seen in public during this period, preferring instead to stay home to feather their own myths. The early 1970s was a crisis period for Dylan, with a couple of badly received albums, *Self Portrait* and *New Morning,* while Clapton was in the middle of one of his token "bluesman-on-the-edge" routines. In fairness to the pair, at least they did show up.

This uncertainty over their participation must have been a source of worry to George, facing as he was being left with Madison Square Garden to fill and only Billy Preston and Leon Russell for company, an enervating prospect if ever there was.

However, even the Bangladesh B-list of Preston, Russell, Ravi Shankar and Badfinger would still probably have beat the motley rabble that gather at the average Grammy Award Ceremony at rock 'n' roll top trumps.

Joining them for the shows was a clutch of the best session men currently working on the planet, including Jesse Ed Davis on electric guitar, Jim Horn on sax, Klaus Voormann on bass, Jim Keltner on drums, a brass section and a "Ben Hur" cast of backing singers.

The idea had been to get together as many people as possible, and with a minimum amount of rehearsal, put on the greatest show on earth. George would later describe the event as "pure adrenaline, and it was very lucky that it came off because all musicians weren't there for rehearsal. We rehearsed bits and pieces with different people but we didn't have everybody all on at one time until the show itself. And we were just very lucky really that it all came together."

The 40,000 tickets for the shows were completely sold out within six hours. This was hardly enough to feed a starving nation in itself, so George employed Phil Spector to record the music and roped in Saul Swimmer to film the event for posterity.

Come the day of the concert, Dylan and Clapton were still causing headaches. Allegedly Clapton was spaced out throughout the whole concert. A deputation sent to find him located him inebriated in a New York hotel room. Luckily they were able to get him to Madison Square Garden where he played note perfectly throughout the whole show.

Dylan, meanwhile, was a nervous wreck, and Harrison was still not sure whether he would actually perform. Initially Dylan had offered George only the *possibility* of his turning up – "I'll consider it man" being the extent of his initial "promise." Dylan did agree to show up for the final rehearsal and sound check and said he would perform, depending on how he felt. Immediately prior to his set Dylan was, according to the event publicist Pete Bennett, hiding in the toilet wracked by insecurity and vacillating as to whether or not he should go on stage.

But perform Dylan did, making the Bangladesh show's billing as "The Greatest Rock Concert Ever," not a bad title after all.

Unlike previous extravaganzas, like the Woodstock, Monterey and Isle of Wight festivals, the Bangladesh show was not staged as a collection of individual performances but as a revue. Another difference was that the concert was not about egos and one-upmanship, and Harrison's presence throughout underlined the notion that this was a one-off gathering of musicians united in a single charitable purpose.

The shows kicked off with Ravi Shankar's "Bangla Dhun." Since the album's track listing was sequenced in line with the concerts, those listening on vinyl had the advantage of being able to skip Ravi's doggerel. The only option open to ticket buyers was arriving fashionably late or having a drink with Clapton in the bar. Ravi is undoubtedly a mesmerising musician and his presence at the concerts was undeniably appropriate, but you know enough already.

After Shankar's set, the main attraction would appear, resplendent in a crisp white suit and orange shirt ensemble, to deliver a powerhouse opening barrage of "Wah-Wah," "My Sweet Lord" and "Awaiting on You All." Thanks to the concert album it is great to be able hear the live versions of "Wah-Wah" and "Awaiting on You All," where, shorn of Spector's drowning wall of sound, George's vocals can be heard with clarity. With the two-drum attack of Ringo and Keltner behind him, the performances were simply almighty. Similarly powerful was "My Sweet Lord," with a particularly precise Clapton solo, and a vocal performance sung by George with the conviction of a true believer.

For such a lack of rehearsal these songs in particular sounded remarkably tight. George was also impressed by the sound, later saying "it sounded really good inside in Madison Square Garden."

After the rousing start, George then introduced Billy Preston to the mike whereupon Preston subjected the audience and future generations of listeners to "That's the Way God Planned It," which is simply generic gospel tosh. Preston's appearance at this point was probably more designed as a way of pacing the show than to any desire on the part of anyone wanting to actually see the man perform.

Next up to the microphone was Ringo to sing his "It

Don't Come Easy" smash. Perhaps the drummer had taken a hit from Clapton's hip-flask prior to his performance because Ringo was notably off key.

George then returned for stabs at "Beware of Darkness" and "While My Guitar Gently Weeps." Inexplicably the former became a duet with Leon Russell who butchered this lovely song with his totally unwelcome redneck hillbilly drawl. Nonetheless, *Rolling Stone* magazine called the vocal duet "a performance of almost stately proportions."

George chose this moment to introduce the dozens of musicians in attendance and the album shows that Clapton received the loudest round of applause on the album, presumably because people thought he was killing himself on smack and this was their chance to say goodbye.

After the spectacle of Leon Russell hamming his way through "Youngblood" and "Jumpin' Jack Flash," George then returned for a superb acoustic version of "Here Comes the Sun," with only the assistance of Badfinger's Pete Ham, who would tragically take his own life before the end of the decade.

This tasteful acoustic segue allowed George to clear the stage, change the dynamic, and introduce Bob Dylan with a minimum of fuss. Though he never committed himself right up until the moment he came onstage, when he finally made it, his insecurities were laid to rest by a ten-minute standing ovation, most of which unfortunately appears on the live album.

Dylan ignored his recent back-catalogue and gave an affecting performance of songs from his peak period: "A Hard Rain's A-Gonna Fall," "It Takes a Lot to Laugh, It Takes a Train to Cry," "Blowin' in the Wind," "Just Like a Woman," "Love Minus Zaro/No Limit" (in the afternoon show only) and "Mr. Tambourine Man."

Rolling back the years with Dylan on these tracks was a very tasteful and sparse backing arrangement from two Beatles (George on guitar and Ringo on tambourine) and the omnipresent Russell on bass.

Dylan rightfully deserved his ovation and his contribution alone must have helped shift units of the live album by the bucket-load, as would Harrison's delicate and moving version of "Something." George seemed comfortable dipping into his Beatle collection, which, after all, was what the punters wanted to hear. By contrast, McCartney could not bring himself to perform Beatle songs in his live performances until several years after the break-up.

The concert then finished off with a spirited group performance of "Bangla Desh," sung with as much feeling and passion as George could muster. After the main body of the song had been completed, George put down his guitar, and left the stage while the rest of the band launched into an extended jam.

As he took his leave, Harrison raised his hand to both salute and reciprocate the audience's applause and acknowledge the teamwork involved in making the concert such a success. The whole show had delivered and done justice, in every respect, to the cause it was aimed to promote and aid.

For the live album, George decided not to tamper with the original tapes, making the record feel like a true musical representation of what happened at Madison Square Garden, with all the bum notes and fluffs captured by the forty-four microphones Spector used to record the songs.

Some critics felt that too much of the album's running time had been devoted to Ravi Shankar, and that far too much of the evening's applause had been preserved on the disc – which meant there was no room for Harrison's concert performance of "Hear Me Lord."

Most, however, felt that the document of such an historically significant event was above criticism. *Rolling Stone* magazine described the concert as "a great show, brilliantly put together by an man who not only knew how to assemble a lot of great musicians but had an instinctive feeling for how best to present them and their music with honesty, dignity, and maturity."

George was typically modest about the whole thing – "I was asked by a friend to help, that's all. This was Ravi's idea. Once I decided I was going to go on the show, then I organised the thing with a little help from my friends."

EMI meanwhile proved to be somewhat less charitable, with an unnecessarily high price for the album, a price inflated by the lavish boxed-set packaging and glossy booklet. In America the record retailed at nine dollars with five dollars per album going to the Bangladesh relief fund, and due to the overwhelming support for the Bengali cause, demand for the album was high when it was released on January 10, 1972. So high in fact that many unscrupulous shopkeepers hiked up the price and kept the difference, completely undermining the spirit of the whole venture.

The album sold huge quantities, taking it to number two in America and number one in England. The problem was getting the money raised to the starving millions.

With the diabolical Allen Klein doing the books, who could say how much made its way to the refugees. This is not libel or mere conjecture: Klein himself had been quoted on February 19 as saying, "I have the ability to think like a thief."

On top of these headaches, Harrison soon learned that his old nemesis, the taxmen (on both sides of the Atlantic) were not convinced that he had set the project up for charitable purposes, believing he had done it for himself and his own profit. In other words, the Inland Revenue was intent on their pound of flesh from George's compassion.

Angered, George set up a meeting with Patrick Jenkin, a high ranking government finance official to try and convince the bureaucrat that the money was indeed needed for the Bangladesh cause.

Jenkin was unmoved by George's impassioned description of the bloody war and the suffering it was causing a developing nation, and instead remained intent on collecting every last cent of the taxes due to the government, which George duly paid out of his own pocket. A facsimile of his cheque to the Inland Revenue can be seen in Harrison's *I Me Mine* autobiography dated July 25, 1973.

In the same book George would lay the blame for the administrative fiasco squarely at Klein's door: "He didn't structure the affairs properly, he went to UNICEF after the event rather than before and since then we have had lawyers trying to solve it with the American tax people." The upshot of all this was that the money was held in an escrow account for many years. Later, when George was asked whether the litigation that resulted from the Concert for Bangladesh had depressed him, he would reply, "Yeah, that is sure enough to make you go crazy and commit suicide."

The dichotomy of the material world and the spiritual world that George wanted to live in was never really put in a starker contrast. You try to do good things and there's always some loser in a dandruff-collared pin-stripe there to bilk some money out of you under the aegis of officialdom. Still it would give George plenty to sing about on his next album.

Harrison himself would later refute the public perception that the project never made any money, saying, "Now it's all settled and the UN own the rights to it themselves and I think there's been about 45 million dollars made."

No matter how exaggerated this might sound, George, in fact, felt that the money raised was a secondary issue, and the main purpose of the concert had been to attract attention to the situation. "The main thing was, we spread the word and helped get the war ended," he would say with pride.

Not even the Conservative government could detract from Harrison's big-heartedness and the people of Bangladesh would never forget. George would later write: "Even now I still meet waiters in Bengali restaurants who say, 'When we were in the jungle fighting it was great to know somebody out there was thinking of us.'"

It's also not out of the question that John and Paul probably wished they had swallowed their pride and participated. It's certainly not out of the question that they were more than slightly jealous.

Though Harrison would later reveal that he felt it was "a poor state of affairs when 'pop stars' are required to set an example in order to solve this type of problem," he nonetheless emerged as an inspirational figure, pop's foremost avatar and conscience.

"The Concert for Bangladesh was just a moral stance," Harrison would later reiterate. "These kinds of things have grown over the years, but what we did show was that musicians and people are more humane than politicians. Today people accept the commitment rock 'n' roll musicians have when they perform for a charity. When I did it, they said things like, 'He's only doing this to be nice.'"

Nonetheless, George had conducted the whole "Bangladesh" exercise with a great dignity and had earned a lot of money without pledges, credit cards or swearing on television. For his efforts George was rewarded with a best album of the year Grammy in March 1973.

In contrast to the first two years of the post-Beatle decade, 1972 would be a relatively quiet annus. Harrison didn't feel the need to push the envelope and he was probably right not to. Not only would following *All Things Must Pass* require time and patience, George would not have wanted any of his releases to interfere with or compromise the commercial via-bility of *The Concert for Bangladesh* album. To their credit none of the other Beatles would release an album to stand in its way until John released *Sometime in New York City* (fea-turing guitar work from George) in September.

If George was enjoying a well-earned break from his nas-cent solo career his serenity would be wrecked on February 28 when he and Pattie were involved in a potentially fatal car crash.

Driving too fast from Friar Park to London, George would wreck their Mercedes on the M4 Motorway near Maidenhead, wrapping it around an out-of-order lamp-post placed inconveniently on a recently opened roundabout, showing that the *Yellow Submarine* cartoon Lennon drew was wrong – some things are Beatle proof.

Both George and Pattie were injured and taken to Maid-enhead Hospital. Pictures of George would circulate the next day, heavily bandaged with blood literally pouring down his face, although the extent of his injuries were nothing a few stitches couldn't fix. Pattie however came off worse, being knocked unconscious and suffering broken ribs, cuts, bruises and a concussion. Pattie was taken to Nuffield Nursing Home in Fulmer, Slough and detained for observation.

On July 12, 1972, George appeared before magistrates to explain himself to the authorities, who were still no doubt peeved about the damaged lamp-post. Charged with reckless driving, George told the court: "I hit a motorway interchange crash barrier because I did not see the warning sign." George was found guilty of careless driving and fined £20, plus penalty points on his licence – a reprimand that I'm sure taught one of the richest men in Britain a stiff lesson!

Meanwhile, money was still pouring into the Bangladesh account, not only through sales of the record, but also via the box office. The film of the concert had received its world premiere in New York City on March 23, 1972, and its London opening over three months later on July 1, 1972. There, the film smashed box office records at the Rialto Cinema in Coventry Street for a single film, due to its round-the-clock screenings.

George would claim the actual filming of the event was a small-scale disaster and putting together the final cut was a matter of making do.

George would later call the cameramen "crazy." Of the footage shot some was out of focus, some of the cameras had cables hanging in front of them throughout, others picked up nothing but black with just a little pin of light in the middle, and others had taped nothing but grainy footage, particularly on the Dylan segment, which apparently Bob liked. George would even go to the extent of giving his guarantee to the artists involved that if they didn't like the film he would take them out of it. Nonetheless, none of George's gripes actually detract from one's enjoyment of the film.

For their efforts on behalf of the refugees of Bangladesh, George and Ravi justly received, in June, UNICEF's "Child Is the Father of the Man" award. What was more surprising was that Klein managed to find his way onto the dais to collect the same award. Given his malfeasant organisation of the event's business affairs, a communal round of pantomime boos would have been more appropriate.

August 1972 would see the first publicly visible signs that the Harrisons' marriage was suffering difficulties. George took a holiday to Portugal without Pattie, staying with his friend Gary Wright and his wife Christina.

George had first met Pattie Boyd on the set of the Beatles' first movie, *A Hard Day's Night,* in 1964, by which time she was already a successful model. Pattie appeared as a schoolgirl in the film's opening scene in which she spoke her only line ("Prisoners?"), though she can also be seen during the Beatles' performance of "I Should've Known Better."

Spotting the attractive Boyd, George invited her to visit his trailer, but as Pattie remembered, "I was loyal, not stupid." It was not long before George asked her on a proper date.

When their relationship became public Harrison stated that: "She's my kind of girl and we like each other a lot, but marriage is not on our minds. We hope to see more of each other when we can. It isn't a sin to have a girlfriend, is it?"

By early 1965, Pattie had moved into George's Esher bungalow and on Christmas day, 1965, George proposed. Pattie would recall in 1968: "We were just motoring along listening to the radio when suddenly he very calmly told me he loved me and wanted us to get married. I think I just said yes or some such nonsense, but believe me, inside I was doing cartwheels. We really were very much in love."

They married soon after on January 21, 1966, at the Epsom Registry Office in Surrey, with McCartney as Best Man and the only Beatle in attendance. For many years theirs seemed a picture-perfect marriage.

However, the already publicity shy George said he didn't want any invasions into their privacy, so Pattie had to give up her modelling career, and ultimately was forced to become "a northern wife," like Cynthia Lennon and Maureen Starkey.

To assuage the boredom Pattie discovered the teachings of the East and it was she who sparked off George's own interest. The Harrisons had taken a trip to India in 1966, and the country fascinated both of them. When Pattie suggested she and George go and hear the Maharishi Mahesh Yogi speak in August 1967, the rest of the Beatles inner sanctum followed suit. However, she would eventually regret this introduction when George fell deeply in love with the religious aspect of the eastern philosophies as this would be a major part in the break-up of their marriage.

While Harrison's solo trip to Portugal indicated how far he and his wife had drifted apart, when quizzed by the press Gary Wright would play the diplomat saying, "George is just driving around Portugal and the South of France, staying with friends and at hotels. He seems to be enjoying himself. He's writing a lot of new things and he seems to be having a good time . . . Sometimes George goes off on his own. Sometimes he takes Pattie with him but I feel he just felt like a holiday and wanted to get away."

This was just covering up the basic facts. Although upon his return George would try to patch things up with his wife, the effort couldn't have lasted.

Pattie dearly wanted to start a family but clearly she was unable to. To get around the problem she had suggested adoption but George would not countenance it. And one must feel sympathy for Pattie in this situation, cloistered and bored at Friar Park like Susan Kane at Xanadu in *Citizen Kane*, and forbidden by her husband to continue her career. Rightly, Pattie defied her husband's objections and did indeed resume modelling.

The main problem was that, in 1972, George's religious fealty was at its most overt, as his next album would certainly show, and this was driving a wedge between the couple. George had by this time become a devotee, though not a member, of ISKCON (the International Society for Krishna Consciousness), to which he donated large amounts of his time and money. In 1973 Harrison's dedication even stretched as far as buying, for the Hare Krishna devotees, a fifteen-room Elizabethan mansion in Hertfordshire renamed Bhaktivedanta Manor. The Manor would serve as one of the most important Hindu temples in Europe.

Explaining his attraction to Krishna Consciousness, Harrison would say, "It was like a door opened somewhere in my subconscious, maybe from a previous life."

Harrison would expostulate on his religious views thus: "If God exists, I want to see him. There's no sense believing in something without proof and meditation. Krishna Consciousness are methods from which to obtain a better perception of God. In that way you can see, hear and play with God. Perhaps this may sound weird, but God is really there next to you."

Pattie felt isolated by George's deep spiritual convictions and must have been utterly desperate for a bit of old fashioned attention.

While his marriage floundered, the trip to Portugal was a creative shot in the arm because George returned to England with a bag full of quality songs with which to make a new album. From October 1972 to January 1973, George would work at Abbey Road on what would become his second solo outing, *Living in the Material World.*

The big question was – with his backlog of Beatles songs now cleared – could George keep up the momentum of his career or had he, as some predicted, put all his eggs in one basket on *All Things Must Pass?*

The strength of his début would be a hard act to follow, bettering it would have been beyond mere mortals and this time there would be no Phil Spector (except on one track) to help. Spector had been scheduled to assist on the album, but unreliability and alcohol consumption rendered him unable to contribute adequately to the project.

In an interview with *Musician* magazine years later, Harrison would relate the story: "Phil was never there. I literally used to have to go and break into the hotel to get him. I'd go along the roof at The Inn on the Park in London and climb in his window yelling, 'Come on! We're supposed to be making a record.' He'd say 'Oh, okay' and then he used to have eighteen cherry brandies before he could get himself down to the studio." In the end Harrison simply felt that continuing to work with Spector 'became more trouble that it was worth.'"

As a result George would not attempt to remake *All Things Must Pass* and this is to his utmost credit. Some critics felt that George had found a sound (on his début) that he should have stuck with, but George wasn't interested in standing still and aurally repeating himself. *Living in the Material World* would succeed in creating a much more intimate and mellow feel that, thankfully, would not replicate the decision to bury George's vocals in the mix. But George had learnt well from Spector and side two in particular would contain some lavish production techniques worthy of the master.

When the album finally appeared it was, like *All Things Must Pass* and *The Concert for Bangladesh,* a beautifully packaged affair that clearly depicted where George's head was at in 1973.

Written, recorded and released on the height of his days of devotion, Harrison was clearly having difficulty combining his desire to attain the spiritual goals he had set himself, whilst simultaneously being one of the most famous and wealthy men in the world. This quandary would be eloquently expressed on the gatefold cover of the album where religious symbols conflict with his band indulging in a gratuitously sumptuous feast, while a stretch-limousine and scantily clad women await their caprice.

The cover showed a symbolic hand-print and came with the dedication, "All Glories to Sri Krishna," while the lyric booklet even came complete with a gaudy image depicting a key scene from the *Bhagavad-Gita.*

In addition, the album's sleeve notes informed us that George would be donating the proceeds from nine of the

album's tracks to charities reflective of their concerns. To this
end Harrison had set up The Material World Charitable Foundation Trust in April, a month before the album's release.

As for the music – all but two of the album's eleven cuts
were in some way an expressions of deep spiritual commitment. *Living in the Material World,* in this way, was the closest George ever came to making a concept album, which of
course was very much the vogue in 1973.

Without Spector, the cast of thousands had been pared
down to a redoubtable nucleus of Nicky Hopkins and Gary
Wright (keyboards) Klaus Voormann (bass), Jim Keltner and
Ringo Starr (drums), Jim Horn (sax & flutes) and Zakir Hussein (tabla), while John Barham would again be responsible
for the string arrangements. Meanwhile, George wisely dispensed with the services of Clapton and handled all the guitar duties himself.

The album kicked off with the heart-felt plea for love and
peace, "Give Me Love (Give Me Peace on Earth)," a spirited
single that immediately answered any questions about George's
continued popularity. The irresistibly catchy chorus, mesmeric
slide guitar solo and lyrically dummed-down version of the
Harrison "message" sweetened the pill for record buyers and
justifiably sent it to number one on the American charts.

Since George was the only guitar player on this album his
slide chops would be very much the order of the day on many
of the album's tracks. Never more so than on the excellent second track "Sue Me, Sue You Blues." A biting diatribe, "Sue Me,
Sue You Blues" deals with his Apple-related legal escapades
with a good pinch of humour – "it's affidavit swearing time/
sign it on the dotted line/ Hold your bible in your hand/ and
all that's left is to find yourself a new band." Indeed, George's
new band really show what they're made of on this track, with
the rhythm section being particularly effective.

The magnificent steel guitar riff on "Sue Me, Sue You

Blues" was a rare, albeit effective foray into blues for George, normally a genre that most 1960s guitarists couldn't keep their ersatz, white hands away from. George perhaps wisely acknowledged that the last thing popular music needed was albums as flawed as Eric Clapton's, Harrison being from a more Carl Perkins-influenced, countrified tranche of stealing from the black man.

His distinctive slide guitar playing was by no means born on *Living in the Material World,* but the album would mark the start of it as George's favoured style of 6-stringed expression. Since George had had no Ravi Shankar equivalent to teach him, he developed his bottleneck technique by trial and error. It's a testament to Harrison's assiduous musicianship that he soon became one of the world's best slide players.

Harrison would claim that the next track "The Light That Has Lighted the World" was actually written for fellow Liverpudlian Cilla Black. In trying to relate to Cilla, George wrote a song dealing with the perception that they'd altered since they'd both left Liverpool, and how this is somehow resented by people who just won't accept change in a person. How could George reasonably be expected to be the jovial mop-top always ready with a lop-sided grin and a "fab" quip after all he had been through?

The sparse piano backing (later joined by a tasteful rhythm section of bass, drums and jangling acoustic guitars) sounded a million miles away from the symphonics of *All Things Must Pass.* What was perfectly in keeping with his début was the beautiful slide guitar solo on the song, showing once again that George had the right stuff to challenge the best of this approach to axe-wielding.

"Don't Let Me Wait Too Long" would be a superlative slice of almost McCartney-esque pop, and once again his exquisite slide guitar is very much to the fore. The hook-filled "Don't Let Me Wait Too Long" could easily have been another hit single and is certainly one of the greatest up-tempo love songs of George's career. And like McCartney says, what's wrong with silly love songs?

Aside from "Sue Me, Sue You Blues," "Don't Let Me Wait Too Long" was the only track on the album not concerned with spiritual bug-bears, and it's interesting to speculate as to who it was written about given that his marriage to Pattie was very much on the rocks.

The bullish mood of "Don't Let Me Wait Too Long" is succeeded by "Who Can See It," a beautiful ballad on which Harrison clearly had Roy Orbison at the back of his mind when writing it. An aching, yearning masterpiece.

Side one closes with the title track which has always posed a problem for me in that I don't like it but can't explain why. On the face of it the song is a fairly straightforward Harrisong, a humorous lyric that relates Harrison's thirty-year life story in the "material" world, name checking each of the other Beatles on the way. That said, in places the lyrics are a trifle guileless.

Jim Horn's brass is also a little overbearing and the complex, powerhouse arrangement is a little out of step with the rest of the more intimate, pastoral mood on the album. Nor is the melody as strong as the rest of the album. The best part of the song is the vaguely Indian middle eight. It has always been interesting why George didn't pursue the Indian theme that he'd kick-started on "Love You To" throughout his solo career. George seemed to reserve his bag of Eastern tricks only for tongue-in-cheek, revisionist songs like this composition and "When We Was Fab," suggesting he had simply moved on.

If the title track was included as a sop to those who found spiritual didactics unpalatable, George need not have bothered – spiritual didactics were at least his original preserve in 1973.

Fortunately, side two would mark a return to the grandiloquent ballad tone of the album that had proved so success-ful hitherto. The second side of *Living in the Material World* is for the most part, almost gospel in feel, and this is where the album sounds most like a concept album. But that is what albums should be: a cohesive whole and George delivered that. The exception to that cohesion was the polished foot-tapper, "The Lord Loves the One (That Loves the Lord)," which has a rocky arrangement that belies its clearly devout message. The drums push the song along nicely but the exces-sively wordy libretto somehow struggles to fit, and certainly doesn't match the rock mood of the composition.

"Be Here Now," meanwhile, is a lesson in understate-ment. This is the sort of song that critics wrote off as a dirge but I find the melody meltingly beautiful. The arrangement is a masterpiece. Behind the soft vocals and acoustic guitar there is the exotic hint of sitars chiming gently in the back-ground, underpinned by a scarcely audible string embellish-ment and faint "George O'Hara Smith" backing vocals. A bucolic tour de force.

The backing track to "Try Some, Buy Some" had original-ly been recorded in February 1971 during the "Ronnie Spector Sessions" when her husband Phil had at least been cogent enough to contribute. As a result, the song is perhaps the most like an *All Things Must Pass* song, with its bank of swelling strings and overblown production. Strangely the song did not chart when it was released in Britain by Spector, although this may be more due to her name than Harrison's – either way she certainly made for a more attractive picture sleeve.

George's yearning vocal on this track is one of the many highlights of *Living in the Material World*, which may have been an accident as the melody sounds a little high for him, a fact George would acknowledge in his "I Me Mine" autobiography.

Ronnie Spector would say that she didn't really under-stand what George's lyrics were about. I've always thought the song was about religion; the song cleverly reiterates George's devotional message in television evangelist terms.

Another highlight on the album is the "The Day the World Gets Round" with its stunning structure and melody twists and an emotional lyric, due to the fact that it was written the day after the Bangladesh concerts. John Barham's string accompaniment complements the song's mood perfectly and the most enjoyable moment in the song is when George lets rip with his vocals on the middle eight. This was another song that would not have been out of place on *All Things Must Pass,* and a strong candidate for the *Material World* album's best song.

The album ended on yet another high with "That Is All," a lush orchestral prayer where George really does prostrate himself at His feet. This is especially noticeable in the song's concluding stanza, in which George almost sounds like he's giving his own testimony in a Salem Witch Trial, but then again, the sentiments are perfectly in keeping with the tone of the whole album.

The hymn-like song cycle of the last three tracks is as strong a sequence of songs as anything on *All Things Must Pass* and peremptorily contradicted those expecting Hari to fail with his stock of songs exhausted.

On *Living in the Material World* Harrison presented a tablet of stone on which he had written the basic attraction of spiritual enlightenment, and the critics and fans alike welcomed the album with open arms. Though some reviewers felt the album a touch *over*-religious in places, few felt that this detracted from the album's charm and the strength of Harrison's song-writing. The spiritual subject matter certainly made for more effective lyrical inspiration than the radical politics of Lennon's *Sometime in New York City,* and the LP has unarguably stood the test of time much better as well.

Rolling Stone magazine described *Living in the Material*

World as "the most concise, universally conceived work by a former Beatle since *John Lennon/Plastic Ono Band*," and called the album "a pop religious ceremony for all seasons and a profoundly seductive record. Harrison's rapt dedication infuses his musicality so completely that the album stands alone as an article of faith, miraculous in its radiance."

Released in May 1973 in the U.S.A. and June in the U.K., record buyers in America would reward Harrison's promotion of his religious beliefs by sending it to the top of the charts, the second and last time that Harrison accomplished this Stateside.

Both *Living in the Material World* and the "Give Me Love" single would be up against McCartney's *Red Rose Speedway* album and its sublime lead single, "My Love." As it happened, all four releases reached number one in America, with "Give Me Love" knocking "My Love" off the top spot on the Billboard Hot 100 in June.

Not that Macca seemed to mind, generously calling "Give Me Love" "very nice" and praising the song's time changes and "ace" guitar solo.

The "Give Me Love" single also had that rarest of all George commodities, a B-side not from the album – "Miss O'Dell" – a playful but throwaway ditty that Harrison somewhat compromises by corpsing throughout and shows how seriously he treats the recording by stating Paul McCartney's childhood phone number during the coda.

Although now somewhat overlooked, *Living in the Material World* is indisputably a lost classic. Contrary to the revision of music historians, the album was actually only an ever-so-slightly inferior cousin to *All Things Must Pass.*

Living in the Material World kept up the standard of good work and, although it didn't necessarily alter the public's perception as to what he represented musically, its success kept Harrison's solo career firmly on the rails.

CHAPTER FOUR

1973-1974

I'd rather she was with him than some dope.
George Harrison, 1974

With *Living in the Material World* completed, Harrison could afford to take time out to help Ringo make *his* first solo album proper.

On March 13, 1973, Harrison met up with Lennon and Starr in Los Angeles, a meeting that had been arranged to discuss their various Klein related headaches. Later that night the three of them would find the perfect aspirin by recording together for the first time since August 1969.

At Sunset Sound Studios in Los Angeles George and John would help Starr record "I'm the Greatest," the song that would become the opening track on the *Ringo* album. Though written by Lennon, the song was a semi-autobiographical account of Ringo's life from Liverpool through to his participation in "the greatest show on Earth." Alongside Klaus Voormann and Billy Preston, the trio would make ten attempts at the song during the session that lasted approximately eighteen minutes. These eighteen minutes would represent the closest thing the Beatles would ever get to a studio reunion in John's lifetime.

Three Beatles in the same room working together, wow! According to producer Richard Perry: "You could really tell that they were excited. There was such a fantastic energy coming out of the room. It was really sensational." And the results successful! Of "I'm the Greatest," *Rolling Stone* magazine observed, "A stunning alchemy occurs. The small matter of John's pungent sardonic backup vocal and a Harrison guitar part that burns . . . energises this song beyond all explanation."

John would say of "I'm The Greatest": "I really enjoyed working with George and Ringo again. Unfortunately, Paul could not come out to the States to work on that record because he could not get a visa. But I think we'll play together again."

Naturally, the press jumped on the story, thinking that it was prelude to a reformation, with Voormann on bass, as per earlier rumours. Billy Preston played down these hopes by saying that John and George "were just looking for something to do, just playing together and having a good time." The truth of it was that John wouldn't see George again for quite some time.

All the Beatles would contribute heavily to Ringo's first fully-fledged solo album. Aside from Lennon's "I'm the Greatest," Paul would donate the saccharine "Six O' Clock," and would contribute an effective imitation sax solo to "You're Sixteen" played on a kazoo.

George meanwhile would be the most generous donor to the Ringo telethon, submitting three compositions, all of which he would play guitar on. There would be the hoedown, "Sunshine Life for Me (Sail Away Raymond)," brilliantly performed with four-fifths of The Band, and the album's syrupy closer "You and Me Babe" (co-written with faithful retainer Mal Evans), on which Harrison provided one of the most effective solos of his career.

The album's stand-out track, however was "Photograph" that George co-wrote with Ringo. "Photograph" was, by a country mile, the commercial high-point of Ringo's career as a composer. The song's "All I have is a photograph to remind me of the places we used to go" refrain spoke of yearning for lost love, one of America's great national pastimes in 1973, as the Vietnam war took many of their young. It's a deep shame that the Harrison-Starkey song-writing team would never write together again.

When "Photograph" was released as a single in September 1973, it would rocket to number one on the American charts; the third and last time Harrison would reach this summit as a composer. It's interesting to note that while George had written three solo American chart-toppers, John Lennon would not scale that peak himself until "Whatever Gets You Through the Night" in 1975. In Britain, Lennon would not have a number one at all until it was posthumous.

Harrison clearly still had quite a lot left in the tank. Two well-received solo albums, a clutch of hits, a Grammy and here he was tossing off number one singles like it was second nature. Who did he think he was, Lennon-McCartney?

Further good news and royalties would arrive when the "1962-1966" and "1967-1970" (commonly referred to as the "Red" and "Blue") double albums were put out by EMI in 1973. Released on April 2, they would sell so quickly that they were certified gold by the RIAA by April 13! The success of the "Red" and "Blue" albums would give EMI the excuse they needed to continue repackaging the Beatles into various compilations *ad infinitum*.

Not that all was serenity and plain sailing in the Beatles camp. Just over a fortnight after the first incarnation of the Threetles had recorded "I'm the Greatest," John, George and Ringo would finally see sense and extricate themselves from Allen Klein's management clutches.

When asked why they had not renewed their contract with the Brooklyn wrangler Lennon would state, "Let's say possibly Paul's suspicions were right!" In November, John, George and Ringo raised an action in the High Court against Klein and ABKCO claiming damages for alleged misrepresentation. Klein, however, responded with a $19 million counter action for unpaid fees, commissions and expenses.

While all this was going on, Harrison had invited soon-to-be Rolling Stone Ronnie Wood and his wife to stay at Friar Park. The idea was that the Woods could dine at a rich man's table, while Ronnie worked on tracks in George's studio, for his forthcoming solo LP *I've Got My Own Album to Do* – an album that was greeted by the public with a resounding "we've got better albums to buy." Wood would repay George's generosity by sleeping with Pattie.

With George away at his rented apartment in Hollywood, supposedly writing songs for Barbra Streisand, Wood and Pattie were given the perfect opportunity to continue their tryst. Unfortunately, nothing can be kept quiet on the "Planet Beatle" for long, and, by late November 1973, Pattie's mental aberration would be common knowledge.

Wood issued the following statement: "My romance with Pattie Boyd is definitely on. Things will be sorted out in a few days. Until then, naturally I can't say very much. We're going to talk it out between us and hope to get a happy arrangement. Meanwhile Pattie has gone back to her home and will be talking to George. I won't be seeing her today."

George angrily denied Wood's statement: "Whatever Ronnie Wood has got to say about anything, certainly about us, has nothing to do with Pattie or me! Got that? It has nothing to do with us – her or me!"

Angry denial or no, there was no smoke without fire and clearly George and Pattie's marriage had gone beyond the point of no return, if she was seeking her jollies from Ronnie Wood!

The end was certainly nigh. Pattie had long felt rejected and ignored by George. The root of the problem appeared to be that George seemed more bothered about meditation and spending his time with members of the Hare Krishna sect than with her. While Pattie often accompanied her husband on his trips to India and was interested in its philosophies and teachings, she did not share George's daily and utter devotion to the cause. As a result Pattie had become increasingly isolated, disillusioned and bored.

As the world knows, it was not Ronnie Wood to whom George would lose his wife. When George bought Friar Park, his decree nisi had, in fact, been living a short drive up the road in the form of Eric Clapton.

George had met Clapton in 1966 and a mutual appreciation society had formed. George recalled their first meeting: "We were in the Hammersmith Odeon, and the Yardbirds were sort of supporting a group on the bill, and I just met him then, but really didn't get to know him . . . And then a couple of years, maybe a year or so later, the Bee Gees, the Cream, were all involved with Brian Epstein originally, so I started meeting Eric and hanging out with him then at Brian Epstein's house. We sort of went out quite a bit with Brian for dinner and stuff, and then the whole Cream thing started happening. Through that period he played 'Guitar Gently Weeps,' and after that he just escaped out of London because some cop was after him. And he bought a house just a bit further out in the country from where I was, and we used to hang out."

Pattie was desperate to get her husband's attention and flirted a lot with Clapton when he came to visit. Though Eric could see from close quarters that things were not good between the couple, he misinterpreted Pattie's cynical ploy to win back her husband's affection and began to fall in love with her.

Clapton would regularly go to the Harrisons' for dinner. According to Clapton, "Every time I left I remember feeling a dreadful emptiness because I was certain I was never going to meet a woman quite that beautiful for myself . . . I knew I was in love. I fell in love with her at first sight. And it got heavier and heavier for me."

In a move of ruthless brilliance calculated to capture Pattie's heart, Clapton began dating her eighteen year-old sister Paula. When that didn't work, he phoned Pattie and asked her if she knew of any girlfriend's who'd be interested in going out with him. Pattie duly obliged and brought a girl down to the studio where George and Eric had been making *All Things Must Pass.* It was there that Clapton played his ace: "Eric was so rude to my girlfriend," Pattie would later recall, "I could hardly believe it . . . he ignored her or made fun of her throughout the evening." The reason behind this masterstroke of smooth operating became apparent when Clapton phoned Pattie and said, "Look, I didn't want you to find me a girlfriend. I meant you." This shocked Pattie, but somehow pleased and flattered her.

As Clapton puts it: "What I couldn't accept was that she was out of reach. OK, she was married to George and he was a mate but I had fallen in love and nothing else mattered."

Clapton was aware that his love for Pattie would threaten his friendship with George. He carried on regardless. "It was an impossible situation," Clapton would concede, "nobody ever steals a Beatle's wife."

Clapton wrote a letter to Pattie saying, "I need to see you and I love you." Clapton was honest enough to acknowledge his difficulty in expressing his emotions to the woman he loved, which is why he put his feelings into songs, such as "Wonderful Tonight" and his most famous pile of lovelorn drivel, "Layla," a deeply anguished and personally heartfelt ditty, that Slowhand co-wrote with his drummer, Jim Gordon.

Pattie says that when Eric played her the song she found "his intensity both frightening and fascinating." What's more frightening to me is that people buy Clapton's records, and what's more fascinating is that Pattie was fooled and flattered by this hokum. Clandestine meetings soon followed at Clapton's home but their affair was brief – despite Clapton's protestations that she should leave her husband, Pattie was not one to carry on extramarital affairs and stopped seeing Clapton.

Clapton had only one card left to play: emotional blackmail. Pattie recalled the experience: "Eric showed me this packet of heroin and said: 'Either you come away with me or I will take this.' I was appalled. I grabbed at it and tried to throw it away, but he snatched it back. At first, I felt guilt. Then I felt anger because it was totally irrational of him to blame me for something he was probably going to do anyway; it was very selfish and destructive." The pressure was too much for Pattie to bear and she went back to George's indifference and superior love songs.

To drown the pain of Pattie's rejection, Eric had decided to embark on a long bout of depression and drugs, a hibernation that would last from December 1970 to early 1973. His drug-fueled seclusion was a necessary thing for the Clapton myth – a man who having pushed himself to the very edge of heroin excess, could then return in a couple of years as a certified rock 'n' roll hero and sell more records. A drug problem was just the injection, if you pardon the pun, that his career needed. As the premier white bluesman in England, did he really have a choice?

With Clapton out of the way with his collection of charbroiled spoons, George did his best to prove how much he cared for Pattie. According to Beatle legend, one night at Ringo's house and in the presence of Pattie and the Starkeys, George blurted out that he was madly in love with Ringo's wife Maureen. It is said that George did consummate his love for Maureen, but since I was not in the room – I wasn't born when this was alleged to have happened – I can't confirm this rumour. The only two people who can are, sadly, now dead.

While George's marriage deteriorated, Clapton was trying to pull himself together. A comeback gig at The Rainbow Theatre with Ronnie Wood and Pete Townshend in early 1973 showed the world that Clapton had finally kicked the drug habit that had taken him to the precipice of death. The man London graffiti artists called "God" was now back and playing guitar in a band that included Ronnie Wood, showing that "God" does indeed move in mysterious ways.

Strange that Clapton should be involved musically with a man who was also soon to be linked with the love of his life. The look on Clapton's face when he heard of the Ronnie Wood developments must have been priceless. I would have given a lot to see how many pharmaceuticals were needed to drown the knowledge that he, Eric Clapton, was only third in Pattie Boyd's affections, behind a man who no longer seemed to care about her and Ronnie Wood! No wonder the man was on his knees.

Pattie, therefore, seemed to have a three-pronged choice, a man who was more interested in meditation, a man who was more interested in medication and a man who was more interested in mediocrity.

After kicking his heroin habit, Clapton set about renewing contact with Pattie and this time he would get his girl. On a visit to Friar Park with Pete Townshend (who kept George talking about their shared interest in spiritual matters), Clapton begged Pattie to leave her husband.

The conversation must have worked because three weeks after Clapton's visit, in June 1974, Pattie decided that her marriage was finally over and left for Los Angeles to stay with her sister Jenny. Before Pattie had even shaken off her jetlag, Clapton would call to invite her join him in Miami.

Pattie's presence seemed to re-energise Clapton and he got his career back on the rails, embarking on a sell-out tour. Pattie was probably grateful to be in the arms of a man who had yearned for her for years and would give her the attention she obviously craved. According to Pattie, George "didn't seem to worry whether I left him or not."

George was not trying to put a brave face on things; he genuinely did not seem too heartbroken about the collapse of his marriage. George would later say, "Pattie and he got together after we'd really split, and actually we'd been splitting up for years. That was the funny thing, you know. I thought that was the best thing to do, for us to split, and we should've done it much sooner. But I didn't have any problem about it, Eric had the problem. Every time I'd go and see him, and stuff, he'd be really hung up about it, and I was saying, 'F*** it, man. Don't be apologising,' and he didn't believe me. I was saying, 'I don't care.'"

Clapton's good fortune was now complete. Having won the love of his life and having kicked his heroin addiction, he celebrated by becoming an alcoholic.

Pattie later recalled her tempestuous relationship with Clapton: "In my naiveté, I believed everything was all right. He wasn't taking heroin anymore, which I thought was the main addiction for him. But, as it turned out, his drug of choice turned out to be alcohol."

At a Press Conference for the Dark Horse tour in 1974, Harrison would claim to be "very happy" about the fact that Clapton had run off with his wife saying Eric was "great" and that "I'd rather she was with him than some dope."

George and Pattie's divorce was not finalised until June 9, 1977, and Pattie and Eric would not tie the knot until March 27, 1979 in Tucson, Arizona. The couple then lived happily ever after until their divorce a few years later.

CHAPTER FIVE

1974

> *The point is, it's all fantasy, the idea of putting the Beatles together again. If we ever do that, I'll tell you, the reason will be that everybody's broke.*
>
> George Harrison, 1974

To say 1974 was a mixed year for Harrison is putting it mildly. While full of surprises and intense activity, 1974 was also a year of negative press coverage and disappointing ticket and record sales. So extraordinarily busy was he during 1974 that the bottom line seemed to be that he simply bit off more than he could chew.

The year would see him stage a full-scale North American Tour, record the worst album of his career, fall seriously ill, and see his marriage irreparably break down.

If that wasn't enough, May 1974 would also see George launch a new record label, Dark Horse. To distribute his new company's product Harrison signed a lucrative contract with A&M Records.

In exchange for $2.6 million, George was required to deliver new acts to A&M and also an album of his own by July 1976, whilst retaining complete artistic control over content. In hindsight, this was a disastrous deal for A&M, coinciding as it did with start of the public's waning interest in Beatles solo releases, and a mystifying one considering the fact that both of Harrison's next two solo albums would still be released on Apple. In fact, A&M would never distribute a single George Harrison album, but that shall be explored later.

The inspiration for Harrison's choice of name for the fledgling label came from the old phrase, as George would explain: "A dark horse is the one who suddenly pulls out from behind the rest and barrels ahead to actually win the race. The one that nobody's bothered to put any money on. That's me, I guess. The very last one anyone would have ever expected to come out a winner." After the success of his first two albums and the Bangladesh concert, Harrison could afford a bit of braggadocio. Could he keep it going?

While George had emerged as the initial front-runner in the solo Beatle handicap, McCartney had gained the ascendancy by 1974, thanks in the main to his confident and assured *Band on the Run* album. After promising starts George and Ringo's commercial stars, at least in England, were now receding faster than Elton John's pre-weave hairline.

So what was George hoping to achieve with his new label, other than tax deductibility? It's strange, that as the fiercest critic of Apple within the Beatles, Harrison had decided to form *another* record company – admittedly one backed by a generous A&M. Alternatively it may just have been an excuse to get his mate Ravi Shankar a record contract, though he would also soon sign the bands Java, Attitudes and Stairsteps, ex-Wings guitarist Henry McCullogh, Keni Burk and the duo Splinter.

Asked what the hopes of Dark Horse Records were, at a Press Conference in 1974, Harrison replied that he wanted it to "be reasonably small. To tell the truth, I've been here just over a week and if I signed all the people who gave me tapes, I'd be bigger than RCA, but fortunately I don't have time to listen to them."

One thing was for sure with Java, Attitudes and Ravi Shankar on his books, Dark Horse wouldn't be giving RCA any sleepless nights. One of his acts, Splinter did, however, have a British top-twenty hit in November 1974 with their Harrison-produced "Costafine Town."

Perhaps George had thrown himself into work to put his personal problems to the back of his mind. And work wasn't the only thing he threw himself into. After the end of his marriage Harrison admitted that he "went on a bit of a bender. I wasn't ready to join alcoholics anonymous or anything; I don't think I was that far gone but I could put back a bottle of brandy and all the other things that fly around."

This little lost weekend may have contributed to the deterioration of his voice, and could only have distracted him from what he should have been doing – making a decent album with which to take on his forthcoming tour of North America.

Sessions for the *Dark Horse* album began in September and only lasted four weeks. During that month George also found time to produce Ravi Shankar's *Music Festival from India* at the Royal Albert Hall, a concert that was also filmed. Though admirable in his desire to further the careers of his label's signings, in 1974, George should perhaps have spent more time concentrating on his own.

Harrison's tour of North America was formally announced to the world in October. Having been the Beatle most in favour of ending touring, who would have predicted that George would be the first ex-Beatle to tour the U.S.A.?

At the press conference at the Beverly Wiltshire Hotel in California, Harrison fielded the usual questions about the other Beatles and the possibility of the Beatles getting together again, even for one night. "If we ever do that," George answered, "the reason will be that everybody's broke." George then went on to say that if he was to play with the Beatles he would "rather have Willie Weeks on bass than Paul McCartney. That's the truth, with all respect to Paul. I don't think the Beatles are that good. I mean, they're fine. Ringo's got the best backbeat I've ever heard and he'll play a great backbeat 24 hours a day. He hated drum solos. Paul is a fine bass player, a little overpowering at times, and John has gone through his scene, but it feels to me like he's come around. I mean, to tell you the truth, I'd join a band with John Lennon any day, but I couldn't join a band with Paul McCartney. But that's nothing personal. It's just from a musical point of view." Sentiments like these could hardly have endeared him to McCartney or, for that matter, to a general public still drunk on the wishful thinking of a Beatles reunion.

Though the tour was a pleasant surprise, there was a problem. The album the tour was meant to promote was far from complete and remained unreleased until over half the tour was over.

In some way George had himself to blame, or at least his concept of time management. Instead of working to ensure the album was ready for the tour, he had busied himself producing the Dark Horse albums: *Shankar Family & Friends* by Ravi Shankar and the underrated *The Place I Love* by Splinter, both released in the U.K. on September 20, 1974.

There was also a bigger problem on the horizon: a sore throat. With an album to record and the start of his tour imminent, the timing couldn't have been worse.

In hindsight, George might have been better off booking an appointment to see a doctor rather than booking a tour. Either way when the tour finally kicked off, his decision handed critics a mighty big stick with which to thwack his backside.

For the *Dark Horse* album and tour George had hired a band of studio hacks: the aforementioned Willie Weeks on bass, Billy Preston on keyboards, Robben Ford on guitar, Jim Keltner on drums, Emil Richards on percussion and Tom Scott on saxophone. The result was an album full of competent, if unexceptional performances.

Because of the spirit of rush release under which the album was recorded, many of the tracks seemed unrehearsed.

"Hari's On Tour (Express)" kicked off both the *Dark Horse* album and the concerts of the tour and though this West Coast sound instrumental was performed brilliantly on the LP, unfortunately brilliant musicians alone do not a good song make.

The first vocal track on the album was "Simply Shady," a song that contained the first indication that George's voice was not at its usual peak. His vocals sound a little throaty and in places his diction make the lyrics hard to decipher. The track is one I've always liked, with its pleasant melody and continuation of the West Coast feel that commenced the album.

Track three was "So Sad," an out-take from *Living in the Material World* which George had donated to Alvin Lee and Mylon LeFevre's *On the Road to Freedom* album released in late 1973. Recording of this track was hardly promising news if George was already having to delve into his reject pile by 1974.

The song was written around the time George was breaking up with Pattie. Harrison would say of "So Sad" in his autobiography, "I like the song a lot as a melody and lyrically, except the only problem with it, is it's depressing." George is right about that, but the song is still one of the highlights of the nine-track *Dark Horse* album.

Certainly the song was a better stab at reflecting the Pattie situation than Harrison's cover of the Everly Brothers' "Bye, Bye Love." Originally written by Felix and Boudleaux Bryant, George added new lyrics to reflect and make light of the Pattie and Eric situation.

The song had been covered more straightforwardly on Simon and Garfunkel's *Bridge Over Troubled Water* monster four years earlier, begging the question: did the world really need yet another cover of this chestnut? If George desperately wanted to draw attention to his broken marriage, a songwriter of his experience and calibre could surely have come up with a better song and something a lot more trenchant himself, as he had proved on "So Sad."

At a press conference George was asked if the song was "a musical rebuttal to 'Layla'." George would respond, "What do you mean, musical rebuttal? That sounds nasty, doesn't it? I'd like to sort that one out. I love Eric Clapton. He's been a close friend for years."

Closing side one, "Maya Love" at least had an energy to it, with some fine playing and a good piano hook. Basically the song is just a blues riff with lyrics sung over the top, rather than the heady cocktail of east meets west the song was probably designed to be. Its vibe and feel, rather than its compositional strengths save the song. Especially nice is the lovely break-down at the end of the song where George's slide accompanies the bass, drums and honky-tonk piano through the fade-out.

Side two kicked off with "Ding Dong," a lightweight New Year singalong, a kind of "Auld Lang Syne" for the 1970s which Harrison allegedly wrote in five minutes. The "Ring out the false/Ring in the true" refrain in the chorus had been inspired by some Tennyson carved over either side of a fireplace in Friar Park.

George is not at his best here. There is very little variety in the saxophone riff played by Tom Scott and this makes the song quite irritating in places. George apparently was inspired to write the song by the chimes of a clock, which is hardly the best conceivable recipe for a melody.

The "Ding Dong" single barely squeezed into the British Top 40 but once again George's voice sounds like it could use a lozenge – the mellifluous authority of his larynx replaced by a throaty rasp.

The album's stand-out track was the title track, even for-giving the "Sesame Street" flutes tootling away in the back-

ground and the fact that Harrison's voice is, again, all but
shot to pieces.

"I was rehearsing to go on the road and I was losing my
voice very quickly," George would explain, "and I hadn't
completed the studio version of 'Dark Horse.' I had almost
finished so I decided, well, as I'm gonna do this live with the
band, I'll rehearse the band, and also then we'll just do it like
a live take of the song, and use that as the album cut."

Harrison defended his tonsils on the track saying he
wished he "could sing like that more often . . . like Louis
Armstrong." In fact, "Dark Horse" would have made an
excellent stand-alone single, backed by, say, "So Sad," a move
which could have kept his solo career on track as opposed to
temporarily derailing it at full speed. Predictably this is the
only song that has really survived from the album, and it was
a joy to hear George perform it live in the 1990s. The *Live in
Japan* album would bring out the song's true potential in a
much more evident way.

The song deals with people's perceptions of himself, as
Harrison brags of being "a dark horse." Unfortunately the
album did not reinforce this definition of himself.

Not that it was all doom and gloom as "Far East Man"
would prove. A willowy, melodic ballad with some nice
chord changes, the song was co-written with Ronnie Wood,
during Wood's ill-fated stay at Friar Park in 1973. Wood also
recorded the song himself on his *I've Got My Own Album to
Do* LP, which only served to prove that even when suffering
from severe laryngitis George could still out-sing Ronnie
Wood, although that is no proud boast.

"Far East Man" was notable for George's genuine spoken
dedication of the song to Frank Sinatra and again the
arrangement is very West Coast, not that that means it sounds
like Captain and Tenille. The bachelor-pad saxophones on
the track are quite tasteful and wonderfully complement

George's slide guitar. Equally tasteful was Billy Preston's electric piano part, sounding not unlike his solo on "Don't Let Me Down."

Like "Maya Love," "Far East Man" came complete with a lovely fade-out and perhaps the album should have ended there because *Dark Horse* reaches its nadir on its final track, "It Is He (Jai Sri Krishna)." "It is He" mainly consisted of Krishna-consciousness psychobabble and the refrain "Jai Sri Krishna" repeated *ad nauseum* over the sound of a wobble board being played by Emil Richards. As a showstopper "It Is He" is clearly wanting.

Even though I dislike the album, I will concede that George's song-writing is still listenable even if the melodies are not too remarkable. The level of preachiness could hardly grow exponentially after *Living in the Material World,* but the subject matter of his lyrics had not really widened. It's interesting to speculate how much of the material on *Dark Horse* would have got through quality control had the album been overseen by Phil Spector's guiding hand. Probably not much!

While the album was released when the tour was nearly over, it didn't seem to affect sales, climbing as high as number 4 on the U.S. charts, which is frankly bizarre. But then, ex-Beatles solo works were appreciated for much longer after the break-up than they were in the country of their birth.

Critics, however, were not as forgiving as the American public and they let him have it with both barrels. *Rolling Stone* was especially scathing about the album. Changing their tune from the praise they'd lavished on *Living in the Material World,* the magazine called "Dark Horse" "an embarrassingly bad record." Their *volte-face* was complete when they said "Harrison's tunes are often formulaic, his melodic talent brittle."

Focusing on what they called the "hardening of his religious attitudes" and the spiritual preoccupations on the album, the magazine damned them as "insufferable . . . His religiosity, once a spacey bauble within the Beatles' panoply, has come to resemble the obsessiveness of a zealot."

It seemed that the good will on which George had built his solo career had evaporated. *Rolling Stone* continued its duck shoot thus: "How long will his fans continue to tolerate such mediocrity? Harrison himself, affecting the stance of the misunderstood artist, claims not to care: 'I don't give a shit, it doesn't matter to me, but I'm going to do what I feel within myself.' His belligerence, however, reveals a fundamental insecurity. In plain point of fact, George Harrison has never been a great artist, as he himself must know. Given his current mood, the question becomes whether he will ever again be a competent entertainer."

All this was a bit strong. "So Sad," "Simply Shady," "Far East Man" and the title track had certainly rescued the album from being the complete waste of vinyl that *Rolling Stone* magazine had insinuated. Their criticism did perhaps show their visceral disappointment at George, whom everyone knew, was capable of so much more. Unfortunately, as far as the public was concerned, the spell had been broken with this album.

The album is the stain on a solo career that is otherwise markedly consistent. Whilst promoting the album George would say that he didn't do personal interviews because there was nothing to say, and suggested that the album would tell people exactly what he'd been doing. If that's any judge he clearly hadn't been writing songs.

Naturally, the album failed to chart in Britain. Song titles like "Maya Love" and "It is He (Jai Sri Krishna)" would almost certainly have alerted the potential record buyer that George's spiritual fascinations were still very much the order of the day – as did the sight of Krishna watching over his flock on the album's cover.

Why did George feel the need to release something so below-par? Had his personal problems so clouded his judgement? After such a sure-footed start to his solo career it is difficult to fathom the fundamental errors of judgement he made on *Dark Horse*.

It's hard to tell exactly what George was aiming for. Maybe the four week long recording session was an attempt at Dylan-esque spontaneity. Or maybe the B-side to "Ding Dong," "I Don't Care Anymore" (which Harrison recorded in one take), was a literal reflection of his attitude, circa 1974.

One magazine inferred that George had buckled under the pressure of composing enough new material to sustain a solo career and the album did suggest that George had run out of ideas. A mystifying proposition considering the gap between *Living in the Material World* and *Dark Horse* was in the region of two years, surely enough time to come up with enough good new songs.

Rolling Stone magazine summed up its vitriol by describing *Dark Horse* as a "chronicle of a performer out of his element, working to deadline, enfeebling his overtaxed talents by a rush to deliver new 'LP product,' rehearse a band and assemble a cross-country tour, all within three weeks." The magazine even questioned whether George Harrison was cut out to be a solo artist.

All that amounted to a very public bottom spanking and the Dark Horse tour would do nothing to quell the tsunami of bile that the *Dark Horse* album had unleashed.

After the album had been completed George was exhausted. He himself would describe this period in his autobiography: "I was doing a Splinter album and a Ravi Shankar album . . . and then during rehearsals I was trying to finish my own album and in the end Denis O'Brien [his manager] carried me out of the studio to my first concert."

The tour kicked off in Vancouver on November 2 and like the Bangladesh concert George arranged the shows as a revue, presenting himself as just one part of the nine-man ensemble, with segments from his featured guests (Ravi Shankar, Tom Scott and Billy Preston) peppered throughout the show. I personally would have felt cheated, had I gone to the concerts, that George didn't confine his buddies to the opening slots when people can hide in the bar.

Faith in one's friends is one thing, as was George's persistent attempts to bring Indian music to a wider audience, but people had bought tickets to see an ex-Beatle, not Ravi Shankar.

The first set in Vancouver contained twenty-four songs: "Hari's On Tour (Express)," "The Lord Loves the One Who Loves the Lord," "Who Can See It," "Something," "While My Guitar Gently Weeps," "Going Around in Circles" (Billy Preston), "Sue Me, Sue You Blues," "Zoon, Zoon, Zoon," "Na Na Dahni," "Cheparte" (all three Ravi Shankar), "For You Blue," "Give Me Love," "Soundstage of Mine," "In My Life," "Tom Cat" (Tom Scott), "Maya Love," "Outta Space" (Billy Preston), "Dark Horse," "Nothing from Nothing" (Billy Preston), "What Is Life," "Anurag," "I Am Missing You," "Dispute and Violence" (all three Ravi Shankar) and "My Sweet Lord."

According to Tom Scott it was only due to Ravi Shankar's urging that Harrison to include the four Beatle songs. "George didn't want to do 'Something' at all," concurred Billy Preston at the time. "I knew he was gonna have to do it, and he started rebelling against it by doing it a different way, rewriting the lyrics. But at least he's doing the song."

"Soundstage of Mine" was a new track written during a sound check – hence the title. Introducing the song at Fort Worth, Texas, George would presage the song as "Just a boogie-woogie tune for you, which we haven't written the words to yet and it's one we made up on the soundstage rehearsal."

On the versions I've heard Harrison vocalises at various stages of the song, suggesting that he planned to add lyrics to it. While there is cohesion and melody to the song, it does still sound like a jam made up during a soundcheck.

The version of "In My Life," meanwhile, was a much more melodramatic re-working of the Lennon-McCartney classic. George changed the words to "in my life I love God more." With the arrangement, it seemed that George had gone out of his way to make his version of this song sound as unlike the Beatles as possible. Indeed, the same could be said of the whole tour.

Keen-eyed readers will note that Harrison clearly only felt that three songs from his newest album ("Hari's On Tour," "Maya Love" and "Dark Horse") were worthy of performing on tour, which was hardly a resounding vote of confidence. The album's delay and the inclusion of "Soundstage of Mine" meant the set-list lacked the overall familiarity factor so beloved of Beatle fans when watching their heroes live.

Sensitive to this fact, Harrison immediately re-tooled the show after the first date in Vancouver: "The Lord Loves the One" and "Who Can See It" were jettisoned, while Ravi's contribution was abridged and grouped together with Scott and Preston's, rather than sprinkled throughout the running order.

The inclusion of his three chums would at least give George the opportunity to rest his voice during the shows, as did his own instrumentals. In some way it was amazing that he had a voice at all after recording, rehearsing, sound-checking and a hectic schedule of back-to-back shows.

However, the only official release of anything from the tour with vocals on it, "For You Blue" (on the first volume of *Songs by George Harrison* in 1988) actually shows that George's voice was on good form, contrary to popular myth.

Nonetheless, whether real or imagined, it was the deterioration of Harrison's vocal skills that the critics used as their main weapon in their attempt to savage the tour. Many critics wittily renamed the tour "Dark Hoarse," and lambasted the presence of Ravi Shankar's name on the ticket stub. Shankar was honest enough to acknowledge that there were "troubles with the half and half combination of Indian and pop music. I suppose only a tenth of the audience came for me and the rest of them were there mainly for George. Neither camp was fully satisfied!"

In defence of his tour George Harrison argued that, "If you don't expect anything, life is one big bonus. But when you expect anything, then you can be let down." Harrison would also deny that he was affected by the adverse criticism: "I know we get ten people who say the show sucks every night. And we get a hundred who, when we ask them did they like the show, say, 'we got much more than we hoped for.'"

Not that this meant that audiences went gaga, their response was, at times, muted, something that Harrison himself conceded. At one show George would announce to the crowd: "I don't know how it feels down there but from up here you seem pretty dead."

At another show when he urged the crowd to chant loudly along with his religious anthems and that "they could blow the roof of this joint" if they did, they didn't! They were there to hear George perform Beatles' hits, not metaphorically buy a pencil from a bald man at an airport.

Still, George seemed in good spirits throughout most of the tour. Most photographs from this period show George smiling from ear to ear, most famously whilst posing for pictures with President Gerald Ford when invited to lunch at the White House on December 13. George would attend with his father, Ravi Shankar, Tom Scott and Billy Preston, the latter sporting the biggest afro ever supported by gravity.

Even so the hectic schedule of the tour, the critical spleen, the state of his throat, the Beatlemania hiding in the shadows, and the fact that George was in charge of the whole damn circus must have been a strain. That George carried it off with a smile and humility is testament to the man's greatness.

And if George needed any more stress in December 1974, there was always an argument to be had with another ex-Beatle. Prior to the tour George had described his relationship with John and Paul as "very good." "I haven't seen John," he would state, "because he's been in the States, although I've spoken to him quite a lot on the telephone, and he sounds to me like he's in great shape. I just met Paul recently and everybody's really friendly. But it doesn't mean we're going to form a band." Nonetheless, the spirit of Glasnost was such that when George met up with John in New York on December 14, Lennon offered to join him on stage at Madison Square Garden five days later.

Sadly, this wouldn't happen, due to Lennon's refusal to sign the agreement to dissolve the Beatles as a legal entity on December 19. Though Ringo had remained in London to avoid a subpoena from Klein, George and Paul were waiting patiently at New York's Plaza Hotel ready to sign the paperwork. John, however, failed to arrive.

Even though he was living in New York, Lennon instead sent a courier delivering them a balloon with a card saying, "Listen to this balloon." George was livid, according to McCartney's recollections to *Playboy* magazine in 1984: "John wouldn't show up! He wouldn't come from across the park! George got on the phone, yelled, 'Take those f***ing shades off and come over here.'"

Though Lennon eventually signed the papers (on December 27), his refusal to do so at the Plaza meeting meant that his offer to appear at George's Madison Square Garden show was inevitably rebuffed. According to John's girlfriend, May Pang, George said, "Tell him I started this tour on my own and I'll end it on my own."

Nonetheless, John and May did attend George's end-of-tour party at New York City's Hippopotamus night-club. Lennon would describe their relationship as amicable that night: "I saw George after the Garden show and we were friends again . . . I respect George but I think he made a mistake on the tour . . . one of the basic mistakes seemed to be that the people wanted to hear the old stuff. George wasn't prepared to do that . . . " Sadly, it is unknown if John and George ever even saw each other again.

And so the tour limped on to its terminus. Harrison would later view the tour as a success, if only from the point of view of the camaraderie that was shared between the musicians and the crew. Ravi Shankar agreed that a good time had at least been had by the band: "Reviews were lukewarm," he would reflect later in his autobiography, "but financially it was not a failure, and in spite of the difficulties we all immensely enjoyed the performing and especially the touring together." However, this was not enough to persuade Harrison to bring the tour over to England.

Before the tour had started George had been quoted as saying, "I either finish this tour ecstatically happy and want to go on tour everywhere, or I'll end up just going back to my cave for another five years." When he got back to England, the cave option looked the more likely of the two.

As Harrison himself says in *I Me Mine:* "When I got off the plane and back home and went into the garden and I was so relieved. That was the nearest I got to a nervous breakdown. I couldn't even go into the house. I was a bit wound up – then when I came in, I looked in the mirror and decided: 'Oh, I'm not that bad after all.'"

Nonetheless, the North American tour would mark the last time that George would wholeheartedly play the pop star. While 1975 would be a better year, it could hardly have been worse than 1974.

CHAPTER SIX

1975-1976

I'll give up this sort of touring madness certainly, but music, everything is based on music. No, I'll never stop my music.

George Harrison

If 1974 had been an *annus horribilis* for George, there was one bright thing to cheer him up and that was his relationship with Olivia Arias, the woman who would later become his second wife. In fact, when put into perspective, being in love beats being in a rock band every time, especially when the press is on your back.

In 1974 Olivia had been working in the marketing department of A&M Records, with whom George had negotiated the doomed distribution deal for Dark Horse Records earlier in the year. Soon she became a secretary for Dark Horse Records and as a result she and George often found themselves chatting on the phone, not only about business but also about the things they had in common. When he finally met Olivia face to face after this brief telephone courtship, George fell in love at first sight. "I fell for her immediately. She's been a very calming influence on me," he would later preen.

Like George, Olivia too had deep religious convictions, and shared George's vegetarianism and passion for gardening, meditation and privacy. Intelligent and beautiful, Olivia was also similarly unmaterialistic. Over the next year, George and Olivia grew much closer, and before too long she moved into his Henley-on-Thames estate.

There was further good news when, on January 9, the 1967 contract that continued to legally bind the four Beatles was dissolved at a private hearing at London's High Court.

The next day McCartney who had fought for four years for this conclusion told journalists: "I'm relieved that the legal links between the Beatles have been separated." (The legal partnership would be finally absolved on April 9, 1975.)

George was probably relieved as well. The settlement seemed to promise a more amicable relationship for the ex-Fabs. By March, George was seen attending a party thrown by Paul to celebrate recording his *Venus & Mars* album aboard the Queen Mary ocean liner docked in Long Beach, California.

With Bob Dylan, Mal Evans and Derek Taylor also in attendance, this party would mark the first time that Paul and George had *socialised* together, since the height of the Beatles' internecine squabbles.

With the traumatic Dark Horse tour and the worst of the Beatles' strife consigned to history, as well as a blossoming new relationship, it seemed that 1975 was already shaping up to be a good year for George.

There were setbacks: in February his Apple film *Little Malcolm and His Struggle Against the Eunuchs* received its West End premiere in February, and despite his own promotional assistance, the film failed to trouble box-office cash tills the world over, although it did win prizes at several film festivals. Nonetheless, *Little Malcolm* must have whetted George's appetite for film production, and he would return to the medium and with greater success before the decade was through.

If *Malcolm* had achieved little, that was nothing compared to the failure of the Dark Horse record label's singles around this period. February 1975 saw the release of two Splinter singles within two weeks of each other: the Harrison-produced "Drink All Day" and "China Light." Both, unsurprisingly, sank without trace.

Not that George was in a position to mock. In February,

his own single "Dark Horse" single became only the second Beatle solo seven-inch to fail to chart in the U.K., Ringo's "Snookeroo" beating "Dark Horse" to that dubious accolade by seven days.

The fact that Beatle solo singles could now longer be guaranteed a top 50 hit in Britain on name or fan-base alone would be a worrying sign of things to come. Harrison was actually not too far away from a time when his singles would have a hard time creeping into the expanded U.K. Top 75!

Undaunted by the dimming of his commercial star (that had once been a supernova) Harrison would begin work on what would become his fourth proper studio album in May 1975.

Most of the album was recorded in Los Angeles with Harrison's usual bunch of studio cronies: Klaus Voormann, Billy Preston, Jim Keltner, Leon Russell, Gary Wright, Tom Scott, Willie Weeks and Jesse Ed Davis. Surely it was about time George ditched these barnacles and their soulless proficiency.

If the sessions for *Dark Horse* the year before had only yielded nine complete songs and one new b-side, George would be even more parsimonious on *Extra Texture (Read All About It)*. *Extra Texture* would contain "You" (and its reprise) that had been recorded as long ago as 1971 and therefore the sessions for his new album would only really amount to eight new songs.

Upon its release, *Extra Texture* revealed a welcome return to form after the disappointing *Dark Horse,* with some gorgeous love songs, a truly commercial lead single, and flashes of the humour that define George Harrison as a songwriter.

The album would also be a departure in some small way – being a very piano-orientated, almost a pop/soul album. The credits listed no fewer than five keyboard players contributing: Russell, Wright, Preston, David Foster and Nicky Hopkins, with a combination of at least two of them on eight of the tracks. George himself would also contribute synthesiser to many of the tracks.

George seemed to believe in the album, granting innumerable interviews around this period, and doing everything he could to make "You," released three weeks prior to the album, a hit single. In Britain it wasn't to be, peaking as it did at number thirty-eight. In America it fared somewhat better, climbing to twenty on the Billboard Hot 100.

The backing track for "You" had originally been recorded at the ill-fated Ronnie Spector sessions. Ronnie herself never laid a vocal down, so George used the instrumental take already prepared, as he had done with "Try Some, Buy Some" on *Living in the Material World*.

George would rightly acknowledge that "it was high for me, singing it, because I wrote it in Ronnie Spector's key and put my vocals on the instrumental track we'd completed."

The song was a credible stab at writing a sort of "Be My Baby" mark two. In spite of the fact that the lyrics are basically Harrison repeating "I love you" for the majority of the song, *Rolling Stone* magazine called it "the best thing he has done since 'My Sweet Lord.'"

If the lyrics to "You" were simple, the rest of *Extra Texture (Read All About It)* would show that George had lost none of his gift for depth. That is, if you can call it a gift, most critics had decided by 1975 that it was George's curse.

One of the album's most thought-provoking numbers was "The Answer's at the End," a gorgeously melodic song of forgiveness, inspired by an inscription on one of Sir Frankie Crisp's Friar Park walls: "Scan not a friend with a microscopic glass, you know his faults now let his foibles pass." I wonder if any of Sir Frankie Crisp's distant relatives ever asked Harrison for song-writing royalties!

The epic sweep of "The Answer's at the End" would not have been out of place on side two of *Living in the Material World*. The five-minute song is pushed along nicely by David Foster's classy string arrangement and a Ringo-esque drum track, for almost three minutes until the song breaks down to bass, piano and the merest veneer of the strings accompanying George's voice. Harrison would say in his autobiography that he was inspired to do this by Nina Simone's version of "Isn't It A Pity," a comment that perfectly describes the feel of the song. This is one of my favourite moments of the entire Harrison back-catalogue, especially when the ensemble returns to see the song through to its conclusion and George's vocals sound a little more impassioned. After the troubles with his voice on *Dark Horse* Harrison sounded fully cured here and throughout *Extra Texture*.

While "The Answer's at the End" would be the first of the piano songs, track three of the album would be one of the few songs on the album that allotted George's slide guitar due space.

Critics derided "This Guitar (Can't Keep from Crying)" for being a lame sequel to "While My Guitar Gently Weeps." Though that doesn't make it a bad song, Harrison made a fatal mistake in making it sound like a sequel. "This Guitar (Can't Keep From Crying)" is a good song in its own right, with excellent lead guitar work from the master, but the title, atmosphere and general structure can't help but draw comparisons with the far superior Beatles number.

The guitar solo is not as tearful or anywhere near as intense and the piano playing nowhere near as creative or as sinister as Paul's is on "While My Guitar Gently Weeps," and "This Guitar . . . " could have benefitted from Ringo's drumming, if it was George's intention to do a Beatle song. It would not be the last time George that would do a sequel to one of his Beatle tunes.

It wasn't just the critics who disliked it, when the song was released as a single four months later, it followed "Dark Horse" into George's growing pile of seven-inch sized misfires.

More successful was the next track, "Ooh Baby (You Know that I Love You)," George's tribute to Smokey Robinson, a solid, hook-filled attempt at white soul.

On his Dark Horse tour, when asked which contemporary artist he most admired, Harrison had replied: "I am madly in love with Smokey Robinson. Smokey Robinson is my favourite."

George would underline this admiration in his autobiography saying "he's probably one of the best song writers around. He writes great lyrics and great melodies and he is fantastic to see in concert because one tends to forget how many good tunes he has written."

Rolling Stone would say of this track that Harrison "fails simply because he isn't much of a melodist," which is patently untrue on this track and pretty much all of *Extra Texture (Read All About It)*. On "Ooh Baby" George pulls off a sincere pastiche of the Smokey Robinson gossamer, and delivers a falsetto vocal coated in velvet.

I would, however, agree with any critic who says, "World of Stone" is a bit ponderous, at nearly five minutes the song could possibly have done with being shorter.

The song consists of two parts: the primarily piano-led first verse followed by a sped up second section that contains guitar, organ and backing vocals, all of which are a bit annoying. George's guitar actually sounds a bit thin and weedy and the change in arrangement seems to hide the fact that the melody doesn't really deviate from its beginnings.

After a 45-second reprise of George's ode to a pronoun ("A Bit More of You") at the start of side two, the album then segues into one of the best songs George ever wrote, "Can't

Stop Thinking about You." *Rolling Stone* magazine seemed to think the lyric was an elegy for his former marriage but it seems more likely that the song was about Olivia, who would of course be the inspiration behind many great Harrisongs to come.

It may sound like hyperbole but "Can't Stop Thinking about You" is right up there with "Something." It's one of those songs where everything comes together – the refined arrangement, Nicky Hopkins' elegant piano, the unmistakably multi-tracked George O'Hara Smith backing vocals, the tender lyric and of course the exquisite lead vocal.

After his much publicised throat problems, George's voice seems, if anything, *better* on this album. Certainly his voice seems more flexible and able to reach the higher notes, as witnessed by Harrison's falsettos on this track, "You" and "Ooh Baby (You Know I Love You)."

If the inspiration behind "Can't Stop Thinking about You" was obvious, "Tired of Midnight Blue" belied a more cryptic subject matter. George would later claim the song was about his depressing experiences hanging out at a Los Angeles night-club with a gang of "grey-haired naughty people." The fact that what was going on in that night club made George "chill right through to the bone," according to the lyric, makes the mind boggle for more information, or at least gossip to sell to a venal divorce lawyer.

The song is actually vaguely funky for a Harrison song, with its popping bass notes and staccato guitar chops. On *Extra Texture* George also finally treats us to a guitar solo worthy of his reputation.

Rolling Stone magazine would call "Can't Stop Thinking about You" and "Tired of Midnight Blue," "the most effective nine minutes of music Harrison's made since his solo career began," which is praise coming from a review that basically denigrates the album.

The penultimate track, "Grey Cloudy Lies," has a melody that seems somehow familiar, though a different arrangement may have made for a more successful song. By different, I mean a backing without the bass moog and Arp strings that seem to soak the song. There's nothing wrong with the song; the problem is the synthetic 1970s sound of these thankfully now obsolete instruments, and we should all be grateful that they are no longer part of our cultural landscape, except when watching Starsky and Hutch re-runs.

Luckily for future owners of the programmable compact disc player, George leaves the real misfire on the album till the end with "His Name Is Legs (Ladies and Gentlemen)," his second parenthetical album closer in a row. Sadly this track is no better than "It is "He" (Jai Sri Krishna)" from *Dark Horse*, and I'm at a loss to second-guess what Harrison was up to with this song!

Primarily the song is a celebration of "Legs" Larry Smith, former drummer with the Bonzo Dog Doo Dah Band. Undoubtedly "The Bonzos," led by the mercurial Vivian Stanshall and featuring Neil Innes were a great cult band, and were clearly a favourite of the Beatles; their contribution to the strip-club segment of the *Magical Mystery Tour* movie is one of the film's highlights. McCartney would produce their "I'm the Urban Spaceman" single, and though Smith would take pride of place in George's inner sanctum for many years, I'm not sure that that warrants the need to write a song about him.

The lyrics seem nothing more than a collection of Smith's zany catch-phrases, without the humour or invention of "The Bonzos" on their best songs.

The arrangement of the song is also a bit of a mess with too much going on. The three-pronged piano attack from George, Preston and Foster, and the dual horns of Tom Scott and Chuck Findlay drown George and Smith's incomprehensible vocals in the muddy mix, making it hard to decipher their punch lines. A quick perusal of the lyrics makes this a blessing, if Harrison is trying to be funny he doesn't succeed.

The virtually non-existent melody is based on a repetitive musical phrase, which would have been acceptable if the song had been brief, but the song is an interminable five minutes, forty-six seconds long. *Rolling Stone* seemed to think the track was Harrison's way of countering charges of being humourless, which, of course, he didn't really need to do.

A more effective joke could be found on the album's inlay sleeve that bore the legend "Ohnothimagain." This self-disparagement showed, if nothing else, that George was aware of his rapid decline from flavour of the month to everyone's least favourite party guest. Keen-eyed George watchers would also have noticed the partly eaten Granny Smith logo (on the label) signifying the end of Apple.

I take issue with those critics who wrote the album off as preachy. I'd love to know in what way "You," "Ooh Baby," "Can't Stop Thinking About You," and "His Name Is Legs" are supposed to be preachy and didactic. Unfortunately George had been labelled. George would later say that he felt that *Extra Texture* was "a grubby album in a way. The production left a lot to be desired, as did my performance. I was in a real down place. Some songs I like but in retrospect I wasn't very happy about it."

Rolling Stone meanwhile would say, "too much of *Extra Texture* relies on a continuation of the vague cant and astral pomposity Harrison's been selling since Sgt. Pepper's 'Within You, Without You' . . . Musically, despite the pleasures of 'You' and a pair of minor successes on side two, the album is sketchy at best, dominated by merely competent keyboard work and Harrison's near total avoidance of any interesting new guitar riffs."

Not content with these epithets *Rolling Stone* would put

the boot in: "Finally, we are faced with the fact that Harrison's records are nothing so much as boring. They drone, and while chants and mantras may be paths to glory in other realms, in pop music they are only routes to tedium. Harrison is no longer a Beatle, as he has reminded us more than we have asked. But if he learned nothing else from his experience in that organisation, it ought to have been that a good guitar player isn't worth much without a band."

Extra Texture (Read All About It) was undoubtedly a massive improvement on *Dark Horse,* which helped Harrison win back some of the prestige he'd lost the previous year, and the album at least charted in his homeland – reaching a creditable number sixteen. Meanwhile, in America, the record was certified gold and reached number eight on the Billboard charts, while "You" climbed to number twenty. All in all, *Extra Texture* was a good basis from which to build for the future.

If "His Name Is Legs (Ladies And Gentlemen)" had failed to sparkle as an exercise in comedy, George's appearance on Eric Idle's *Rutland Weekend Television Christmas Show* would be a triumph.

Pre-recorded, but screened on British TV on Boxing Day 1975, Harrison appeared in two segments – first as "Pirate Bob" in a comedy sketch and then hamming his way through an exclusive rendition of "The Pirate Song" (co-written with Idle). The song's intro is basically that of "My Sweet Lord" before it becomes a Python-esque sea shanty.

The song has yet to be officially released and while the song is not a lost Harrison gem it's worth tracking down on bootlegs, if only for Harrison's salty sea-dog vocal delivery.

The *Rutland Weekend Television Christmas Special* was arguably the first real public indication of George's relationship with Idle, a relationship that would bear more fruit in the years to come. Not only would Idle direct the promo videos for a couple of George's singles, he would also cajole George into appearing in the Rutles' *All You Need Is Cash* film. On top of that, their friendship would also directly lead to the formation of Harrison's HandMade Films.

George would surely have been grateful for more diversions of this sort in the early months of 1976 when Bright Tunes Music's copyright infringement action against George finally came to court in February.

Bright Tunes claimed that Harrison had plagiarised their 1963 song "He's So Fine" (composed by Ronald Mack), and to counter the allegation Harrison would appear in court himself to demonstrate how he wrote the song.

George would tell the court that "My Sweet Lord" had been conceived while "vamping" some chords on his guitar, playing along to vocalised refrains of Hallelujah and Hare Krishna, whilst on tour with Delaney and Bonnie in 1969.

When the tour was over Harrison had returned to England to supervise Billy Preston's *Encouraging Words* album during which "My Sweet Lord" was finished, with a little help from Preston.

Subsequently, Preston's own version of the song was released, selling a few records without threatening chart longevity. Indeed, had George not released his own version that may have been the end of the "My Sweet Lord" story. After all, why would Bright Tunes wish to sue for a share in the royalties of a Billy Preston album track? Why go to all that trouble for a few bucks?

When Harrison's version became a world-wide number one, the blue torch paper was lit and Bright Tunes were quick off the mark. The original action for unauthorised plagiarism had been instigated as early as March 1971.

"The first thing I knew was when Klein said something," George would recall. "He said, 'somebody has made a recording,'" referring to the Jodie Miller version, which had the lyrics to "He's So Fine" sung to the chords of "My Sweet Lord," with a slide guitar part over the top, a version that George called "putting the screws in."

To try to resolve the dispute without litigation, Allen Klein (who was still Harrison's manager at this point) met with Seymour Barash, the president and major stockholder of Bright Tunes.

On George's behalf, Klein suggested to Barash that his client would be willing to purchase the entire Bright catalogue. Unfortunately this ploy did not wash with the greedy Barash who wanted the copyright to "My Sweet Lord" owned by his company, from whom George would receive half of the proceeds derived from the song. Since no settlement agreement could be reached at this juncture, both sides prepared to go to court, a case that was delayed when Bright Tunes were placed in receivership, not long after these settlement negotiations.

It was during this delay that Klein's business association with George, John and Ringo acrimoniously came to an end when, in 1973, the trio declined to renew his contract, effectively sacking him as their manager. Klein would seek his revenge via the "My Sweet Lord" court case.

After the affairs of Bright Tunes had been put in order to enable them to continue the case, settlement negotiations between Bright and Harrison resumed. In January 1976, a few week's before the trial, Harrison offered a settlement of $148,000 (representing 40% of the writer and publisher's royalties earned so far in the U.S.A.) providing he retained the copyright for "My Sweet Lord."

Prior to the trial Bright's attorney described Harrison's settlement offer, as "a good one," though it in no way matched Bright's exorbitant demands of 75% of the worldwide receipts, plus the surrender of the "My Sweet Lord" copyright.

Predictably, the man behind the rejection of this offer was Allen Klein. Klein had attempted to outbid George and buy Bright Tunes for his ABKCO company. To ensure that Bright accepted his offer rather than Harrison's, Klein gave Bright information regarding the royalties generated by "My Sweet Lord," and his own estimate on the present and future value of the copyright. As it turned out, neither Harrison nor Klein could reach a settlement with Bright before trial.

The trial on the issue of liability was conducted from February 23 to 25, 1976, and Judge Richard Owen was called upon to make an analysis of the music of both "He's So Fine" and "My Sweet Lord."

Both sides called expert witnesses to support their contentions. Though George himself testified about the process involved in writing "My Sweet Lord," Judge Owen nonetheless found that "My Sweet Lord" did indeed infringe upon the copyright of "He's So Fine."

George's own experts testified that the musical leitmotifs inherent in both songs were common enough to be in the public domain and all attempts to point out the differences in the two songs fell on deaf ears.

The judge found that while there may have been modest alterations to accommodate different words and syllables, the essential musical piece was not significantly changed.

In court Judge Owen would even go as far as saying that it was "perfectly obvious" that "the two songs are virtually identical." Although he was satisfied that George had not consciously set out to appropriate the melody of "He's So Fine," this could not be used as a defence.

George did concede that he had obviously heard "He's So Fine" prior to writing "My Sweet Lord," and as a result the Judge stated, "his subconscious knew it already had worked in a song his conscious did not remember . . . That is, under the law, infringement of copyright, and is no less so even though subconsciously accomplished." Terming this "subconscious plagiarism," Judge Owen found that the case should be re-set for a trial on the issue of damages.

George appealed on the grounds that it was unsound policy to allow a finding of plagiarism based on subconscious copying, as there was no evidence that he done anything wrong on purpose.

Unfortunately, this appeal fell on deaf ears and the ruling was upheld on the basis that a copyright infringement could be established when the second work is substantially similar to the protected work and the second composer had "access" to the first work, as George had admitted. The Copyright Act did not require the person who holds a copyright to prove that any infringement was intentional to support a finding of infringement.

With that established, the real cruelty to George came in the amount of damages awarded to Bright Tunes. In deciding the award, the Judge had to work out how much money "My Sweet Lord" had made and had to decide how much of its success was due to the "He's So Fine" melody, a calculation that was never going to be an exact science.

Up to 1976 "My Sweet Lord" had earned $359,794 in performance royalties and another $67,675 in sheet music sales. Bright's lawyers also falsely contended that the enormous success of the "My Sweet Lord" single had generated revenue for the other compositions on *All Things Must Pass* beyond that which they would otherwise have earned.

The judge agreed and noted that of the album's other twenty-one songs, only "What Is Life" had achieved any significant degree of popularity.

The judge devised a very specious formula to determine how much revenue "My Sweet Lord" had boosted the sales of *All Things Must Pass* using, as a gauge, the amount of American airplay received by each of the album's songs. This was misleading, as the album's lead single "My Sweet Lord" would obviously get more airplay, especially since it was a number one hit.

The Judge eventually ruled that 70% of the single's royalties were attributable to it's A-side, and also ruled that 50% of the record sales of *All Things Must Pass* were due to "My Sweet Lord."

The decision that 50% of the *All Things Must Pass* songwriting royalties were the direct result of "My Sweet Lord" was simply baffling. Had the Judge done no research into the climate of 1970 and the goodwill the public felt towards Harrison at that time? Did he not read any of reviews praising *all* the songs on the album? "My Sweet Lord" could have been left off the album and *All Things Must Pass* would have seen little or no diminution in sales or quality. People don't usually hear a single and then automatically go and buy an expensive boxed-set triple album on the off chance.

The Judge did not, however, apply the same test to the earnings of *The Best of George Harrison,* since he was not satisfied that the inclusion of "My Sweet Lord" had not disproportionately enhanced sales of the compilation, probably because it contained Beatles songs and other hits. An argument that could equally have applied to *All Things Must Pass.*

Nonetheless using the judge's "formula" the gross earnings for each of the three releases attributable to "My Sweet Lord" were $54,526 for the single; $588,188 from *All Things Must Pass;* and $6,887 from *The Best of George Harrison,* making a total of $646,601.

There was also the matter of the money Apple records had made from its distribution deal with Capitol Records to take into account. Apple paid Capitol Records a sum of money for the pressing of its records, while Capitol's Distribution arm in return paid Apple a significantly higher price for the right to distribute the Apple product.

The Judge applied his rationale to Apple's earnings from the above deal and found that the earnings attributable to "My Sweet Lord" were $130,629 from the single, $925,731 from *All Things Must Pass,* and $21,598 from *The Best of George Harrison,* making a total of $1,077,958. Adding all this together the judge's figures for the total gross earnings of "My Sweet Lord" in the U.S.A. and Canada were $2,152,028, a sum reduced to $2,133,316 by the court after offsetting some agent's fees which George had already paid.

Whilst Judge Owen acknowledged that Harrison was an internationally known artist and that he did provide new lyrics for the song, he still found that three-fourth's of the success of "My Sweet Lord" was due to the plagiarised tune. The judge's blithe ignorance of Harrison's enormous popularity, his status as an ex-Beatle with millions of fans, Spector's amazing production, the lyrical content, George's superb vocal and slide guitar performance was staggering.

The Judge even went on record to state that the intro was a minimal factor in the popularity of this song, and pointed out that the unique melody of "He's So Fine" had already demonstrated its appeal.

"He's So Fine" is a good song but unique is pushing it a bit. If the melody was that good, why was Billy Preston's version not a sizeable hit? The Judge also failed to take into account that the lawsuit boiled down more to emptying a Beatle's notoriously deep pockets than any righteous indignation over copyright infringement.

Therefore, Judge Owen concluded that $1,599,987 (representing three quarters of the $2,133,316 gross earnings) was attributable to the music of "He's So Fine." Owen said, "had it been shown that Bright Tunes and Harrison were realistically close to a specific figure in their settlement negotiations, I could have utilised that figure for the resolution of the issue here." The primary reason that Harrison and Bright

Tunes were not closer together was the fact that Klein was outbidding Harrison, without his knowledge. It was only when Klein offered almost twice that which Harrison had put on the table that Bright Tunes realised that Harrison's offer was inadequate. In essence, what Klein had been trying to buy was a lawsuit in which a millionaire ex-Beatle would have to pay damages! Revenge, in other words, for being fired as Harrison's manager.

The damages portion of the case was delayed until February 1981, because in 1978 Bright Tunes sold its copyright and its rights in this litigation to ABKCO for $587,000. Klein asked that the full amount of damages, $1,599,987, be paid to him. Instead, George asserted that Klein had acted improperly in purchasing Bright Tunes, and therefore should be disqualified from recovering anything from him.

The Judge ruled that Klein was not entitled to profit from his purchase of the rights to "He's So Fine," and that George needed only to prove that Klein's intrusion into the settlement of the lawsuit prior to the trial on the issue of liability was to his "probable detriment." George was not required to show that a settlement would have been reached had Klein not intervened.

The court found that Klein had acted improperly in giving financial information about "My Sweet Lord" to Bright Tunes prior to the decision on the question of liability. Judge Owen determined that Klein's attempt to buy the copyright of "He's So Fine" from Bright Tunes destroyed Harrison's ability to negotiate a fair settlement. Consequently, Owen held that the court would not reward Klein for his breach of the fiduciary duty owed to Harrison, a duty that continued even after the principal-agent relationship had ended.

However, rather than just have Klein hand over his ill-gotten gains, the judge ordered that Klein hold the rights to "He's So Fine" in trust for Harrison, and those interests would be transferred to Harrison upon payment of $587,000, plus interest, thus allowing Klein to "break even" on his purchase. This decision was upheld on appeal.

Klein's role in the whole story was, therefore, rendered pointless. His original offer to Bright Tunes not only scuppered an early resolution to the litigation by encouraging them to reject George's generous settlement offer, the subsequent ruling in Bright's favour on the issue of liability drove up the purchase price that Klein ended up paying. Hardly the actions of a shrewd business brain!

By purchasing the rights from Bright Tunes Klein had surprisingly not recognised that by doing so he was in breach of his duty to George, meaning that ultimately he would not profit from the deal. Aside from huge legal fees, Klein, it would seem, ended up with little to show for his participation in this dizzy affair.

On November 5, 1990, a U.S. Federal Court in New York ruled that George would own song rights to both "My Sweet Lord" and "He's So Fine" in the U.S.A., the U.K. and Canada, and ABKCO would continue to own the rights to "He's So Fine" everywhere else, whilst receiving a percentage of royalties from "My Sweet Lord."

Of Klein's participation Harrison had this say: "The thing that really disappoints me is when you have a relationship with one person and they turn out to betray you, because the whole story of 'My Sweet Lord' is based upon Allen Klein. When they issued a complaint about 'My Sweet Lord,' he was my business manager. He was the one who put out 'My Sweet Lord' and collected 20% commission on the record and he was the one who got the lawyers to defend me, and did an interview in *Playboy* where he talked about how the song was nothing like the other song. Later, when the judge in court told me to settle with them, because he didn't think I'd consciously stolen their song, they were doing a settlement deal with me when they suddenly stopped the settlement, some time elapsed, and I found out that this guy Klein had gone around the back door. In the meantime we'd fired him. He went round the backdoor and bought the rights to the one song 'He's So Fine' in order to continue a lawsuit against me. He, on one hand, was defending me, then he switched sides and continued the law suit and every time the judge said what the result was, he'd appeal, and he kept appealing and appealing until it got to the supreme court. I mean this thing went on for sixteen years or something, eighteen years, and finally it's all over with and the result of it is I own 'My Sweet Lord' and I now own 'He's So Fine' and Allen Klein owes me like three or four hundred thousand dollars because he took all the money on both songs. It's really a joke, it's a total joke."

In the same interview George would claim that the court case didn't affect his song-writing, but in reality his confidence had taken a severe battering and 1977 would see him make the first semi-retirement of his solo career.

CHAPTER SEVEN

1976-1978

The world is very serious and at times a very sad place. But at the same time it's such a joke. It's all Crackerbox Palace.

George Harrison

With George's copyright infringement case on the immediate horizon, 1976 would start with bad news for all *four* Beatles when, on January 4, Mal Evans, their long-time friend and roadie, was shot and killed in a Los Angeles motel.

To make matters significantly more tragic, Evans' shooting, by Lieutenant Charles Higbie of the LAPD robbery and homicide division, was completely unnecessary. A drunken Evans had become violent towards his girlfriend Fran Hughes (with whom he was living after separating from his wife). When the police arrived on the scene of what they'd expected to be just a routine domestic quarrel, they found Evans wafting a rifle and apparently in the middle of attempting suicide. In self-defence Lieutenant Higbie shot Evans four times.

Of the Beatles inner circle, Evans had arguably taken the break-up the hardest. After virtually a lifetime looking after the four most famous men in the world, by 1976, of course, they no longer needed him. George had settled down into a new relationship and a lower profile, John had retired, Paul had severed his links with the Beatles many years previously, and even Ringo didn't need a drinking partner *all* the time. While Neil Aspinall's position as director of Apple was a job for life, with more than enough lawsuits to keep him occupied, what could "Big Mal" do to replace his significant role in the greatest story ever told? Evans had been working on a book *Living with the Beatles Legend,* and was probably waiting for a Beatles reunion, when his services would once more be required.

Indeed, when the Beatles' nine-year contract with EMI finally expired on January 26, 1976, the chances of a reunion looked at their likeliest since the break-up. And with the contract expiry, EMI and Capitol now had the unfettered opportunity to exploit the Beatles legacy, a chance they seized with a zeal that would have made Elton John look like dignified.

A task force was immediately assembled to dream up ways of repackaging previously released material in new sleeves, such as the rather unimaginative double album, *Rock and Roll Music* (remastered by George Martin). Unfortunately such releases seemed to be motivated by greed more than anything else.

Alongside the repackaging task force, EMI assigned another team to listen to the unreleased Beatles studio material stored in the Abbey Road vaults; the first time such a thing had been attempted.

Apparently only song titles which hadn't been released were considered, ignoring the hundreds of hours of rehearsals, demos, and alternate takes. As a result, their initial research only yielded about a dozen titles considered worthy of attention. Since EMI had made the mistake of doing in-house compilation cassettes of this material, it wasn't long before these tracks found their way into the hands of the bootleggers.

At irregular intervals between 1976 and 1985, EMI staff (notably Geoff Emerick), worked on mixing and compiling a single album of this previously unreleased material and this was *nearly* released as an album called *Sessions*.

Another not missing a trick was Bill Sargent, a Los Angeles promoter, who offered the group a guaranteed $50 million for one reunion concert, anywhere in the world for at least twenty minutes. Sargent aimed to broadcast the concert via CCTV to cinemas throughout the globe from which he planned to recoup $150 million.

The Beatles did not respond officially to Sargent, prompting the promoter to double his offer and add a share of the profits incentive scheme. After a swift round of "no comments" the plan was dropped. In September Sid Bernstein, a promoter of their early Beatles tours in America, went a step further, publicly offering $230 million dollars if the Beatles would reunite to do a concert for charity. Again the offer was rejected.

Paul would be quoted as saying, "The only way we could come together would be if we wanted to do something musically, not lukewarm just to get the money. That would ruin the whole Beatles thing for me." Not that Paul needed the money, the attention or a band. His *Wings Over America* tour was the biggest box-office success since . . . well, since the Beatles.

Curiously, around this time John seemed the keenest on the idea of a reunion and Ringo the most opposed, ensconced as he was in recording his Ringo's *Rotogravure* album. *Rotogravure* had been conceived as a sort of *Ringo* mark II, with all three Beatles contributing songs. John would proffer "Cookin' in the Kitchen of Love," Paul would donate "Pure Gold" and George would submit "I'll Still Love You."

Ringo recalled that "I'll Still Love You," "was an old song of George's. I remember the song from 1970 . . . I always loved it and no one ever did it."

Though Ringo liked the song, there was no escaping the fact that, by 1976, neither Paul nor George were prepared to give up anything from their top drawer. Consequently, each of their tunes was pedestrian in comparison to those that appeared on the eponymous 1973 album that *Rotogravure* was trying to emulate.

Paul and John would both play on the album, though this time George would not, busy as he was making his own new album. It was a shame that George couldn't play on "I'll Still Love You" because he disliked Ringo's melodramatic version of this rather dull ballad so much he felt compelled to take legal action against his old friend, although the matter was quickly resolved.

Reunion rumours continued unabated throughout 1976, and clearly the individual Beatles seemed on much friendlier terms. Aside from the *Rotogravure* sessions, the renewed *entente cordiale* would see John and Paul hanging out quite regularly at John's Dakota residence, while George and Ringo were both spotted at Paul's Maple Leaf Gardens gig on May 9, 1976, in Toronto.

Nonetheless, it should be stressed that a 1976 reformation was never likely. Lennon was already one year into his five-year hiatus of self-imposed house-husbandry. Ringo, meanwhile, was already well on his way to becoming perhaps the world's most famous lush, a title that had been his to contest with Keith Moon since the death of Judy Garland in 1969. That left just Paul and George to challenge for the ex-Beatle top spot.

Free from EMI, Harrison would begin work on *Thirty-Three and 1/3* in May 1976. The original plan was for the album to be distributed by A&M records. Unfortunately, George would renege on his agreement with A&M by failing to deliver the album on time, citing a two and a half month bout of hepatitis, that prevented him meeting the July 26 contractual deadline. Unwilling to trust modern doctors, George's hepatitis was eventually cured by the Chinese acupuncturist Dr. Zion Yu, whom he had visited at Olivia's insistence.

"The regular doctor just said to stay in bed," Olivia recalled. "Our Los Angeles doctor sent herbs that we boiled and ate every morning. It really worked." Within weeks of treatment George had regained his vitality.

Another possible reason for the delay of *Thirty-Three and 1/3*, however, was the "My Sweet Lord" trial. Not only had the court case been a drain on George's time it had also made him insecure about his song-writing abilities.

While that case continued Harrison would be rocked by *further* litigation, when on September 28, 1976, A&M tried to sue George for $10 million. Aside from the fact that Harrison had not completed his album by the July deadline, he hadn't returned A&M's £588,000 advance either. A&M sought an injunction against Harrison releasing any music until their case was heard.

According to George, "What happened was, we had a deal for Dark Horse and I had a deal for myself, which didn't happen until this year because I was with EMI and Capitol. They were trying to get together over the two years to finalise all the details. The attorney who was with them when they made the deal was not the one with them when they were filling in the details. He read the deal and he said they were going to use my money to offset Dark Horse. We said, 'No, no. It's in the contract. It has been there for two years. You don't cross-collateralise me and Dark Horse.' And the attorney said, 'I can't believe the other attorney did this to you.' So, in effect, what happened was they realised they had not made themselves such a good deal. Instead of phoning up and saying, 'Now, look, George, we have made ourselves a bad deal. Let's talk about it and work it out,' they found the only legal grounds they had was that I had had hepatitis, so my album was two months delayed. We had in the original contract, that I would give it to them around the July 25. And so they picked on that legal point and said, 'Okay, we'll get him on that.' I arrived in LA with my album under my arm, all happy, and I was given this letter saying, 'Give us back the million dollars,' which was an advance, 'and give us the album and when you give us the album, you don't get the million back.'

Now I turned down a great deal from Capitol and EMI which was of more value, from the money point of view, and guarantees, than what I took with A&M. But I took that because of the relationship we were supposedly going to have, which it turned out we never did. And that was it, I couldn't live with that sort of situation so I left." It wouldn't be the last time that a record company tried to screw him.

The matter was swiftly resolved, and according to George, "almost overnight, me and Dark Horse Records were transferred from A&M on one side of Hollywood Hills to Warner Brothers on the other and a new album, *Thirty-Three and 1/3* was soon in the racks in the record stores."

As the first George Harrison album to appear on Dark Horse Records, *Thirty-Three and 1/3* was something of a new start for George. So-called because it was George's age at the time it was recorded, the LP was a much lighter sounding record than anything Harrison had hitherto released. Olivia's influence seemed to have brought Harrison a more serene outlook on life, and in 1976, he seemed less inclined to pontificate on the horrors of the material world. *Thirty-Three and 1/3* would include songs about Smokey Robinson, Jim Keltner's car, a comedian's house, and a humorous take on his "My Sweet Lord" court case.

For *Thirty-Three and 1/3,* Harrison had modified, if not departed from, the formula of his previous records, being a much livelier record, full of up-tempo and catchy songs that have aged well. In the wake of the disappointing sales of *Extra Texture,* it sounded as though George was consciously trying to return to commercial popularity.

In an interview with *Melody Maker* earlier in the year, Harrison had talked about hiring a producer to help him with his next album, "I'd like someone to produce me, either that or a co-producer or just a friend working with me. I've found there's no way that you can judge your own work. Maybe I should get Ry Cooder to produce me. I've always liked his work. But the nearest I've got to him was waving to him when we were watching Bob Marley and the Wailers." George would stick true to his promise and to share production duties hired . . . er . . . Tom Scott! Given that Cooder has one glass eye it's feasible that he missed George's come on.

Whether due to Scott's assistance or not, the arrangements on *Thirty-Three and 1/3* were a lot simpler and contemporary. *Rolling Stone* magazine, however, disagreed saying, "Harrison's concept of the popular . . . leads him to use Tom Scott as an 'assistant' in producing the album, and the overall sound of *Thirty-Three and 1/3* hums with Scott's presence: it is music with the feeling and sincerity of cellophane." I don't know if this is true, since it's only really on *Crackerbox Palace* that Scott's "saxophonic" influence comes through significantly.

Alongside Tom Scott's saxophone, Emil Richards' marimba and Willie Weeks on bass had been retained from the Dark Horse Tour, while old faces Gary Wright and Billy Preston would still be on hand to handle the eighty-eights. This would, however, be the first album without the rhythm triumvirate of Ringo, Jim Keltner and Klaus Voormann, and the first on which Willie Weeks would be fully represented, alongside Alvin Taylor on drums. George's new rhythm section brings to the table a much more fluid approach and it's difficult to argue with why George was so impressed by Weeks' bass chops.

David Foster had also been retained from *Extra Texture (Read All About It)* and on *Thirty-Three and 1/3* Foster and Richard Tee play some fantastic Fender Rhodes keyboard, the sound of which I've always found hard to resist.

As with *Living in the Material World* in 1973, there would be no supplementary guitarists on *Thirty-Three* and

Harrison's 6-string work is as playful as it had ever been, ably backed on the treble clef by Richards and Scott. Indeed, it was good to hear George get his guitar out of its case after the piano heavy *Extra Texture.*

The bluesy and funky "Woman Don't Cry for Me" got the album off to a rollicking good start. On the track's sexy intro, George's brooding slide guitar had never sounded so good, and the band showcase how tight they would be throughout. "Woman Don't Cry for Me" particularly brought out the best in the rubbery bass of Willie Weeks and the funky drumming of Alvin Taylor.

The song had been written whilst on tour with Delaney and Bonnie way back in 1969 and had almost been included on *All Things Must Pass.* It would have been interesting to have heard what Phil Spector would have done to it. With Voormann and Keltner as a rhythm section, it's my guess that it wouldn't have been anywhere near as soulful. Unfortunately, like *All Things Must Pass,* Harrison's vocals are a little buried in the mix.

The second track, "Dear One" is a melodically simple tune, especially on the verses where it's practically bereft. The chorus is more colourful and exciting even, with its affecting change of pace and curious almost pump-organ feel going on somewhere in the background. According to George, the song was a musical tribute to Paramahansa Yogananda, author of *Autobiography of a Yogi* and one of his favourite gurus.

Things pick up on "Beautiful Girl," with its enchanting melody and swirling organs. Once again the song had originally been written for *All Things Must Pass* but was strangely discounted from inclusion at an early stage. Strange because the song is one of the prettiest ballads George ever wrote. Perhaps its comparatively happy-go-lucky quality made it unsuitable for George's monolithic début and the 1969 demo shows the lyrics not quite finished. When it appeared on *Thirty-Three and 1/3,* George had transformed it into a masterpiece, complete with a thrilling conversational guitar solo, where two axes interweave and answer one another. Appropriately, George would dedicate the song to Olivia.

The jaunty "This Song," meanwhile, with its sarcastic lyrics made light of the "My Sweet Lord" plagiarism case. If George had hoped to offset the costs of the litigation via the royalties gleaned from "This Song" when it was released as a single he would be disappointed, seeing as it didn't chart. Ironically the intro to "This Song" stole the riff from "I Can't Help Myself" by the Four Tops much more blatantly than "My Sweet Lord" had plagiarised "He's So Fine."

"See Yourself" was the first track on *Thirty-Three and 1/3* to return to George's preachy formula. Unlike some critics, I don't have a problem with Harrison's preaching, especially when elegiac arrangements, fresh insights and worthwhile lyrics justify it. But the lyrics to "See Yourself" suggested that Harrison had lost some of his bite, and besides, he'd visited this subject before on "Run of the Mill." Maybe he was just mellowing as he approached thirty-four.

The song had been written in 1967 about McCartney's candour when he revealed he *had* taken LSD in response to being asked by some journalists looking for copy. Nonetheless, "See Yourself" was clearly not completed for qualitative reasons in 1967, aside from the fact that the Beatles would never have recorded it, which I think I can say without fear of contradiction.

Side two kicks off with "It's What You Value," inspired by Jim Keltner's request for a Mercedes 450 SL instead of financial payment for his part on the Dark Horse Tour. The tune also celebrates George's love of motoring and the song has a "drive-time" feel with its funky arrangement, slap bass work and honky-tonk piano. In fact, the song is actually vaguely reminiscent of 1974's "Maya Love," inasmuch as it's a rare rock-out for George.

"True Love," meanwhile, would represent the first time that Harrison had *seriously* attempted a cover version since "If Not for You" on his first album. I've always loved this old Cole Porter chestnut, famously sung by Bing Crosby to Grace Kelly in the 1956 film *High Society*. Harrison's arrangement is not as stodgy as Crosby's and George delivers a much more energetic vocal (actually wringing about seven syllables out of the title refrain "True-ooo-uuue-ooo-uuue-oo Love"), and the song is given a uniquely up-tempo treatment, drenched in George's trademark slide guitar careens.

For a man who was allegedly trying to win back his commercial footing, this was a curious song choice, which perhaps said more about George's record collection and attitude to modern music – a "they don't write them like that any more" statement.

On the appropriately soulful "Pure Smokey," George simply bathes in good feeling and I think the sun shines out of this song's proverbial. "Pure Smokey" wasn't the first time George had expressed his admiration for the Motown genius – he had done so on "Ooh Baby (You Know That I Love You)," and had praised him several times in interviews. Though specifically the song is dedicated to Smokey, more generally George would say it's about telling people you like them before it becomes too late.

From the start of the long shimmering guitar fade-in the song is a class act: melodic and tastefully arranged. Along with the album's closing tune "Learning How to Love You," Harrison shows his skill at writing white soul, and once again it's a pity he didn't pursue writing more songs in this direction.

Sandwiched between the two soul numbers came "Crackerbox Palace," the song that had been clearly earmarked as the album's "big single." This song was inspired by the name of 1960's comedian Lord Buckley's house in Los Angeles, although George widened the subject matter to use "Crackerbox Palace" as a metaphor for the material world. In the lyric George rejects the obligation to be like everyone else, singing the lyrics so querulously the song becomes a celebration of non-conformity.

It's clear that George Harrison had a keen sense of not doing "what the rest all do" from an early age and over the years this had blossomed into an uncompromising eccentricity. This was most visible not only in his music, or his sense of humour, but also in the fact that he would often claim to prefer gardening to being a pop star. The very fact that he would later become honorary presidency of the George Formby Appreciation Society clearly distinguished him from virtually every other rock god there has ever been. Indeed, his own Crackerbox Palace, Friar Park, was itself an entire thirty-eight acre monument to non-conformity.

The song is performed with tongue in cheek and it was good to hear George making such a confidently light-hearted recording, which was deservedly a big hit in America – reaching number nineteen on the Billboard Hot 100.

The album closes with the sleazy bachelor-pad tune, "Learning How to Love You." Originally written for Tijuana Brass main-man Herb Alpert, "Learning How to Love You" was Harrison's (successful) attempt to write a Burt Bacharach type of song, a sort of "This Guy's in Love with You" for the 1970s. Naturally, George recorded it himself, with the Fender Rhodes and clavinet sound complementing Harrison's laid-back vocal performance and equally assured Spanish guitar solo – all of which fused together to make "Learning How to Love You" a beautiful love song that once again underlined Harrison's mastery of the ballad form.

By covering "True Love," and by digging deep into the recesses of his memory for "See Yourself," "Beautiful Girl" and "Woman Don't Cry for Me," George was clearly indicating how few new songs he had in 1976, certainly too few originals to be giving away gems like "Learning How to Love You" to trumpet players.

A further indication of the paucity of new material was the fact that no unreleased songs have surfaced from the sessions for this album. Explaining this writer's block, Harrison would say in *I Me Mine*, "This Song" had been written to "exorcise the paranoia about song-writing that had started to build up in me."

Nonetheless, *Thirty-Three and 1/3* was, and is, a hugely enjoyable album, one that is long overdue a critical revision. With an album of pure pop music, George Harrison showed that he was not a man to be stylistically pigeonholed, although a return to former sales levels was not forthcoming, particularly in Britain where the album charted at a disappointing number thirty-five. Possibly people were put off by the fact that George is wearing arguably the worst pair of sunglasses ever known to man on both the front and back cover. As a further kick in the teeth, none of the four singles ("It's What You Value," "Crackerbox Palace," "True Love," and "This Song") would crack the British Top 50. The latter three would be backed by glossy and amusing promotional videos, a medium George embraced with perhaps more innovation than the other ex-Beatles did.

Perhaps George *should* have taken his new band out on the road to further promote the album. Instead, he would go on a year-long hiatus from the music industry, something his fans would have to get used to in future years.

While *Thirty-Three and 1/3* was struggling to make an impact on the charts, EMI released *The Best of George Harrison* in November 1976.

Quite where EMI thought Beatles fans would find the money to buy *all* their reissues is anyone's guess. During this period EMI released umpteen compilations to compensate for the loss of revenue they could have earned, had the Beatles continued as a recording entity.

Ringo and John were also given the greatest hits treatment, but only Harrison's contained Beatle material (the entire side one). This was a completely unnecessary public humiliation for Harrison. The implication being that his solo material to date had not been good enough and therefore had to be backed by "Something" and "While My Guitar Gently Weeps" to be commercially viable. Had EMI forgotten the great songs on *All Things Must Pass?*

When asked about the release, Harrison would contend, "I did have a suggestion, which I made to Capitol early in the year, as to a title and a format of songs. What they've done is take a lot of songs which happen to be me singing lead on my songs which were Beatle songs, when there was really a lot of good songs they could have used of me separately, solo songs. I don't see why they didn't do that. They did that with Ringo's *Blast from Your Past,* and John's *Shaved Fish.* It wasn't digging into Beatle records." *The Best of George Harrison* of course gave the impression that Ringo and John had had more successful solo careers when, in reality, the opposite was the case.

If EMI were going to put Beatle material on a George greatest hits, they should have gone the whole hog and released an album of all twenty-two of his Beatle compositions, and, if not then, they should certainly have done it on the CD re-issue many years later. Such an album could have been a huge success and would have certified how underrated Harrison's talent had been within the Fab Four. As it was, when *The Best of George Harrison* failed to chart in England, a trend seemed to be emerging.

Harrison was, thus, hardly given hope that relentlessly pursuing a solo career was worthwhile if his only reward was diminishing returns. Further damaging to his confidence was the damages award of $587,000 to Bright Tunes that coincided with the same day of *The Best of George Harrison* release. Who'd be a rock star!

To escape these irritations, George threw himself into his promotional duties for his new album in America, appearing on the top-rated American comedy show *Saturday Night Live* filmed in New York.

George would tape two performances with the show's guest host Paul Simon – his own "Here Comes the Sun" and a fantastic version of "Homeward Bound" on which the duo's finger-picking and harmonies were simply exhilarating, making the *Nobody's Child: Romanian Angel Appeal* charity compilation an essential purchase when the performance was included on it fourteen years later in July 1990.

"It must have seemed as strange to him to be harmonising with someone other than Lennon or McCartney as it was for me to blend with someone other than Art Garfunkel," Paul Simon would recall after Harrison's death. "Nevertheless, it was an effortless collaboration. The mesh of his guitar and voice with my playing and singing gave our duet an ease and musicality that made me realise how intrinsic and subtle his contribution was to the Beatles' brilliant creative weave. He made musicians sound good without calling attention to himself."

Ironically, the segment with Simon was not actually live. Due to fears about Beatlemaniacs descending *en masse* to the studio, the segment was pre-recorded to avoid any such incident. Those fortunate enough to be in attendance were actually treated to a mini-concert, as George and Paul Simon performed several other songs to the delight of the stunned audience.

If George was concentrating his promotional energies for his latest album in the U.S.A., the ploy worked when *Thirty-*

Three and 1/3 peaked at number 11 on the American album charts.

And there was more good news when, at the turn of the year John, George and Ringo settled all remaining legal disputes with Allen Klein that had been dragging on for what must have seemed like an eternity. Peace of mind came at a premium however: Apple Corps had to pay Klein a staggering $5,009,200 to get him out of their hair.

Though this meant that the Beatles were now legally free to reunite, Paul was quick to quash such speculation, preparing a limerick in the style of Muhammad Ali: "The Beatles split in 1969, and since then they have been doing fine. And if that question doesn't cease, ain't no one gonna get no peace. And if they ask it just once more, I think I'll have to bash them on the jaw."

George too would cast doubts on the possibility, though he was more circumspect. In a lengthy February 1977 interview with *Crawdaddy* magazine, Harrison would describe the idea of a reunion as "like going back to school again, really. The four of us are so tied up with our own lives, and it's been eight years since we split. And time goes so fast. It's not beyond the bounds of possibility, but we'd have to want to do it for the music's sake first." Instead, George would take 1977 completely off, later claiming that he wrote not one single song throughout the whole year.

Maybe George was taking a leaf out of Lennon's book, and after the intensity of the past few years who could blame him? When you consider the high profile court cases, the decline of his solo career, the break-up of his marriage and his serious bout of hepatitis, if anything, it's amazing he hadn't taken an extended break earlier.

A lengthy sabbatical gave him the chance to indulge himself in holidays, follow his beloved formula one motor racing around the globe and devote more time to Olivia.

But even though George was taking 1977 off he still managed, in May, to find himself part of yet another number one album when *The Beatles Live at the Hollywood Bowl* topped the charts in England and reached number two in America.

Remixed and edited by George Martin from the August 1964 and August 1965 Hollywood concerts, these tapes had not originally been deemed good enough for release, due to the lousy equipment on which they were recorded, and the noise made by 17,000 screaming girls.

George Martin had initially been unsure whether he could make them into a releasable record but once he had heard the "rawness and vitality of the Beatles singing," he decided to try and make something of the tapes. Sadly Martin was unable to disguise the fact that the Beatles can't hear enough of what they are playing to deliver quality performances of the familiar material presented on the album. The album proved emphatically that: a) the Beatles were always a better *studio* band, and b) they could still shift truck-loads of vinyl.

When Martin and Geoff Emerick had finished the clean-up job, he sought permission from the four Beatles to release the album. When Martin visited John personally, he told him that he himself had initially been sceptical but having heard the tapes, had become "very enthusiastic," thinking the album would be "a piece of history, which should be preserved." According to Martin, Lennon was "delighted with the album." George, by all accounts, was not so smitten but gave his blessing anyway.

Shortly afterwards, on June 9, 1977 George and Pattie's divorce finally came through after eleven years of marriage, George gallantly consenting to the decree nisi.

In early August George would underline his reputation as the Beatle with the keenest sense of humour by appearing in

All You Need Is Cash, a genuinely hilarious parody of Beatles mythology, written and directed by Eric Idle and produced by *Saturday Night Live* creator Lorne Michaels.

Tracing the exploits of the Rutles, the Pre-Fab Four (Ron, Dirk, Stig and Barry), the TV film was originally intended as a piece on NBC's *Saturday Night Live* in America. NBC was so taken with the project that it was instead expanded into a 70-minute prime-time mockumentary. *All You Need Is Cash* took milestones from the Beatles' history and subtly inverted them for comic effect. The Rutles' attention to detail is astonishing.

The template for the film was the 1976 rough-cut of *The Long and Winding Road* that George leant to ex-Bonzo Dog Band alumni Neil Innes, who would compose the soundtrack of well-crafted Beatle-lite parody songs. Innes would recall, "The Beatles were very good about it. They allowed us to use lots of their old footage, stuff that eventually became the bones of the Anthology series, and intercut it with newly filmed Rutles sequences to give it more authenticity."

The George figure in the Rutles story, Stig O'Hara, was played by Rikki Fataar (ex of the Beach Boys) who after the group's split becomes an air stewardess for Air India, a none too subtle lampoon of George's passion for the East.

George, naturally, saw the funny side and was happy to help debunk the Beatles myth by appearing in the film as an ageing TV reporter (heavily moustachioed and sporting a grey wig) alongside such other luminaries as Mick Jagger, Ronnie Wood and Paul Simon.

All You Need Is Cash co-director Gary Weis recalled, "George Harrison was involved almost from the beginning. He was around quite a lot, even when he didn't need to be there. We were sitting around in Eric's kitchen one day, planning a sequence that really ripped into the mythology and George looked up and said, 'We were the Beatles, you know!'

Then he shook his head and said, 'Aw, never mind.' I think he was the only one of the Beatles who really could see the irony of it all."

When *All You Need Is Cash* was premiered in March 1978, it was greeted enthusiastically and has been a consistent seller on the home video market ever since, a perfect companion to the Beatles' own films. George was so impressed with the film he introduced Idle to Mo Ostin (Warner Brothers' President), an introduction that would dovetail nicely with George's future career as a film producer.

It's interesting to speculate whether the Rutles project encouraged Harrison to go back to work. It certainly seemed to put him in a Beatles frame of mind when it came to writing his next album, which would arguably be the most Beatle-esque of all his solo records.

In December Harrison even had an impromptu gig at the Row Barge Pub in Henley near his home, his first live appearance for three years. The concert, however, would be a one-off because George and Olivia would head off to Hawaii for a two-month Christmas and New Year vacation.

The trip to Hawaii was obviously beneficial to George's muse. After a year of allegedly not writing a single song, Harrison would write, in Hawaii, half of the tracks for his next album: "Love Come to Everyone," "Soft-Hearted Hana," "Here Comes the Moon," "Dark Sweet Lady" and would finish the lyrics to "If You Believe." It is also rumoured that he penned the unreleased comedy song "Sooty Goes to Hawaii" during this vacation. George obviously loved Polynesia; two years later he would buy a property in Maui.

George would commence recording his stock of new tunes in April, although sessions would be disrupted when in May, George's father, Harry, died from emphysema at Friar Park. George would later say that the night before his father's death he had a dream about his dad saying goodbye.

On a happier note, May 1978 was also the month that George was first approached by the Monty Python team to help finance their *Life of Brian* film after they had run into financial difficulties. EMI had pulled out of the deal to make *Life of Brian* just two days before the actors and crew were set to leave for location shooting in Tunisia. Sir James Carreras (a member of the EMI board) said the film was blasphemous and that EMI's name should not be attached to it. George would not be as faint-hearted.

John Goldstone (the film's producer) went to United Artists who only came up with half the money for the $4 million budget and time was running out. As luck would have it, Eric Idle came up with the idea that George would cough up the money. Even though George had never personally invested in movies, he did have experience as a producer, thanks to 1974's *Little Malcolm and His Struggle Against the Eunuchs.* As a very rich man and Python's main proselytiser, it was a natural step.

Harrison had long been a fan and friend of the comedy troupe. George played Monty Python's "Lumberjack Song" at the beginning of each of his Dark Horse Tour shows, and even donned the Canadian Mountie costume to sing the song live on stage with the Pythons at New York's City Centre in April 1976.

According to Goldstone, the Python representation descended on Friar Park and George said words to the effect of "talk to my business manager Denis O'Brien and he'll sort it out." And, as a result, HandMade Films was born.

When the Pythons went to see O'Brien he said, "Yeah, George wants to do this, but we've never done films, and we don't really know much about film contracts or anything, you're really going to have to help me through this." Goldstone then presented O'Brien with the draft contract drawn up between EMI and Python that gave the troupe final cut and artistic control. Reportedly, O'Brien said simply, "Fine we'll use that as the basis of our contract."

Arguably this was the quickest and easiest bit of business George ever did in his life, and brought about not only one of the best British comedy films ever, but would also give Harrison a new career as a movie mogul.

Harrison was happy to help his friends. He had often claimed that the Flying Circus television shows had been a real fillip during the dark days of the Beatles break-up. Maybe funding *Life of Brian* was his way of repaying the enjoyment they'd given him, or maybe Harrison just needed a pick-me-up after the trauma of his father's passing. The finance took two months to arrange and obtain, and in July, Harrison was able to give the Pythons the green light.

"We borrowed the money from the bank and formed HandMade films. I did it because I wanted to see the film. I couldn't stand the idea of it not being made," George would say in 1988, prompting Monty Python member Michael Palin to call George's investment "the highest price paid for a cinema ticket ever."

Weeks later, on August 1, Olivia would make 1978 a year to remember when she gave birth to George's first and only child, Dhani (named after the Indian word for wealthy), who weighed in at a fragile five pounds, although he has since put on weight.

To get over the strain of childbirth, George took Olivia for a trip to Amsterdam, after which the couple were finally married in a secret ceremony at Henley-on-Thames registry office on the September 2. Only Olivia's parents were there as witnesses, and in fact, the wedding was so secret that the happy couple wouldn't tell the press until a week *after* they'd tied the knot.

Not that there was time to enjoy the afterglow of newly wedded bliss because there was a film to produce and an album to record. In October, George and Olivia would fly out to Tunisia to check out how his substantial investment in *Life of Brian* was being spent. As he could have predicted, the film was going swimmingly, with the Pythons in good spirits and pulling together as a tight working unit. While there, George would even be persuaded to take a blink-and-you'll-miss-it role in the film as Mr. Papadopoulis.

"I got shoved into wardrobe and make-up and before I knew it I was dressed up as an Arab," George would recall. "There's just one little shot, it's probably about twelve frames."

Life of Brian tells the story of a contemporary of Jesus Christ who is mistaken for a messianic figure. Though John Cleese would rightly claim that the film doesn't attack religion itself but makes fun of "the way people follow religion," the parallels between Brian and Christ were deemed blasphemous and the release of the film in 1979 was followed by a huge furore. The devil in George must have watched the whole absurd reaction with amusement and a certain pride in his role in offending such ludicrous people.

Several people did spot the irony of how the man behind "My Sweet Lord" could produce such a supposedly sacrilegious biblical farce. Later Harrison would tell Timothy White of *Billboard* magazine: "All it made fun of was people's stupidity in the story. Christ came out of it looking good! Myself and all of Monty Python have great respect for Christ. It's only the ignorant people – who don't care to check it out – who thought that it was knocking Christ. Actually it was upholding Him and knocking all the idiotic stuff that goes on around religion, like the fact that many folks often misread things and will follow anybody."

Although local councils in certain parts of the country banned the film, the controversy and protests from religious types everywhere actually helped publicise the film in ways the marketing men could never have dreamt of.

As a result, the film was a huge smash and made everyone involved very rich men. The film grossed receipts of $21 million in North America alone. This achievement must rank high on George's curriculum vitae: from a mere punt to help some friends, he helped make a comedy film as seminal in its field as his own contributions to music.

Although HandMade Films was originally only set up to make *Life of Brian,* the company would go on to executive produce another twenty-two movies, establishing itself as the daddy of the British independent production houses. In its eleven years of film-making, the company rightly garnered a reputation for financing innovative and challenging projects such as *Time Bandits, The Long, Good Friday, Mona Lisa* and *Withnail and I,* to name but four. Not many rock stars can claim such multi-media hegemony.

After Harrison died, his dear friend Michael Palin said, "When you look at that HandMade slate, they are really very good films." If HandMade had been Harrison's *only* contribution to the twentieth century popular culture, it would still have been one hell of a legacy.

CHAPTER EIGHT

1979-1980

*This is the first time I've done a birth, a marriage
and a death during the making of a record. We had
a lot of stoppages, but I don't think it really took
any longer than any other album to record.*

George Harrison

With all the activity in his personal life it was amazing that
George found the time to record his subsequent *George Harrison* album, an LP that marked a stunning return to form.
George had obviously been refreshed by his hiatus, whether
he took stock of himself and his career only he could say.
Whatever he did, it seemed to work!

His sabbatical had also allowed him to sleep through the
majority of punk and new wave, a move that no doubt suited him down to the ground. In an interview in 1979, Harrison dismissed punk as "rubbish, total rubbish. Listen to the
early Beatles records, they were simple too, but they still had
much more depth and meaning. It was innocent or even trivial but it still had more meaning than punk which is deliberately destructive and aggressive." This would not be the last
time that George would rail against the latest trends in popular music.

The compositional paranoia felt at the time of making
Thirty-Three and 1/3 had been carried forward however.
When it came to writing *George Harrison*, George would say,
"I hadn't written anything for a year since *Thirty-Three and
1/3*. F***, what happens if I can't write anymore?" He needn't
have worried, as evinced by his prolific burst of song-writing
in Hawaii, a place that certainly contributed to the subsequent album's sunny disposition.

Unfortunately, when *George Harrison* was released in

1979, at the height of new wave when interest in Beatle product was probably at an all time low. Ringo couldn't give away his records, Lennon was still in retirement and Paul's *Back to the Egg* was critically massacred.

In 1979 the second post-break-up Beatles renaissance (due to Lennon's death) was nearly two years away, and Harrison's personal stock and fan base had dwindled dramatically since his initial solo career highs. This was a shame because his 1979 LP featured his best work since *All Things Must Pass*, indeed it was reported that George had listened repeatedly to his début for inspiration in the run-up to making *George Harrison*.

If Harrison was waiting until he had the songs to justify an eponymously-titled LP, then it was certainly worth the wait. The devout, pontifical tone of the early 1970s seemed long gone and it was great to hear George sounding so happy and relaxed, a mood that continued during the promotion of the album.

Publicity for the album chores did, however, take a knock when Harrison had an accident on his tractor. When the brakes failed, George was thrown from the vehicle and the back wheels ran over his foot. After being rushed to Reading hospital X-rays revealed that his foot was not badly injured. That did not stop George turning up at Heathrow before departing to promote the album in America in a wheelchair.

In a 1979 Los Angeles Press Conference to promote the album, Harrison even seemed more comfortable dealing with the inevitable Beatle questions saying, "I did resent it for a while but not anymore. Now I face it. I must admit, it was a privilege to have that experience, to have been one of the Fab Four because there were only four of us who had that experience." When asked, "Do you ever foresee a time when the Beatles would actually reunite?" George suggested the Beatles reunite for a cup of tea together: "Get the four people together and just put them in a room and have tea and satellite it all over the world and charge $20 each to watch it. We could make a fortune."

While people probably *would* have paid to see the four ex-Beatles drinking tea, Harrison would acknowledge that this idea "would be just as difficult because everybody's left home and they're living their own lives. I haven't seen John for two or three years." He would never see him again.

George even went so far as to speculate (on a hypothetical level) on what a reformed Beatles album might sound like in 1979, "If it did happen, and I'm telling you it won't, then you'll never know what it would be like. If it did happen, there's no way we'd do a mediocre album. It would be very, very good. Maybe that's what people want. Maybe people want them to all get together and they all fall over and everyone can say, 'Yeah, well, I told you they would.'"

In fact, in 1979, a reformed Beatles album might have sounded like *George Harrison*. Asked what his feelings were about his new LP, Harrison would say with satisfaction: "I feel happy about it. It seems the response to it is really nice. I mean, sometimes it's like you can do something and it's like swimming against the tide. You know no matter what you do, it just doesn't have that natural flavour with it, whereas with this one it just feels like the timing, everything, the songs, but it's all as if it's just being supported by positive reaction which is very nice."

George also reflected on the changes he had gone through in his life since *Thirty-Three and 1/3* and how this had affected the new record: "I think what happened between this album and the last album is that everything has been happening nice for me. My life is getting better all the time, and I'm happy, and I think that it's reflected in the music."

To co-produce, Harrison selected Russ Titelman, who had produced albums by a wide variety of artists, such as James Taylor, George Benson, Rickie Lee Jones, Randy Newman and Ry Cooder.

Harrison would explain, "I wanted a co-producer, somebody to give me a hand for years. It's very important to the selection of somebody because I'm sure a lot of people would come and produce me but you have to live with someone for a long time. It's important not only that musically you see eye to eye as personalities you get on." Harrison would say he chose Titelman because, "at the time I felt I really didn't know what was going on out there in music, and I felt Russ, who was in music day by day, would give me a bit of direction."

Titelman pared down the "Spector-esque" tendencies of earlier albums and totally dispensed with Tom Scott's horn-heavy production of parts of *Thirty-Three and 1/3*. The result? A light-hearted album, with tight unfussy arrangements that gave the songs more room to breathe.

Recorded between April and October 1978 with the help of Dark Horse Tour mainstays – Andy Newmark, Willie Weeks and Emil Richards – *George Harrison* kicked off with the laid-back "Love Comes to Everyone," a song which also featured cameos from Stevie Winwood and Eric Clapton.

With its sophisticated melody and chord changes "Love Comes to Everyone" is a glorious piece of work, despite Clapton's mediocre guitar intro and the healthy dose of synthesisers (that sound like a paper and comb) in the song's coda. The song was released as a single although it failed to trouble the charts on both sides of the Atlantic, a mystifying turn of events given that it seemed perfect for AOR radio stations the world over.

Track two was a re-working of "Not Guilty." Originally written, recorded for and omitted from *The White Album* in 1968, the song expressed the growing disenchantment and mistrust within the Beatles around that time. Unfinished though it was, the Beatles version was a tad heavy-handed compared to the softer version found here.

Harrison would later explain the song's birth to *Billboard* magazine's Timothy White: "It was me getting pissed off at Lennon and McCartney for the grief I was catching during the making of *The White Album*. I said I wasn't guilty of getting in the way of their career. I said I wasn't guilty of leading them astray in our going to Rishikesh to see the Maharishi. I was sticking up for myself, and the song became strong enough to be saved and utilised."

The song is generally regarded as the finest Beatles' song ever finished and not included on an album, though the original version would finally see the light of day when it was released on *The Beatles Anthology 3* in 1997.

George was also asked in a press conference whether the song was written specifically about Paul. "No," he replied, "it's just about that period in 1968. It's a complete joke, the lyrics, in fact, if you go back on all the records, there's a lot of comedy in it. You just have to look for it."

Its inclusion on *George Harrison* makes the album that little bit *more* "Beatley" and the arrangement here is a lot less dense. The *George Harrison* version is slick in comparison and, dare one say, better. At least everyone's heart seems to be in it. George would describe the new arrangement as "kind of jazzy."

The Beatles theme is continued with "Here Comes the Moon," another song sequel, like "This Guitar (Can't Keep From Crying)" on *Extra Texture*. This time Harrison attempted a remake of "Here Comes the Sun," and although an excellent song, it is obviously not in the same league as its precursor. Though critics seemed to dislike George attempting sequels to Beatles songs, surely if anyone was allowed to rip-off the Beatles, it was the fabs themselves.

"For 'Here Comes the Moon,'" Harrison would explain, "I think I was on LSD or mushrooms at the time and was out sunning in Maui. The sun was setting over the ocean, and it gets pretty stunning even when you're not on mushrooms. I was blissed out, and then I turned 'round and saw a big, full moon rising. I laughed and thought it was about time someone, and it may as well be me, gave the moon its due."

"Here Comes the Moon" is, in essence, a lengthy suite with the title reprised for what seems like an eternity, almost like a mantra.

The next track, however, would be a departure for George with a lyric on a subject he had definitely not written a song about before. "Soft-Hearted Hana" was a very whimsical ode to a magic mushrooms trip indulged by George while in Hana, on the Hawaiian island of Maui. The appropriately hurdy-gurdy, vaguely psychedelic arrangement also marked a departure for George, as did the atypically jazzy guitar solo.

Discussing the song George would explain, "I hadn't had any psychedelic drugs for almost ten years, so I thought maybe I should have it to just see if it reminds me of anything. You have to be careful with mushrooms because they're so good. You feel great, and everything is in perfect focus, even the physical body feels good; I kept eating them all day. Because I felt so good I kept eating them all day. I nearly did myself in; I had too many. I fell over and left my body, hit my head on a piece of concrete – but they were great."

The last track on Side One was the album's lead single, the ultra-commercial "Blow Away" that in many ways typified the spirit of the entire album. Recalling the song's genesis George would say, "I wrote 'Blow Away' on a miserable day, it was pouring down with rain, and we were having a few leaks in the roof. To tell the truth I was a bit embarrassed by it! It was catchy and I was embarrassed to play it to any-body, it was too obvious." It seems surprising that George should have been embarrassed by such a strong song, which deserved to climb much higher than number fifty-one in the British charts. Again it was strange that this song didn't capture the public imagination given that its chorus is so irresistible. "All I've got to be is be happy," George sings on "Blow Away" and he certainly sounded it.

Side Two opened with "Faster," a song expressing Harrison's love for very fast cars and the Formula 1 circus. "Faster" was inspired by Jackie Stewart, who had written a book with the same title, and was dedicated to the memory of Swedish driver Ronnie Petersson who died in a car crash at Monza in 1978.

For all that, the song sounds a bit contrived and the Formula 1 sound effects are a bit annoying. Without putting too fine a point on it, the lyrics are also a trifle lame, and the chorus was clearly not enough of a hook to take the song into the charts. While a more explicable chart miss than "Love Comes to Everyone" and "Blow Away," the failure of "Faster" was more frustrating because it had been released primarily to raise money for the Gunnar Nilsson Cancer Fund. Nilsson had been a Swedish racing driver who had died of the disease.

Things improved dramatically on "Dark Sweet Lady," a delicately beautiful ballad about his equally beautiful wife Olivia. It was great to hear George writing a love song to someone other than God again, especially a song as classy as this. Lacking the gaudy bombast of a "Layla" or the cheap tawdriness of a "Wonderful Tonight," "Dark Sweet Lady" was a master class on how to write a love song. The crystalline Spanish guitar solo is especially delightful, and the track is truly one of the highlights of Harrison's entire solo career.

George was up to his old tricks on "Your Love Is Forever,"

singing about God. Of this song George would say, "If you push 'My Sweet Lord' down people's throats too much, they jump back and try to bite you. And in a way, that message has become a bit more subtle. 'Your Love Is Forever' on the new album is just really saying the same old story. It's 'My Sweet Lord,' really. It's just done in a way which maybe is less offensive to people or through me getting a bit older. And you know just being a bit more laid back."

Either way the song is still gorgeous and George thought it as good as "Something," but admitted it "might not be as popular because it was the Beatles who made 'Something.'" Willie Weeks' bass playing is especially McCartney-esque on "Your Love Is Forever" and the song comes with a lovely slide-guitar solo by the master of the technique.

"Soft Touch," meanwhile, would be a little more up-tempo, although the song is slight in comparison to its two predecessors. Again the song is given a commercial arrangement with lashings of acoustic and Hawaiian guitars and an attractive melody. There's also a vague sense of the tropics which is hardly surprising given that George had written it while in the Virgin Islands. George would say the lyrics reflect the island with "the wind, the cool breeze blowing, the palm trees, the new moon rising." With over half of the album's ten songs being composed in tropical climes, no wonder the album sounded so upbeat.

However, the final track, "If You Believe," was composed in England (with Gary Wright), and it shows. Though this ranks among my least favourite George songs of all time, it's hard, uplifting message and catchy chorus to is hard to resist, much like the rest of the album. That said, the lyrics are a trifle prosaic.

Released in mid-February, the whole album sounded exactly like an album an ex-Beatle *should* have been making in 1979. Unlike Paul's *Back to the Egg* (which, I hasten to add, is an album I've always adored), *George Harrison* did at least sound anachronistically "Beatley," and the nostalgia is seductive.

Rolling Stone would pick up on this, describing *George Harrison* as "nothing at all to do with the Seventies, its deft combination of the quaint and the slick makes the Sixties seem a trifle less remote." With such a well-rounded album burning a hole in his hip-pocket, critics couldn't carp that *this* album lacked emotional and melodic variety. And on the whole the album was very well-received.

Rolling Stone magazine would say, "After several highly uneven LPs that saw the audience for his mystic musings dwindle dramatically, Harrison has come up with his finest record since *All Things Must Pass*. A collection of ten catchy pop songs, *George Harrison* reminds us that this artist was always a much better tunesmith than priest. *George Harrison* is refreshingly light-hearted."

1979 would prove that all his faculties remained intact. Such was his renewed enthusiasm for his song-writing craft that the *George Harrison* sessions would leave three songs on the shelf. Namely, "Flying Hour" which would be resurrected for the rejected version of *Somewhere in England,* "Circles" which would see the light of day on 1982's *Gone Troppo* and "Mo," one of the most obscure songs in the Harrison canon. Written for Warner Brothers' President Mo Ostin, the track would later only be available on the 6-CD box-set, produced by the artists and staff of Warner Brothers Records to commemorate Ostin's retirement after thirty years' service to the company. Entitled "Mo's Blues," only 600 copies were pressed and most of these were given to the company's employees and attendees of the farewell dinner in December 1994, though copies of the boxed set can occasionally be found floating around cyberspace and changing hands for astronomical amounts of money.

It's worth tracking down "Mo" if you haven't come across it. With acoustics competing with slide guitars, "Mo" is vaguely reminiscent of "Faster." The lyrics are also gently amusing and for such a minor release George invested the song with a surprising amount of effort. Likewise "Flying Hour" is another great lost George song, again showing off the sort of quality he was writing in 1979.

A month after the release of *George Harrison,* on March 27, 1979, Pattie and Eric Clapton were finally married in Tucson, Arizona. George was no doubt happy for both of them.

Nearly two months later, on May 19, Clapton threw a huge party to celebrate the marriage at his Hurtwood Edge home in Surrey and managed to create a little piece of Beatle history in the process. George, along with Ringo and Paul, joined Eric Clapton and put on an impromptu concert in the marquee tent alongside Mick Jagger, Ginger Baker, Denny Laine and Lonnie Donegan. The extemporised throng ran through various rock 'n' roll oldies and even a few Beatles tunes, including "Sgt. Pepper's Lonely Hearts Club Band!"

This was the closest the former Beatles had come to a live performance since the break-up. John Lennon would even say, "I would have come if I had known." Another fascinating might-have-been! I don't know, Clapton runs off with George's wife, marries her and all but reforms the Beatles!

Rather than going to ground for another prolonged hibernation after *George Harrison,* in August 1979 George released his *I Me Mine* autobiography, published by Genesis Publications. *I Me Mine* was an expensive, leather-bound affair limited to 2000 signed copies containing facsimiles of his original hand-written lyrics. Dedicated "to gardeners everywhere" the book was primarily aimed at serious collectors. Boy would their faces be red when George sanctioned the release of a mass-market version some time later.

While *I Me Mine* was largely uninformative with regard

to his life story, the lengthy photograph section and his commentaries on his songs made it a very worthwhile venture.

One person who wasn't impressed, however, was John Lennon. Lennon was reportedly livid because he felt George did not mention him enough in the book. Lennon would later declare, "I was hurt by George's book . . . He put a book out privately that, by glaring omission, says that my influence on his life is absolutely zilch and nil. In his book, which is purportedly this clarity of vision of his influence on each song he wrote, he remembers every two-bit sax player or guitarist he ever met in subsequent years. I'm not in the book."

John's rancour would continue in his famous last ever interview with *Playboy* magazine: "That's another reason why I was hurt by his book. I always felt bad that George and Ringo didn't get a piece of the publishing. When the opportunity came to give them five percent each of Maclen [John and Paul's publishing company], it was because of me they got it. It was not because of Klein and not because of Paul but because of me. When I said they should get it, Paul couldn't say no. I don't get a piece of any of George's songs or Ringo's. I never asked for anything for the contributions I made to George's songs like 'Taxman.' Not even the recognition. And that is why I might have sounded resentful about George and Ringo, because it was after all those things that the attitude of 'John has forsaken us' and 'John is tricking us' came out – which is not true."

While resentful, Lennon missed the point that George used the book to mainly talk about gardening, motor racing and spiritual matters, not John Lennon. Nonetheless, in August 1980 George would phone John at his Dakota home, but a still embittered Lennon ignored the message. This would be George or John's last known attempt to contact one another.

In 1980 John, Paul and George all busied themselves

writing songs for Ringo's forthcoming album. Neither of Ringo's last two studio albums, *Ringo the 4th* and *Bad Boy* had included any assistance from the others and consequently Ringo had robbed himself of the only reason people might continue to buy his albums, especially when the quality of his music had dipped to new lows. Into the new decade Ringo would attempt to avoid making the same mistake. The album (tentatively entitled *Can't Fight Lightning*) was tabled to include virtually an entire album of songs written or produced by Ringo's "three brothers," with the filler tracks being written by the Bacharach and David of the bargain bin, Ringo and Ronnie Wood.

In July 1980 Paul produced four tracks (the McCartney-composed "Private Property" and "Attention," Carl Perkins' "Sure to Fall," and the ultimately rejected Starkey composition "Can't Fight Lightning") in France, helped by what remained of Wings. Later in November, John Lennon submitted demos of "Life Begins at Forty," "Nobody Told Me," and "I'm Stepping Out" for inclusion on the album and plans were made to record these in the new year.

By this time Lennon had ended his self-imposed five-year exile of house-husbandry, caring for his and Yoko's son Sean. In 1980 he released his and Yoko's critically acclaimed *Double Fantasy* album and was looking forward to a period of artistic rebirth.

Sessions for George's contributions to Ringo's album took place in November at his Friar Park Studio, where the two Beatles were joined by George's studio band of Herbie Flowers, Al Kooper and Ray Cooper. There they recorded two George songs, "Wrack My Brain" and the backing track to "All Those Years Ago," as well as the Harrison-produced "You Belong to Me." "You Belong to Me" was another song from Harrison's record collection – a tune that pre-dated the rock era by several years. This unlikely song choice was a good one, and George's arrangement was certainly a radical reworking of some of the cornball versions of this song that I personally have heard, although George couldn't resist swamping the song with his favoured early 1980s synth sounds. Harrison may have chosen the song thinking it could have been a hit like 1973's "You're Sixteen."

The backing track of "All Those Years Ago," meanwhile, would go through various stages of completion and Ringo made several attempts at recording a vocal. However, the melody was in too high a register for Ringo to sing and so the song was rejected. Later, of course, the song would be slightly rewritten and released on Harrison's own *Somewhere in England.*

When Ringo's album was finally released in October 1981, it had been shorn of the Lennon tracks because Starr felt that their inclusion was inappropriate. It had also been renamed *Stop and Smell the Roses,* although many of the tracks certainly did not smell as sweet – the album won *Rolling Stone* magazine's worst album of the year award in 1981.

Harrison's "Wrack My Brain" was easily the album's standout track. Written about the frustration of trying to please Warner Brothers and the fickle record buying public, the jaunty arrangement belied the bitterness of the lyric.

Short and snappy with funky guitar chops, "Wrack My Brain" would also be the album's lead single and amazingly peaked at number thirty-eight on the Billboard Hot 100. Amazingly, because even as a huge Beatles fan, I can't fathom how Ringo could still be having Top 40 hits in America in 1981! Allegedly a completed version with George on lead vocals does exist and maybe he should have released the song himself on his next LP, the difficult seventh album, *Somewhere in England.*

George had actually started recording the album as early

as October 30, 1979, returning to it periodically throughout the next year. When *Somewhere in England* was submitted to Warner Brothers (Dark Horse's parent label) on November 2, 1980, Warner Brothers rejected it, deeming its content – "too laid back for today's market, that is, below standard and not commercial enough." Although this was unfair and inaccurate, George had to suffer the humiliation of having to go away and record four replacement songs that lived up to Warner Brothers' expectations of modern pop music.

Tragically, one of the replacements would be inspired by the death of John Lennon five weeks later.

CHAPTER NINE

1980-1982

After all we went through together I had and still have great love and respect for him. I am shocked and stunned. To rob life is the ultimate robbery in life. This perpetual encroachment on other people's space is taken to the limit with the use of a gun. It is an outrage that people can take other people's lives when they obviously haven't got their own lives in order.

George Harrison, 1980

On Monday, December 8, 1980, New York City time, John Lennon was shot and killed as he entered his Dakota apartment building on Manhattan's Upper West Side, across the street from Central Park.

What can you say that hasn't been said before about this senseless, pointless assassination at the hands of twenty-five year-old Hawaii resident Mark Chapman?

Chapman had arrived in New York City a week before with the sole intention of murdering his so-called idol. Chapman was seen several times hanging around the Dakota in the days leading up to December 8, asking about Lennon, and he was there again on Monday evening when Lennon and Ono left their apartment to go to a recording session at the Hit Factory studio.

When Lennon and Ono returned from their evening's recording, shortly before 11 p.m., they walked up the driveway toward the courtyard to the Dakota's entrance. Chapman stepped out of the shadows, came up behind them and called out, "Mr. Lennon!" As Lennon started to turn, Chapman emptied his .38 revolver, containing five bullets, three of which hit their target.

Lennon staggered up six steps into the hallway and said, "I'm shot," before collapsing on the floor. He was then rushed in a police car to St. Luke's-Roosevelt Hospital Centre, where he died shortly after arrival, despite all efforts to revive him.

George was at Friar Park when he became the first Beatle to hear the news. It was George's brother Peter, as Friar Park's estate manager, who received the news via a phone call from their sister Louise (who had long been a U.S. resident). Peter put the call through to Olivia, who had the unpleasant job of informing George that John Lennon had been shot and killed. George would later recount that he immediately went back to sleep, presumably in a state of stunned narcolepsy.

After aborting further work on "Only a Dream Away," it wouldn't be until late the next day that Derek Taylor was able to persuade George to formulate some form of public statement. Not the easiest thing to do in moments of deep shock, as Paul's misinterpreted "it's a drag" comment would prove.

George's statement to the press was as follows: "After all we went through together I had and still have great love and respect for him. I am shocked and stunned. To rob life is the ultimate robbery in life. This perpetual encroachment on other people's space is taken to the limit with the use of a gun. It is an outrage that people can take other people's lives when they obviously haven't got their own lives in order."

Insensitively, a crowd formed at the gates of Friar Park. The gates were locked shut, which is how they would remain for the rest of Harrison's lifetime. George would say, "That guy Chapman cast a very dark cloud over any fan who happens to be standing on the pavement when you come by. You don't know who's crackers and who isn't."

Following Lennon's death, Harrison stepped up his security arrangements ten-fold and gradually became more and more reclusive. It was rumoured that Harrison spent more than £1m upgrading the security at Friar Park – razor wire was placed along the perimeter of his property (after being granted permission from his local council) and infra-red sensors, security lighting, CCTV cameras and electronic gates were all installed during the subsequent years. Friar Park's alarm system was also linked to the nearby police station, which would come in handy twenty years later. If the razor wire didn't spell it out clearly enough, signs in ten languages installed on the gates to Friar Park, requesting people to *Keep Out.*

Spiritually George seemed better equipped than most to deal with the grief, due to his deep religious views on the subject of death and re-incarnation. When Brian Epstein, the band's manager, died of a drug overdose in 1967, Harrison told reporters: "There is no such thing as death, only in a physical sense." In 1987 Harrison would say, "death is only like changing your suit."

Much, though, would later be made of the fact that George was never able to make up with John over the *I Me Mine* contretemps before John was murdered. But Lennon and Harrison often fought throughout their long relationship and always kissed and made up soon afterwards. George would have been able to sleep easier knowing that there was no reason to believe that this would not have been the case over this matter as well.

Lennon would close the subject in his famous 1980 *Playboy* magazine interview by saying, "I am slightly resentful of George's book, but don't get me wrong – I still love those guys. The Beatles are over, but John, Paul, George and Ringo go on. I mean, just because I'm upset about George's book doesn't mean that's all I feel. Do you understand? I like them and it's over. Get it? I don't want to start another whole thing between me and George just because of the way I feel today. Tomorrow I will feel absolutely different."

Harrison would be the first ex-Beatle to release an album

since the nightmare of December 8 – the re-tooled *Somewhere in England.*

In light of John's death this must have been a tortuous album for George to remake. Warner Brothers' decision to stand by their initial rejection of the album was a highly insensitive act, or was it a cynical ploy to wait and see if George could write a money-spinning Lennon tribute.

Surprisingly Harrison would complete the recording of the four new tracks by January 16, 1981. Though it was unavoidable, there was a inappropriately upbeat tone to the majority of the album, since most of it had obviously been recorded long before the awful events of December 1980.

The original track listing for *Somewhere in England* was "Hong Kong Blues," "Writing's on the Wall," "Flying Hour," "Lay His Head," "Unconsciousness Rules," "Sat Singing," "Life Itself," "Tears of the World," "Baltimore Oriole" and "Save the World."

The four rejected songs "Flying Hour," "Lay His Head," "Sat Singing," and "Tears of the World" are all good songs and have a lyrical strength and maturity to them slightly lacking on the replacements.

"Flying Hour" (co-written with Mick Ralphs, ex of Mott the Hoople and Bad Company) was almost a self-parody, all of George's lyrical idioms in one song. The verse is a retread of the "be here now" theme, while the middle eight is a "why are we here, who created us" philosophical treatise. Nonetheless, had "Flying Hour" been included on *Somewhere in England* it could easily have been a contender for the album's best song.

"Lay His Head," "Sat Singing," and "Tears of the World," meanwhile, all sound adequately commercial to my ears – featuring great lyrics, impressive vocals and generous helpings of Harrison's trademark slide guitar. Thankfully all four would later see the light of day.

The replacements: "Blood from a Clone," "Teardrops," "That Which I Have Lost," and "All Those Years Ago" were certainly *more* commercial but were also more throwaway and unbalanced than Harrison's original vision of the album. *Somewhere in England* could have been an album of greater spiritual depth, had Warner Brothers released the November version of the album and jettisoned the ephemeral replacements, "All Those Years Ago" excepted.

Somewhere in England, therefore, marked the first time Harrison or indeed any of the Beatles, had made an album on someone else's terms. George was forced into making a modern pop album and it's a suit that doesn't quite fit him.

Undeniably the songs are uniformly catchy and enjoyable, and it's difficult to be too hard on the album. In the final analysis, *Somewhere in England* turned out to be a creditable stab at making a 1980s pop album, which is what Warner Brothers wanted.

The revised album's opening salvo, "Blood from a Clone" was a riposte in the tradition of "Taxman," "Sue Me, Sue You Blues" and "This Song." The song's lyrics criticised the music industry in general while describing how Warner Brothers had asked Harrison to add some "oomphpapa" to *Somewhere in England.*

George rails against misguided, demographic-chasing record companies and the "awful noises" that masqueraded as music in 1981, calling new wave "crap" in the process. It was good to hear Harrison taking a stand although I'm pretty sure no one was listening.

"[Warner Bros.] were telling me: 'Well, we like it, but we don't really hear a single.'" Harrison would complain. "And then other people were saying, 'Now, look, radio stations are having all these polls done in the street to find out what constitutes a hit single and they've decided a hit single is a song of love gained or lost, directed at 14-to-20-year-olds.' And I said, 'Shit, what chance does that give me?' So anyway, I went in and wrote that song just to shed some of the frustrations."

"Blood from a Clone" is kinda fun, though perhaps George should have given it to Ringo and kept "Wrack My Brain" for himself. Since the songs deal with similar themes he obviously felt he could not include both on the same album.

"Unconsciousness Rules" was another return to one of George's favourite themes – cautioning against the material world, using the temptations of the discotheque as the backdrop. George always seems to be horrified by what he sees in the clubs (witness "Tired of Midnight Blue" on *Extra Texture*). Maybe he should have stuck to gardening!

"Life Itself" is a big song and the critics seemed to like it. Harrison himself certainly had a soft spot for the song, including it on *The Best of Dark Horse* compilation and putting a demo version on his *Songs by George Harrison 2* EP. It is, however, a religious ballad and once again finds George throwing himself at the feet of Him. Harrison had stated around the time of *George Harrison* that he would stop pushing "My Sweet Lord" down people's throats, and here he was doing exactly that. "Life Itself" is a paean to Him in all His guises.

As the first Beatle to release a record in the wake of John's death, George would be the first off the mark with an elegy to his murdered ex-colleague. To help with the tribute Ringo drummed on the track and Paul (and Linda) McCartney pitched in on backing vocals, the sessions for which were co-produced by George Martin in Montserrat.

"All Those Years Ago" wasn't quite the "reunion" the tabloids cracked it up to be. As mentioned earlier, the basic instrumental track was taped *before* Lennon's murder for Starr's "Can't Fight Lightning" album. After the track was re-written to reflect the assassination, Harrison replaced Ringo's vocals with his own as he had done when superimposing his vocals onto the backing tracks of "Try Some, Buy Some" and "You."

Nonetheless, "All Those Years Ago" represented only the second time that three Beatles had been heard on the same record since the break-up (the other being Ringo's "I'm the Greatest"). The song benefits from the McCartney backing vocals and Ringo's drums and some great slide guitar work by George. Sang with genuine emotion, this song was a deserved number two hit on the American charts.

Of course the revelation that Paul McCartney and Ringo Starr had participated in the recording obviously helped push it up the charts. However, given the subject matter there were some who felt that George's tribute to John should have been a more sombre affair.

In his *I Me Mine* autobiography, Harrison recalled having been turned on to music at the age of four by Hoagy Carmichael's "Hong Kong Blues," and thirty-four years later he finally got around to releasing his own version as well as a matchless version of "Baltimore Oriole" by the same composer.

Though the smoky "Baltimore Oriole" was, in my opinion, one of Harrison's greatest ever recordings, critics were unkind to both "Hong Kong Blues" and "Baltimore Oriole," suggesting that George had run out of song-writing ideas. Some critics even suggested that the songs didn't suit George's voice. I myself disagree completely with this view and wish he'd done more of these songs. Perhaps he should have released a *George Sings Hoagy* album as a charming insight into the sort of music that he listened to and also as an interesting take on the long playing format popularised by Sinatra and Ella Fitzgerald.

The infectious "Teardrops" that began Side Two was probably tossed off by George in his sleep. This is George singing disposable pop and the song is noticeably lacking in effort or passion. Harrison was better than this sort of thing, disposable pop not really being his bag. That's not to say that the song is not enjoyable, because it avowedly is.

"That Which I Have Lost" is a pleasant enough steel guitar number, even though George drenched his axe in a chorus effect predominantly found in Christian Rock. Harrison described the lyrics to "That Which I Have Lost" as "right out of the *Bhagavad-Gita*. In it I talk about fighting the forces of darkness, limitations, falsehood and morality."

"Writing's on the Wall," meanwhile, with its sparse arrangement sounds unfinished, although its discreet use of Indian instruments make it a pleasant, if slight number. If he was going to use Indian sounds why not go whole hog *à la* "Within You, Without You?"

Somewhere in England concluded with the ecological "Save the World." Unfortunately, Harrison wasn't going to save anything with this song's rather annoying lyrics. At least the song wasn't as pretentious as the songs of other artists who covered this topic throughout the CND decade. Nonetheless, *Rolling Stone* magazine were possibly right when they said, "veering uncertainly between whimsy and dour warnings, the song ultimately fails either to galvanise or amuse."

George looks cheerful on the cover of *Somewhere in England,* in spite of the original album's rejection, and it's amazing that George didn't stand up for himself. Either way, the success of *All Those Years Ago,* that immensely helped to push sales of the album, accidentally vindicated Warner Brothers' decision.

The album has its limitations. To include so much synthesiser was contradictory given that Harrison would always preface every promotional interview with a "my music doesn't change to suit the times" type quote. The amount of synth couldn't have been motivated purely by Warner Brothers' assertion that the original album had not been commercial enough, so, as producer, the blame must be laid at Harrison's door.

When it was released in June 1981, *Somewhere in England* was given the benefit of the doubt by critics and snapped up by fans desperate for some Beatle product after December 9. One Swedish music critic was not so impressed, reviewing this album in one word: "Zzzz . . ."

Rolling Stone magazine were also harsh saying, "Social commentary and ironic wit clearly remain outside the scope of Harrison's very real talents, as does the ability to belt out a convincing rocker. The most paradoxical of the ex-Beatles, George Harrison is an enigmatic mixture of exquisite craftsmanship and heavy-handed hack work, touching sincerity and plain disingenuousness. As it stands, *Somewhere in England* is neither here nor there."

As I asserted earlier, the album *could* have been better if Warner Brothers had gone with the original version of the album, or if they had more fancifully encouraged George to make an entire album of Hoagy Carmicheal songs. I guess that I'll have to add that to my list of George Harrison "what might-have-beens."

Shortly after the completion of *Somewhere in England,* Ringo married Barbara Bach on April 27, 1981 at Marylebone Registry office, London. Meeting for the first time since Lennon's death, George and Paul were both in attendance (alongside Olivia and Linda) and happily celebrated the union at a post-ceremony party at Rags nightclub in Mayfair. Photographs of the three Beatles looking happy with their partners and various progeny was syndicated across the globe – a comforting gesture in light of Lennon's death.

The three of them, of course, joined in for the obligatory all-star jam with Ray Cooper providing percussive assistance on the spoons. Naturally the jam and the pictures fuelled further speculation of reunions.

A mere month after the release of *Somewhere in England*, another Harrison song would see the light of day, "Only a Dream Away," that would play over the closing credits of the HandMade film *Time Bandits* which opened in July. The song, which featured the strong backing vocal presence of Syreeta (Stevie Wonder's ex-wife), was arguably better than anything on *Somewhere in England* and it's curious that George didn't release it as a single, or even include it on the album. Surely this was exactly what Warner Brothers had in mind when they said they wanted catchy pop music. As it was, "Only a Dream Away" would have to wait a year before its official release on Harrison's next album.

George would do the rounds publicising *Time Bandits,* which is strange when you consider he could barely be bothered to properly promote his own albums half the time. When he appeared on *Good Morning, America* to promote the film, it marked the first time George had granted an American television interview in the ten years that had elapsed since his appearance on *The Dick Cavett Show* in November 1971.

George and HandMade would be rewarded when *Time Bandits,* directed by Terry Gilliam, became a huge hit with kids and adults alike.

Off the back of the film's success surely Harrison should have immediately released "Only a Dream Away" in some form. Another opportunity for a hit record was missed.

The rest of 1981 would be largely uneventful. While on holiday with his family in Australia for Christmas and New Year, George would grant an interview to *Good Morning, Australia* on which he would describe himself in 1982 "as a middle-aged ex-pop star, peace seeker, gardener, ex-celeb."

This definition suggested that 1982 would be another year of the ostrich for Harrison. As it turned out this would not be the case when sessions for his next LP began in May and continued through to August.

Released in October in the U.S.A., and November in the U.K., *Gone Troppo* is the album you're supposed to hate if you're a George Harrison fan, and is certainly the one you're least likely to have heard of, if you're not.

Recorded with the same spine from *Somewhere in England*, *Gone Troppo* also featured cameos by Joe Brown and his wife Vicki (on the title track), Deep Purple's Jon Lord (on "Circles") and Billy Preston. The credits read like a who's who of musicians who will work for food. Billy Preston, for one, must have been particularly in need of a square meal around this time. It was also pleasing to see that Harrison had finally dispensed with most of his now unfashionable side-kicks from the previous decade.

Many reviewers complained that *Gone Troppo* was not that much different from *Somewhere in England*, the only difference being that they felt the songs were, if anything, even more boring.

On the plus side, the production on *Gone Troppo* is certainly slicker than its predecessor and in fact the album now sounds less dated than *Somewhere in England* with that record's heavily chorused guitar and overtly 1980s synth sounds. Reviewers did note that the songs themselves were generally happy and joyful.

Gone Troppo is a unique album in the Harrison canon for its almost throwaway nature, it's so casual and the song selection screams: "I can't be bothered!" That's possibly why it's quite fun. *Rolling Stone* called the album "So offhand and breezy as to be utterly insubstantial, the LP is made up of throwaway ditties, instrumental fragments and formulaic love songs." For all that the album does at least prove that Harrison is still listenable, even on his poorest records.

The album's first track "Wake Up My Love," was in

many ways a sequel to "Teardrops" from *Somewhere in England* with its lightweight synthesiser chops. Unlike "Teardrops," "Wake Up My Love" was buoyant enough to take it to the fringes of the Billboard Top 50 when it was released as a single, an impressive achievement without the aid of any concerted promotion.

"That's the Way it Goes" also sounded like a potential hit single. With *Gone Troppo* George seemed to be hitting his stride as a pure pop merchant.

Equally suitable for release as a single was the title track. "Gone Troppo" was a song about hanging out in the tropics and sounded for all the world like the soundtrack to a soft-drink commercial, possibly a drink that contains a subtle blend of grapefruit and mango. It's bizarre that George should write such a song after spending most of his song-writing life trying to put the world to rights and here he was writing about sitting "mucho in de sunshine" and "counting de fruit bat." Of the album *Rolling Stone* magazine generally felt that "writing de good song" hadn't been on George's agenda.

The instrumental "Greece" and a cover of "I Really Love You" (a 1961 hit for the Stereos) and another stab at "Only a Dream Away" from *Time Bandits* did suggest that George had not taken a great deal of time to write new songs for the album. Likewise, "Circles" (on Side Two) had been started in 1968 for potential inclusion in *The Beatles* (as "Colliding Circles"), but had never been finished. It is, for my money, Harrison's worst-ever composition. A heavy, spiritual dirge, somehow redolent of "Blue Jay Way," but different inasmuch as it's nowhere near as good. "Circles" does indeed go round in circles and you can almost hear the song-writing barrel being scraped.

One unkind reviewer derided *Gone Troppo* as sounding like it had been "written by an average songwriter in a drug-induced coma." I wouldn't go this far, although I concur that Side Two is a trifle bland, particularly "Baby Don't Run Away" and "Unknown Delight."

Side Two is saved by the excellent "Mystical One," one of my all-time favourite Harrisongs. Though the title could be perceived as a nod to how George himself was perceived, "Mystical One" is clearly another paean to God, although the personal lyrics could equally be interpreted as a love song to his wife. With its wonderful melody and passionate vocal, "Mystical One" ranks high as one of Harrison's most underrated songs.

Little heard because the album was not promoted at all by either Harrison or Warner Brothers, and consequently it sold miserably. Harrison specifically refused to be involved in any promotional activities for the album whatsoever. According to the man himself, "It's one thing writing a song, taping it and then making a record, but I wasn't interested in promoting it myself after all that had happened with the Beatles. I'm not into myself in that manner, and I think you have to be an egomaniac to go touring and promoting yourself all the time. Sometimes you release an album and the record company just about ignores it, and so many people don't even know it's out. And I'm not about to jump up and down shouting, 'Hi folks, look at me I'm cool and groovy!' That's not what George Harrison is all about."

It's curious that he even made the album at all if he wasn't bothered by its outcome. Would *Gone Troppo* prove to be the proverbial "contractual obligation" album?

Rolling Stone described *Gone Troppo* as "passable stuff, though it's hardly a day at the beach." Which is a shame because for all its faults several of *Gone Troppo* tracks do leave the aural impression of a sunny day on tropical landscapes. Another reviewer called it *"Somewhere in England* without the memorable riffs." This was ill-informed, "Wake

Up My Love," "Only a Dream Away" and "Mystical One" were all strong pop ditties that McCartney, say, might have had big hits with around this time.

The release of the TV-advertised Beatles' *20 Greatest Hits* and *The John Lennon Collection* albums didn't help either. Both naturally sold by the shed-load, leaving precious little "Beatle" money left over for *Gone Troppo* during stocking-filler season.

Truth be told, neither *Somewhere in England* nor *Gone Troppo* were *bad* records, but by 1982 music had simply taken on a different direction to Harrison's style, with all sorts of fads and one-hit wonders dominating the charts. If ever there was a less promising era for a 1960s refugee and self-confessed "ex-pop star" to release an album containing a barber shop cover version and a Mediterranean-inspired instrumental, it is difficult to think of one.

Consequently George probably felt the time was right to take a dignified leave of absence from the business. As Harrison himself would explain: "I was fed up with people saying, 'Oh, maybe you should do this kind of song.' It's time to give up when you're not allowed or expected to be yourself."

There seemed genuine reason to believe that *Gone Troppo* marked the end of George's recording career. For the next four years Harrison would devote more of his time and energy to HandMade Films, and to indulging his love of gardening and motor racing.

Between 1979 and 1982 George had released three albums and he must have felt a little burnt-out by this comparatively prolific spree. With Lennon's death and the rejection of *Somewhere in England* George probably asked himself, did he need any of this?

His obvious lack of interest in *Gone Troppo* suggested he was simply disillusioned by the music business. In 1983 he would tell Barry Norman of the BBC that he wanted to "just try and live the life of a normal human being. If I have a hit record, they're all knocking on the door again, phoning me up. I've had that concentrated in the '60s and early '70s. I've done that and it's boring."

And so he once again quit *full-time* recording as he had in 1977. Contrary to popular myth, the intervening years between *Gone Troppo* and his next album could in no way be described as a retirement. Either way, when he returned, he would do so with a bang.

CHAPTER TEN

1983-1986

It's time to give up when you're not allowed or expected to be yourself.

George Harrison

Having decided to take an unofficial leave of absence from the music business, George had every reason to believe that he would be able to enjoy his hiatus away from the rat race when, in late 1982, construction of a house was completed on the Maui real estate he'd purchased in November 1981.

Yet, even while George was lying low in the heart of Polynesia, he still couldn't escape chart success when "Love Me Do" was re-released in October 1982 to coincide with the twentieth anniversary of its original release as a U.K. single.

The single would better its original chart placing of number seventeen by peaking at number four second time around, and would be the first of yet another re-release of all the Beatles' singles on each of their respective twentieth anniversaries.

The success of "Love Me Do" would ultimately mean that no *official* Beatles single would chart below number four in the British charts, a record unlikely to be beaten by credible recording artists.

The years 1983 and 1984 would be the lowest profile of George's entire career.

Later, in 1987, Harrison reflected on his self-imposed retreat from and disillusionment with the music business, saying, "I got a bit tired of it, to tell you the truth. It's one thing making a record, but if nobody plays it on the radio, what's the point of spending months in the studio? To be honest, I just got tired of having all the responsibility of writing, performing and producing everything myself. And then when the record business went into that recession and started getting weird back in the late '70s and early '80s, I just decided not to make another record for a bit, and to lie low for a while."

With music put on hold, Harrison was free to pursue his other interests – his passion for motor racing, his gardening, and of course HandMade Films. The early to mid-1980s would be HandMade's glory years and almost single-handedly revitalised the British film industry, something for which Harrison would only really receive credit after his death.

HandMade Films (Production) Ltd. had officially been incorporated in 1980, and a distribution arm was founded in October of the same year. Harrison watched the growth of HandMade with keen interest although he distanced himself from the day-to-day running of the company. Harrison would tell Barry Norman on the BBC's *Film '83* show, "I don't want to be a film star, I don't even want to be a pop star."

"I can't let it become too serious," he commented about his involvement with Handmade, "otherwise it'd become work. And once I'd got myself out of that star rat-race, I promised myself I'd never work again. Well I do work, but I want it to be enjoyable, not just a slog."

Bizarrely, February 1983 would see the release of "I Really Love You" as an American single. There couldn't have been any serious hope that this light-hearted piece of fluff would have charted. Perhaps Warner Brothers thought that a doo-wop cover version by George Harrison would have novelty value. Interestingly, Harrison claimed that he felt the song had been the inspiration behind "Do You Want to Know a Secret" – the Lennon-McCartney song he'd sung on the *Please Please Me* LP.

Alongside "I Don't Want to Do It" and "Got My Mind

Set on You," "I Really Love You" would be the start of three consecutive U.S. singles by George that were cover versions, classic symptoms of an imperilled creative muse.

His U.K. record company was not as ambitious, where "I Really Love You" was not even released, even though this was in a climate of the staggered twentieth anniversary re-release of the Beatles' original singles, virtually all of which became minor hits.

The success of "Love Me Do" in October 1982 had in fact signalled a second wave of Beatles repackaging by EMI, which this time promised to be more interesting than albums like *Love Songs* and *The Beatles Ballads*. In 1983, EMI scheduled for release was a *new* Beatles single: a double A-side of "How Do You Do It" and "Leave My Kitten Alone."

In the early 1980s, Abbey Road engineer John Barrett had been was given the task of cataloguing and listening to all the Beatles session tapes, keeping an eye out for interesting takes. Although the planned single didn't materialise, Barrett's work did lead to EMI taking its first steps towards letting the public actually hear this priceless stuff.

During a 1983 summer renovation, Abbey Road's Studio Two would be opened to tourists – the highlight being a visual history of the Beatles recording career, accompanied by a soundtrack featuring outtakes and alternate mixes.

The Beatles at Abbey Road video presentation would bring to an end years of fanciful speculation as to exactly what the Beatles had left in the vault. On July 11, 1983, Abbey Road confirmed that they certainly had four unreleased gems, namely, "How Do You Do It," "Leave My Kitten Alone," "If You've Got Trouble," and "That Means a Lot." A week later, on July 18 and until September 11, Abbey Road opened its doors to a salivating public.

Billed as "Abbey Road Studios Presents the Beatles – Come and experience the magic of Studio Two where the

Beatles recorded from 1962-1969," tickets for the thrice daily presentation were priced at a highly reasonable £4.50.

"The whole event was a huge success," recalled Abbey Road's then manager, Ken Townsend, "We had something like 22,000 visitors, from all over the world. There were three shows a day, with 135 seats at each, and it was fully booked for the whole duration."

For their money the public could tour Abbey Road's Studio Two (set up exactly as it always had been for Beatles recordings with some original equipment on display), and listen to "How Do You Do It" and "Leave My Kitten Alone," albeit in incomplete versions. There was, however, no sign of "If You've Got Trouble" or "That Means A Lot," or other titles from the vaults like "Come and Get It," "What's the New Mary Jane" and "Not Guilty."

In fairness, the audio visual programme was a curate's egg: stripped-down versions of "Because" and "Strawberry Fields Forever" sat next to less interesting trinkets such as early takes and false starts of "Don't Bother Me," "I Saw Her Standing There," "She's a Woman," and "A Hard Day's Night." Meanwhile, some songs like "Rain," "Hello Goodbye," and "Penny Lane" were presented in radically remixed form. For EMI to have sifted through four hundred hours of tape, and only come up with this was slightly embarrassing.

McCartney, however, was so impressed with the presentation (having slipped in unrecognised one night to observe proceedings) that he informed George and Ringo, who were treated to a private viewing. George would similarly be impressed enough to ask EMI to release his demo of "While My Guitar Gently Weeps" as soon as possible, according to EMI, that is.

Throughout 1983 and 1984 work had continued on the Beatles outtakes. Veteran Beatles engineer Geoff Emerick had been entrusted with the re-mixing of the tapes.

Having heard the various bootlegs this seemed to have involved severely editing some of the tracks, chopping up others, and assembling new versions, which in some cases scarcely resembled the original takes.

By August 1984 a final track listing was set: "Come and Get It" (Paul's demo for Badfinger), "Leave My Kitten Alone" (*Beatles for Sale* outtake), "Not Guilty" (Harrison's *White Album* outtake), "That Means A Lot" (McCartney's *Help!* outtake), "I'm Looking Through You" (an alternate take), "What's the New Mary Jane" (Lennon's avant-garde *White Album* outtake), "How Do You Do It" (a song given to the Beatles by George Martin to try, written by Mitch Murray), "Besame Mucho" (from the Beatles' first EMI session with Pete Best on drums), "One After 909" (1963 version), "If You've Got Trouble" (another *Help!* outtake), "While My Guitar Gently Weeps" (Harrison's glorious demo version), and "Mailman, Bring Me No More Blues" (from the 1969 *Let It Be* sessions).

EMI would decide on *Sessions* as the title and had hoped to release the album in November 1984. All systems seemed to be go. Sleeves for the LP were designed, catalogue numbers were assigned, and even a release date had been finalised.

Unfortunately EMI hadn't told the Beatles. Quite frankly – how stupid is that? Here is EMI sitting in their offices for the fifteen years since the group broke up, watching them sue anyone who dared to trespass against them, including each other, blindly thinking that they could get away with releasing an album of this importance without telling them. It defies belief!

It was only due to the fact that McCartney had released his *Give My Regards to Broad Street* soundtrack that EMI decided not to compete with him by releasing *Sessions* in the same lucrative Christmas market. When Paul, George and Ringo found out about the project, naturally they put an end to it.

An article published in May 1985, quoted EMI's damage limitation as follows: "We're now discussing the matter with the remaining Beatles and representatives of John Lennon's estate with an aim to releasing an album sometime. The format that EMI suggested was not acceptable, but one obviously has to start somewhere. And then we move on from there. We move on to other formats now, other suggestions and discussions."

Not that it mattered to Beatles fans. The much circulated *Sessions* tapes were pressed into bootlegs by early 1986, and some of the mixes prepared for the album would eventually appear on *The Beatles Anthology* collections.

Unlike 1977, when George claimed he did not write a single song, 1984 would see George working on the soundtrack for *Water*, the HandMade film released in 1985 starring Michael Caine and Billy Connolly.

George would contribute "Focus of Attention" (written with Mike Moran and screenwriter Dick Clement) and "Celebration" (written with Moran), both performed by Jimmy Helms on the soundtrack. George would even go a step further, by appearing in the film's finale as part of the Singing Rebels Band, behind Billy Connolly, and alongside Ringo and Eric Clapton.

In November 1984, when George joined Derek Taylor at a press conference in New Zealand to promote his friend's limited edition book, *Fifty Years Adrift*, he was asked how actively involved in music he was at that time.

George would reply, "Well, I don't *have* to make records any longer, which is a relief to go because I'm not really of the competitive nature. I don't want to have to go out there doing all this stuff which is necessary now. Let's face it, it's a cut-throat business and I'm not really into that, so I no longer have to make records. Since I don't have a commitment to the music industry, I've been writing much more music than in the past. For instance, the last couple of months I've written about twenty-eight songs and I made demos, which are better because they can be of good quality. When you get to making a record, though, it's something serious."

On another occasion Harrison would claim of his fallow years, "All the time I wasn't making records, I've always written songs. I've got a twenty-four-track studio here, where I can write a song and get it down on tape in an evening. I got so used to doing that – either making up tunes or recording old songs or whatever – that I lost a lot of the patience required to make a proper album."

The only glimpse the public got of what Harrison was recording during this period was the booming, organ-drenched "I Don't Want to Do It," a natty cover version of a Dylan song donated to the soundtrack of the American "frat" film *Porky's Revenge* (released in March 1985), and released as an American single (in slightly re-mixed form).

Harrison shows once again how much he loved performing Dylan's music by delivering his most impassioned vocal performance on record for several years. Unfortunately, the single didn't chart, and nobody went to watch the film, let alone bought the soundtrack. "I Don't Want to Do It" remains yet another lost gem of the Harrison discography, and is now almost impossible to find anywhere except on bootlegs.

Another song that crops up regularly on George bootlegs is "Abandoned Love," another cover of a Dylan song, recorded during the sessions for *Gone Troppo*. "Abandoned Love," is, if anything, the stronger song, and is long overdue an official release.

Throughout 1985 Harrison continued to content himself with only sporadic recording. June 1985 would see the release of *Greenpeace – The Album,* to which George donated a re-mixed version of "Save the World" with a re-recorded vocal, plus a few more guitar licks and ever so slightly altered lyrics, while in December 1985 George also recorded the rather anodyne ballad, "Shelter in Your Love" with Alvin Lee, the gurning guitar maestro behind Ten Years After. Rumours have circulated that George also recorded "Sooty Goes to Hawaii" (an instrumental apparently written in early 1978) around this time. Both songs have yet to be released, and although the overall blandness of "Shelter in Your Love" would probably do little to enhance Harrison's legend, it would still be nice to see its inclusion on a Harrison solo Anthology Boxed Set – should one ever appear.

If anyone did think that Harrison had retired from the music business, those fears were more comprehensively dispelled in October 1985 when he appeared on the Carl Perkins cable TV special, *Blue Suede Shoes: A Rockabilly Session.*

When Britain's *Q* magazine asked George in 1987 what had made him decide to appear on the programme, he replied, "Well, he was a big influence on me as a kid. I met him, of all places, in Alma Cogan's flat in Kensington, years ago, and he was so nice. He sent me this special video of a little hot rod coming down the road with 'Matchbox' playing in the background, and then he pulled up, got out the car and said, 'Hey George Harrison! Hi, Carl Perkins here. I'm going to do a TV Special and I want you to be on it. In fact it won't *be* a Special unless you're on it!' Then I never heard any more for about six or nine months and then Dave Edmunds got involved and it came together suddenly, that Autumn of '85. We did it like Carl Aid! I thought, if I want to get over my fear, my inhibitions about going on and playing or whatever, if I can't play Carl Perkins songs there's not much chance of me ever playing *anything*!"

Filmed before 250 invited guests at The Limehouse Studios, in London, George joined old friends like Dave

Edmunds, Eric Clapton, Roseanne Cash, and various Stray Cats all keen to pay tribute to their mutual idol. Also on hand was Ringo Starr, although Paul McCartney declined to appear, even though he *had* been invited.

When it was George's turn to emerge from the wings Perkins yelled, "George Harrison, everybody. Don't he look good?," and the audience exploded with applause. George would perform "Glad All Over," share lead vocals (with Carl) on "Your True Love," contribute backing vocals and guitar to "Blue Suede Shoes," "Gone, Gone, Gone," "Whole Lotta Shakin' Goin' On," and joined in on a medley of other oldies. It was obvious to everyone that George was having the time of his life.

"His wife, Olivia, was just so happy." Carl Perkins would later report. "She told me in the dressing room after the show, 'Carl, I don't know what to say to you, because I saw my old George so happy tonight. I saw something there that I hadn't seen in a long time.'"

The show was premiered on Channel 4 in Britain on New Year's Day, 1986, and Harrison looked great in a new grey suit that clashed pleasantly with his iridescent orange Eddie Cochran "Country Gent" guitar.

In a press conference in Los Angeles, 1987, George would talk about his participation in the rockabilly session: "The Carl Perkins show was really for me. It was done because I like Carl and I ought to do something. Otherwise, I'd get so out of it I might never want to do that kind of thing again. It's hard to step back out after you've not done any shows. So I did it thinking, 'Well, Carl Perkins' music is so enjoyable and such fun it's the kind of thing I should be able to do without too much worry."

"Carl Perkins is just such a nice man," Harrison continued. "That's the main reason why that show came across so well. I mean, everybody's out there with their egos, but at the same time it's all concentrated for the love of Carl. I thought that really came across."

In an interview with *Guitar World* magazine some years later George would credit Perkins' rockabilly style as his main influence as a guitarist. "Carl was playing that simple, amazing blend of country, blues and early rock, with these brilliant chordal solos that were very sophisticated," Harrison would genuflect, confirming that George always had been a country gent at heart.

In March 1986 Harrison would be back on stage at the Birmingham NEC for the *Heartbeat '86* charity concert. The concert was part of a series of events that were raising £1million for the Birmingham Children's Hospital. George shared lead vocals on "Money" and "Johnny B. Goode," alongside Robert Plant and Denny Laine. This appearance would actually mark George's first live performance in front of paying customers in England since the 1969 Delaney and Bonnie tour.

1986 would also give the world the first glimpse that Harrison might be ready to release some *new* material, when he went back into the studio to work on the soundtrack for *Shanghai Surprise,* a project for which he returned, in May 1986, to Abbey Road for the first time since February 1971, because his own FPSHOT studio was not big enough to accommodate the large orchestra that was required.

HandMade must have thought they'd hit the jackpot when they secured, for the film's leading roles, the services of Hollywood's golden couple, Sean Penn and Madonna, whose fame and popularity was at its peak.

From the start the film was beset by problems, mainly emanating from the poison Penns' relationship with the press, who seemed hell-bent on following their every move, to the couple's precious dislike. The bellicose Penn's enmity towards and penchant for lashing out at journalists had caused such negative publicity that Harrison himself was called in to personally diffuse the situation, much to the surprise of the British tabloids who had previously been content to paint George as an eccentric recluse.

A press conference was hastily arranged at Shepperton Film Studios for George and Madonna to face the media, during which his female lead described him as "a great boss, very understanding and sympathetic."

Rather than calm things down, however, George spent much of the press conference criticising the paparazzi for acting like "a bunch of animals" when he and Madonna had arrived at Shepperton by car, asking them, "Do you just want us to get torn apart and beaten up?"

Ultimately, the adversarial relationship between the *Shanghai Surprise* production and the press can't have helped reviews because upon its release the film was "torn a new one" by critics, eager to bring the narcissistic Penns down a peg or twelve. One reviewer called the film, "Awesome in its awfulness, momentous in its ineptness and shattering in its stupidity."

Regardless of schadenfreude and journalistic spite, the film *is* a dog and the film bombed at the cinemas and fared little better when it went to video, with all due haste. Harrison would later slam Madonna, calling her a superficial brat! "Stars", Harrison would say, "I don't like people who think they're big shots."

Still, the film did get Harrison back in the studio and, in October, fans in Britain were treated to an ITV documentary showing Harrison working on the soundtrack with Jeff Lynne and Michael Kamen. The film would contain five Harrisongs: "Shanghai Surprise," "Hottest Gong in Town," "Someplace Else," "Breath Away from Heaven," and the instrumental "Zig Zag" (a straightforward trad-jazz tune co-written with Jeff Lynne that eventually surfaced as the B-side to "When We Was Fab" in 1988).

The "Shanghai Surprise" title song, was, for my money, the best thing Harrison had written in years – another of the great "lost" George tracks. A duet with Joe Brown's session-singer wife Vicki, the song is full of hooks, great lyrics and a fantastic lead vocal from George. With its evocation of crowded streets, evil crooks, opium and rickshaws and its simulated south-east Asian f/x, the track was, in fact, a more faithful representation of 1937 Shanghai than the film's labyrinthine plot.

"Hottest Gong in Town," meanwhile, was an authentic stab at making a 1930's style jazz tune complete with muted trumpets and ukulele, and George can briefly be glimpsed crooning the song in the movie, costumed as a brylcreamed lounge singer. Harrison's lyrics showed that he was returning to peak form at exactly the right time. The track would later be officially released on the EP that came with the second *Songs by George Harrison* book, published by Genesis Publications in 1992.

"Someplace Else" and "Breath Away from Heaven" had clearly been earmarked for inclusion on his next album, albeit in a re-recorded form. While "Breath Away from Heaven" would not be radically re-worked, I personally prefer the "Shanghai Surprise" version. It's sparser arrangement highlighted the Asian instrumentation to a much greater extent and is essentially more atmospheric.

The *Shanghai Surprise* version of "Someplace Else," meanwhile is more cinematic, that is, more histrionic and not as heart-meltingly subtle as its *Cloud Nine* sister, and certainly George's vocals are not as effective.

While it was a shame that there was no soundtrack album, George clearly had bigger fish to fry, namely his first studio album in five years.

CHAPTER ELEVEN

1987

People think in terms of a comeback but I really haven't been anywhere. I've been here the whole time.

George Harrison

Having enjoyed working on the *Shanghai Surprise* sound-track, Harrison evidently decided it was time to make a new album, the *Shanghai* songs showing that he certainly still had the goods. Sessions for what would become *Cloud Nine* would begin in January 1987.

The timing was also right for a George comeback. 1987 would see for the first time the release of the Beatles albums on Compact Disc, the most successful of course being the *Sgt. Pepper's Lonely Hearts Club Band* re-issue that was pushed to number three in the U.K. album charts by the overwhelming media interest in its twentieth anniversary.

Harrison would also surprise everyone by making several, relatively high profile live appearances in 1987. On February 19, alongside Bob Dylan, John Fogerty and Jesse Ed Davis, George joined Taj Mahal in an unplanned jam session at the Palomino Club in North Hollywood. "It was a bit raggedy to say the least," George would deprecate, "but we had a laugh." Similarly impromptu would be his appearance at Bob Dylan's Wembley Arena concert on Oct 17, 1987, assisting his good friend on a version of "Rainy Day Women # 12 & 35."

The most exciting of these 1987 cameos was undoubtedly Harrison's June appearance at the annual Prince's Trust Concerts at Wembley Arena, with Ringo. Since each Beatle had been contacted separately, without knowing about the other's involvement, George was initially wary: "Ringo phoned me up, saying, 'Somebody's asked me if I'm doing this Prince's Trust, and of course, I can't really do it without playing on it with you.' I said, 'Ooh, I don't know about that.' I mean Ringo will always be my friend, but just that made me nervous. I felt straightaway, somebody's trying to set this [a 'Beatles' reunion] up again. You know, it's one thing going on as me, but if I'm going on as the Beatles, I want to be able to have some sort of control over it."

Despite this neurosis, George and Ringo inevitably did the show, a nerve-wracking experience that George described as "like going to the electric chair, waiting to go on." Alongside the usual crowd of Phil Collins, Elton John and Eric Clapton, George would perform "Here Comes the Sun" and a particularly stinging "While My Guitar Gently Weeps." On the latter George wiped the stage with Clapton, a resounding away win that could be heard on the subsequent "The Prince's Trust Concert" LP, released in August 1987 in the U.K.

Back in the limelight after such a long break, it was a safe bet that whatever George had released in 1987 would have been a hit. The fact that *Cloud Nine* would represent, after *All Things Must Pass,* his second solo masterpiece made the plaudits all the sweeter.

His near five-year break between albums had been just the tonic for George's muse because *Cloud Nine* was a masterful comeback, an album to catapult him back to the stratosphere of super-stardom. Whether this was by design it's hard to say, though if he didn't want the attention and spotlight he shouldn't have released such a good album.

George would say of his return, "People think in terms of a comeback but I really haven't been anywhere. I've been here the whole time. And this record is very much the music I wanted to make. I don't think it's right to mould what you do to the current market. It's like the old song says, 'Take me as I am or let me go.' This is me; I hope I fit in, but I'm not going to lose any sleep over it."

This was clearly a veiled comment about *Somewhere in England* and *Gone Troppo*. With *Somewhere in England* he had been forced to contemporise and on *Gone Troppo* his heart clearly hadn't been in it. This time he was making a record on *his* terms, full of songs that *he* wanted to record.

Having decided, in 1985, that it was time to make a new album, Harrison decided he needed a producer, and though he had never met him, George's thoughts turned to ex-Electric Light Orchestra main-man Jeff Lynne: "Just from the records, I thought he would be good, if we got on together." Harrison explained. "It was really a question of finding somebody to get in touch with him and then meeting with him, without saying, 'Well, look, right down the line from now I'm going to try to make a record, and you're it,' and frighten the fellow away. But that was in the back of my mind."

Harrison's choice turned out to be inspired. Lynne had long been an ardent admirer of the Beatles, reflected in the stylistic plagiarism of their sound by his former band. "Choosing Jeff was part of a long process." Harrison expanded. "I tried to think of someone who could complement my music without overpowering it and also somebody I had respect for as a producer or as a songwriter."

Via their mutual friend Dave Edmunds, the approach was eventually made. "I was in Los Angeles, actually, at the time," Lynne recalled. "Dave Edmunds said to me, just matter-of-fact, 'Oh, by the way, I forgot to tell you, George Harrison would like you to produce some stuff with him.' You know, 'by the way.' If I could've picked one guy I wanted to work with, it would have been George. I was stunned, really." When Lynne visited George at Friar Park for a casual dinner, thankfully the two men got along famously. Harrison then followed up their initial meeting with a phone call and suggested they start making some music together. After working together effectively on the *Shanghai Surprise* soundtrack, it was clear that the partnership were ready to tackle something a little more full-scale.

In early January, Harrison and Lynne laid down the basic rhythm tracks at Harrison's Friar Park studio, allegedly for seventeen songs before narrowing it down to the eleven songs that ended up on the album, to which the usual mix of old retainers and famous faces added their cameos: Ringo, Jim Keltner, Jim Horn, Gary Wright, Ray Cooper, Eric Clapton and, for the first time on a Harrison album, Elton John.

"Eric Clapton plays on four tracks," Harrison detailed. "Eric has the end solo on 'That's What It Takes,' he plays on 'Devil's Radio,' 'Wreck of the Hesperus,' and on the title track. And then Elton John plays electric piano on 'Cloud Nine,' and he plays piano on 'Devil's Radio' and, I believe, 'Wreck of the Hesperus' also. Just to complete the list of people who's on it, Gary Wright plays keyboard, the piano, on a song called 'Just for Today,' And he also plays on 'When We Was Fab.' All the remaining stuff: bass is Jeff, keyboards, Oberheim, and guitars are me and Jeff. All the little twiddly parts that just crop up, like autoharps, is just me and Jeff, and we also do all the backing voices."

But it was Lynne's immaculate production work that most caught the ear, creating a clean, fresh sound that set Harrison squarely in the 1980s, yet without pandering to trends. The drums are crisply recorded alongside the trademark layered guitars on which George was in especially impressive form; it was great to hear him letting loose and cutting up rough. Synths are, of course, much in evidence but are tastefully arranged and this time didn't really detract, unlike some of the bland stuff on Harrison's previous two studio albums. From start to finish *Cloud Nine* showed how revitalised George was.

To some extent George was under more pressure to come up with something worthy of his talent than at any time in his career since *Living in the Material World,* albeit for different reasons. Whereas *Material World* had followed a classic, George was now trying to erase memories of a five-year-old dud. Did he still have it in him, at the age of forty-four, to make music that people wanted to hear?

The tension was unbearable as I put *Cloud Nine* on my stereo for the first time when it was released in November. After all, his last two albums had opened with the pop fluff of "Blood from a Clone" and "Wake Up My Love." I needn't have worried, from the opening bars of the first track "Cloud 9," with Clapton chasing George's slide around a really cool little groove, the album meant business. It had also been a long time since George had had a band this tight, and as a result he raised his game. His brooding, authoritative vocals on this track sounded absolutely fantastic, answered by Jim Horn's baritone sax on the verse.

Harrison himself described the track as "a good opener" and would add that "Cloud 9" was "the kind of song that is not expected from me." "Cloud 9" was, in fact, a *great* opener – creating a sort of "J.J. Cale meets the East" atmosphere that George could have used as a springboard for later albums.

"If That's What It Takes" would be the first of three songs on the album co-written with Jeff Lynne, a song to which "If You Believe" collaborator, Gary Wright, would also contribute.

Describing the genesis of the song George would say, "We [Harrison and Lynne] started writing 'That's What It Takes' together and we did about five middle parts but weren't sure about any of them. Then Gary Wright was over at the house and I said, 'Gary, have you got a middle bit for this?' He said, 'Oh, I've got these funny chords and I don't know what to do with them.' He played these strange chords and we sort of welded them into the middle of the song. It's like a little Beach Boys bit in the middle."

"If That's What It Takes" sounds exactly how the Beatles themselves might have sounded had they stayed together until 1987, especially with the patented guitar arpeggios that permeate the song. Special highlights on this track are George's assertive lead vocal on the chorus and the beautiful extended lead guitar solo over the fade-out.

Whilst "Fish on the Sand" sounded very contemporary in terms of its glossy production values, Lynne's fealty to the Beatles' sound is never more proudly evident than on this up-tempo song. The *déjà vu* being especially evident on the answering harmonies, the descending guitar part on that begins the middle eight and on George's lovely, almost vulnerable vocal. I'd love to have heard the Beatles tackling this song in their pomp. "Fish on the Sand" was clearly written by a man on a roll – an expertly crafted pop song.

Explaining why the song was so atavistic, Harrison would say, "I wrote it in the mood of an old rock 'n' roll song. On the track I used my old Rickenbacker twelve-string, which was probably last used on 'Ticket to Ride' or 'A Hard Day's Night' . . . Ringo plays drums on it."

One critic hailed Jeff Lynne's restraint of Harrison's kitchen sink style and this can be heard best on "Just for Today," a wonderful but dark ballad with George singing in a lower register than I've ever heard him sing. In fact, on certain lyrics he almost sounds too low for the human ear to hear. The minimal production is complemented by Gary Wright's piano playing, and there are some terrific choral backing vocals (multi-tracked by just George and Jeff), unerringly reminiscent of *All Things Must Pass*.

Of "Just for Today" George would say, "I had these three friends who were all in AA at my house one night back in 1983, and this guy showed me a brochure that was called *Just for Today*. It seemed nice to try and live through this day only. I mean it's not just for alcoholism. It's good for everybody to remember we can only live today and the only thing that exists is now. The past is gone, the future we don't know about. So it's like an extension of the 'be here now' idea. I thought it would make a nice song, so I wrote it." Many would speculate that one of these three friends was none other than Ringo Starr, whose battle with the bottle would later become common knowledge.

If the mood on "Just for Today" was sombre, "This Is Love" was full of optimism. "This Is Love" was especially upbeat for a man who had a reputation as a musical curmudgeon, and this may have been Lynne's influence since he co-wrote the song, after Harrison commissioned Jeff to write him a tune. "'This Is Love' was basically his," Harrison would say, "but I helped put it together and I wrote some of the lyrics." The song sounds like George is stretching for the notes in a couple of places like "Fish on the Sand," but that adds to the passion of the piece.

The first side of the album concludes with "When We Was Fab," Harrison's typically laconic send-up of, and tongue-in-cheek tribute to his Beatle days. Conceived by Harrison and Lynne while on holiday in Australia, earning the song the working title, "Ozzy Fab." "I had this guitar that somebody had loaned me," Harrison recalled, "and, I don't know why, I thought I'd like to write a song like that, period. And I could hear Ringo in my head, going, one, two . . . *da-ka-thump, da-ka-thump*."

The song name-checks the "Taxman" vendetta and contains randomly chanted "mop-top" phrases like "fab" and "gear." The arrest by Sgt. Pilcher in 1969 is also mentioned in passing and describes the press coverage that followed the break-up as "the microscopes that magnified the tears." Harrison also manages to sneak in other 1960s references by including the following song titles in the lyrics: "You Really Got a Hold on Me," "Strangers in the Night," and "It's All Over Now, Baby Blue."

On "When We Was Fab," Lynne pulled out all the tricks learnt during his time with ELO to create a sonic recreation of the 1967 Beatles era. A mood heightened by a cello part that could have been arranged by George Martin, a fade-out of sitar sounds and Ringo's distinctive drums.

Once again Harrison chose to include sitar only on his "retro" songs, rather than taking the bull by the horns and picking up from where *Wonderwall Music* had left off.

"I decided to write about the Beatles after all this time because we all go through cycles," Harrison would explain. "For years after the Beatles, I didn't want to talk about it. It was all too close, the pain and the suffering, 'cause that was what was in my mind at the time. Then after years way from it, I thought, 'No, we had fun and had a good little band and had more laughs than misery. It's just that the misery got broadcast more than the fun.' So I forgot the unhappy times. It was part of exorcising all that and bringing it back to a positive thing."

Side Two opens with the "Gossip, Gossip" refrain of "Devil's Radio," one of the album's most instantly accessible tracks, though surprisingly, it was not chosen as a single. "Devil's Radio" sounded ideal for AOR radio, with the honky-tonk piano chops of Reg Dwight and the Beatles feel of its "oh yeah" backing vocals on the bridge.

The song came about by serendipity. "That was a tune I hit on accidentally," George explained, "I passed a little church in England . . . there was poster on the side of this church saying 'Gossip! The Devil's Radio! Don't Be a Broadcaster!' I just thought it was dead ringer for a rock tune."

The song dealt with one of George's favourite bugbears: the intrusive media. Perhaps the song had been influenced by his recent experiences on *Shanghai Surprise,* and less specifically by the experiences of his entire adult life. The song decries the gossip columns and the endless proliferation of tabloid nonsense; blaming the media for his reclusive nature and incisive aim is true. If ever Dylan is in the mood to do a Harrison cover version, this one would be a perfect choice, which Harrison himself would acknowledge saying, "The only thing missing is it should be Bob Dylan singing it."

Angst is then replaced by tenderness on the truly wonderful ballad, "Someplace Else." Salvaged from the *Shanghai Surprise* soundtrack, the version here would come with a fuller production, more in tune with a hit album than incidental film music.

"The producer of the film at the time said, "I want you to write a song like 'Stardust,'" Harrison would recall. "And I said, "That would be nice. Who wouldn't like to write 'Stardust.'" So this isn't exactly like 'Stardust' but it was an attempt at a very melodic love song." George, typically, was being far too modest. "Someplace Else" was another ballad that was the equal of "Something" in every department.

The lyrics and George's sensitive vocal delivery convey a sense of vulnerability, infused superbly by some majestic guitar playing. For the umpteenth time on the record, the delightful backing vocals remind one of the Beatles, close your eyes and you can make believe it's McCartney harmonising. Alongside Ringo's drumming, the song sounds like a harbinger of Threetles things to come.

The album again shifts gear from ballad to pounding R&B stomper, "Wreck of the Hesperus." On this track, Harrison playfully justifies his place in the current music scene despite his age.

"It's really a funny song," Harrison would say of "Wreck

of the Hesperus." "When I started writing it, I just opened my mouth and those first two lines came out. I thought, 'Oh, okay,' and continued along that theme, until you get to the middle eight, and I suddenly go into a vicious attack on the press!"

Once again Harrison aims a doughty rabbit punch at the temples of the journalists he'd slaughtered in "Devil's Radio" and similarly again hits the bullseye. Superb stuff!

Alongside "Devil's Radio" and "Cloud Nine," "Wreck of the Hesperus" was a surprisingly hard-edged rocker and again this was great to hear, since it had been a long, long, long time since George had written anything like this.

The penultimate track was the eastern influenced "Breath Away from Heaven," like "Someplace Else" a refugee from the *Shanghai Surprise* soundtrack.

"I never did a soundtrack album," George would explain to *Billboard* magazine's Timothy White, "because the film got slagged off so bad and we had such a rotten time with them while making it. I didn't want to lose the songs, especially 'Breath Away from Heaven,' which has nice words." Though "Breath Away from Heaven" was not the most effective love song ever written by Harrison, the lyrics are indeed poetically evocative.

Of the album's closer "Got My Mind Set on You," *Billboard* described the single as "catchy," and predicted that "it will deliver," which was something of an understatement. Backed by "Lay His Head" (the *Somewhere in England* reject) the song would become George's first American number one in fourteen years, taking his tally to three as a solo artist (one more than both Ringo and John, though several behind Paul).

"Got My Mind Set on You" was a rather obscure choice of cover version. Written by Rudy Clark, the song had been an American hit for James Ray in the late 1950s. "The tune has been stuck in my head for twenty years," Harrison would explain, "although this version is quite different from the original. It rocks along quite nicely."

Harrison and Jeff Lynne *substantially* updated a rather straightforward rock 'n' roll song, allegedly for a laugh, and turned it into a transatlantic monster. George's energetic vocal was simply superb.

And so there it was: a triumphant return, one that few of his contemporaries could have pulled off without compromise or pandering to trends and fashions. "I particularly wanted to keep it sounding like a rock band," Harrison would say, "with live drums and piano and proper guitars, so it was great to have guys like Ringo, Elton and Eric help out," Harrison says. "I'm really not a fan of all this current fascination with computer music and electronic drums, because it all sounds the same to me. On the other hand, I'm up on all that stuff, and I didn't want the record to end up sounding dated or faceless."

With *Cloud Nine* he'd stuck to his guns, stayed true to himself and had been rewarded with the second best album of his career, and easily one of the best Beatles solo albums ever.

Knowing that he had something good in his hip pocket, this time George threw himself wholeheartedly into the promotion of the album.

Discussing the album in interviews, Harrison was typically modest about his achievement, but inside he must have known that *Cloud Nine* would silence the critics who had doubted whether he could still be a viable recording artist.

Reviews of the album were glowing and almost overnight Harrison was hip again. *Rolling Stone* magazine described *Cloud Nine* as "an especially heart-warming return to form" and an album that "powerfully reaffirms Harrison's considerable charm as a singer, songwriter and guitarist." Noticing the special thank-you dedication on the album sleeve to John,

Paul and Ringo the magazine called the gesture "only appropriate, because *Cloud Nine* is a totally fab record that lives up to the legacy of all those years ago."

This time around, Warner Brothers knew they had a masterpiece on their hands and, in stark contrast to the early 1980s, they put all their promotional weight behind Harrison's product.

Not surprisingly, sales for *Cloud Nine* were impressive, going platinum in America within three months. In Britain, the "Got My Mind Set on You" single peaked at number two (as it did in Canada and Australia), staying there for four weeks, giving Harrison his first homeland top ten since "Give Me Love" in 1973.

The second single taken from the album was "When We Was Fab," though it would not have the same impact on the charts (peaking at number twenty-three in the States and number twenty-five in Britain). The "When We Was Fab" promo video has long been a source of debate among Beatle fans. Alongside George (wearing his, by now, ill-fitting Sgt. Pepper suit) and Ringo, the video would feature a left-handed bass player in a *Magical Mystery Tour* walrus costume. Was it Paul? Prior to filming Paul had told BBC1's *Going Live* that he would like to appear in the video and that he would like to dress in a walrus costume!

Although George did reveal that "the walrus was Paul" the pair were probably just indulging in a private joke. Of course, this suggested that their relationship was a healthy one around this time, a view undermined by the next important date in the Beatles story.

Though George and Ringo would both be at Manhattan's Waldorf Astoria on January 20, 1988, to accept the Beatles' induction into the Rock 'n' Roll Hall of Fame, alongside Yoko, Julian and Sean Lennon, McCartney would not attend!

McCartney claimed that he had wanted to be there but

gave his reasons for his non-appearance thus: "After twenty years the Beatles still have some business differences, which I had hoped would have been settled by now. Unfortunately they haven't, so I would feel like a hypocrite waving and smiling with them at a fake reunion."

According to Linda McCartney's friend and biographer, Danny Fields, "Paul was aligned on one side against Yoko, Ringo and George on the other, in a dispute about recording royalties." "Paul doesn't feel like pretending everything is fine," Linda McCartney would tell Fields, "when they're all getting up a legal case against him."

Believed to be a further cause of grief for McCartney was the fact that Yoko had allowed "Revolution" to be used in a Nike commercial. George too was piqued at the Nike advertisement saying, "Four of us were a partnership and it's daft when people and the company are trying to set certain precedents and establish certain things and one of them is going off on the side and doing a deal. It makes everyone look stupid."

Discussing the Nike controversy further Harrison would say in 1987, "We have to do certain things to safeguard the past. The other thing is, even while Nike might have paid Capitol records for the rights, Capitol records certainly didn't give us the money. It's one thing if you're dead, but we're still around! They don't have any respect for the fact that we wrote and recorded those songs, and it was our lives."

Nonetheless, George was still happy to attend the Waldorf party, so perhaps the real reason behind Paul's absence was the success of "Got My Mind Set on You." Since Macca hadn't had an American number one since "Say, Say, Say" in 1983, maybe he simply didn't like the idea of being upstaged.

Harrison's friend John Fogerty of Credence Clearwater Revival described Harrison as being in gregarious form that night: "He was seated at a table, and there was a buzz of people around him. He'd had so much success, but it was happening all over again, this time in the MTV age, with videos and everything. It was thrilling. As a fan, you just love to watch your heroes get to ride the shooting star again. I walked up to him and said, 'How's it feel to be the hottest guy in showbiz?' And he said, 'It's a bloody nuisance!'"

Despite Macca's non-appearance the night was a high-profile one with George accepting the award on behalf of the group with the words: "I don't have much to say because I'm the Quiet Beatle. It's unfortunate Paul's not here, because he was the one with the speech in his pocket."

George would go on to say, "We all know why John can't be here and I'm sure he would be. It's hard to stand here supposedly representing the Beatles. It's all that's left I'm afraid. But we all loved him so much, and we all love Paul so much." Pictures of the event were sold all over the world.

Afterwards George and Ringo took part in the obligatory all-star jam with Dylan, Mick Jagger, Bruce Springsteen, Little Richard and Elton John. Paul must have regretted not being there, especially when the all-star band performed "I Saw Her Standing There" to a terrific reception.

If the Hall of Fame suggested that Paul was not on the best of terms with George and Ringo in 1988 after all, they were able to put their differences aside long enough to unite to successfully sue Capitol/EMI Records for a reported $80 million of unpaid royalties, and for their unconscionable, though Yoko sanctioned licensing of the Beatles' original master of "Revolution" to Nike.

"In a nutshell," Harrison would protest, "there are all these people who have the rights to everything, or believe they have the rights to everything. The fact that the original master is used – I think we ought to have some say in that, seeing as it was our lives. The complication comes from the fact that Yoko, when she heard that they wanted it, insisted that it be the Beatles' version. The further complication is that Yoko is now – as John's estate – in effect a quarter of the Beatles, or Apple. The history of the Beatles was that we tried to be tasteful with our records and with ourselves. We could have made millions of extra dollars doing all that in the past, but we thought it would belittle our image or our songs. But as the man [Bob Dylan] said, 'Money doesn't talk, it swears.' Some people seem to do anything for money. They don't have any moral feelings at all."

"It's like the Beatles were the most ripped-off people of all time," Harrison would justifiably complain, "and, as for the record company, they should be ashamed of themselves – it's one thing to treat some artist who's here today and gone tomorrow with your crummy little royalty rate and treat 'em like trash, but a band like us who survived twenty-some odd years, sold a billion records for them at the lowest royalty rate you've ever heard of, and then still steal from you?! I'd be ashamed, I couldn't do it. And to have to argue and fight with them and say, give us a break, man, you're lucky to have anything. But if this thing with Capitol comes to court they'll be lucky to end up owning the masters. There's a good chance we'll get back all our masters and everything. And the Beatles have never been greedy; we've never received huge royalties like some people now. You know, you get over a dollar fifty, at least, for an album. We get one old penny. One old English penny per album."

Asked whether he thought the Beatles would win the case, Harrison would reply, "There's no way we can lose. Because if you just put all the cards on the table and see what we've got and what they've got, I think a blind man on a galloping horse would say that Capitol isn't being fair. It's just the balance: the law of nature demands that all things be equal, and this isn't equal."

Inevitably, the Beatles triumphed and it was this more

than anything that cleared the way for future collaborations in the next decade.

For the meantime George would have his hands full with another supergroup: The Traveling Wilburys.

CHAPTER TWELVE

1988-1990

*As far as I'm concerned, there won't be a Beatles
reunion as long as John Lennon remains dead.*
George Harrison, 1989

The success of *Cloud Nine* was such that demand for a fol-
low-up was high. Instead, Harrison had other ideas. After
Cloud Nine had been completed, George was asked by Warner Brothers to create a new bonus track for the twelve-inch
of "This Is Love." It is curious that George agreed to this
request when he clearly had several completed songs ready to
supply. In February 1988 *Songs by George Harrison Volume
One* had been published. The limited edition book featured
sixty of Harrison's song lyrics with watercolour illustrations
by artist Keith West, who had to trek regularly from his home
in North Wales to Friar Park to discuss with George the inter-
pretations of his lyrics. Pencil sketches were submitted for
George's approval and from these the finished paintings were
produced.

The lavish product was available only via mail order at
the princely sum of £235. Each copy was signed by George
himself and came with an EP, housed in a sliding drawer
inside the two-tray solander box. The disc on *Volume One*
(available on either CD or 7" vinyl) contained a remix of
"Lay His Head," "For You Blue" (live from 1974), "Sat
Singing" and "Flying Hour" (two further *Somewhere in England* rejects).

Although one couldn't quibble at the quality of the Genesis publication, the autograph or the unreleased tracks, Harrison fans still had to be, at least, *relatively* wealthy to get the
new songs. "It's expensive, yes," Harrison excused, "but in a

world of crass disposable junk, it's meant to be a lovely thing."

Rather than giving Warner Brothers any one of these otherwise unrealeased songs ("Lay His Head" having appeared on the B-side of "Got My Mind Set on You"), or anything else from his vaults, Harrison set to work on the especially recorded new track. To help with the new song Jeff Lynne dropped all his other commitments that included working with Tom Petty and on Roy Orbison's *Mystery Girl* album.

When Harrison arranged a lunch date in Los Angeles with Lynne to discuss the new song, Roy Orbison showed up too. To George's delight, Roy eagerly volunteered to sing with him on the recording. The story goes that George was impressed that Roy knew so much about Monty Python.

Harrison wanted the recording wrapped up quickly. "I just thought I'll just go into the studio tomorrow and do one," he would explain, "and it happened that Jeff was working with Roy and Roy wanted to come."

Harrison then realised that he had left his guitar at Tom Petty's house, "and I had to go round and get it," as George puts it. As a result of this visit, Tom Petty was also conscripted to help with the recording.

Harrison was faced with the problem of having to find a studio at short notice: "The only studio that we could find available was Bob's. So we thought, Bob's got one, we'll just call him up." The Bob in question was Bob Dylan, and so the "little Ampex" recording console in the corner of Dylan's garage at his Santa Monica house was booked for the following day.

Initially Dylan's role was merely that of a spectator but with the composition only half-finished George asked Dylan to "give us some lyrics, you famous lyricist." George suggested the title when he found a cardboard box with the words "Handle with Care" printed on it behind the garage door, and after he'd added what he called "a lonely bit" for Orbison to sing, the song was complete and recording could commence.

"And so everybody was there," Harrison would later recall, "and I thought I'm not gonna just sing it myself, I've got Roy Orbison standing there. I'm gonna write a bit for Roy to sing. And then as it progressed, I started doing the vocals and I just thought I might as well push it a bit and get Tom and Bob to sing the bridge."

When the song was completed that seemed to be both the beginning and the end of the collaboration. The next day everyone went their separate ways – Orbison left for a gig in Anaheim near Long Beach, Dylan carried on preparing for his summer tour and Harrison played the tape to Warner Brothers.

Warner Brothers' verdict was that the song was too good to be hidden away as an extra track on a twelve-inch and the idea of making an entire album was proposed, which Harrison discussed with Lynne over a quantity of Mexican lager. When the two suggested the idea to Petty, he, not surprisingly, jumped at the chance.

That evening, Jeff, George, Tom and their wives drove to Anaheim to ask Orbison to participate personally. Orbison naturally replied, "That'd be great," though I dare say any career opportunities would have been an improvement on playing the "oldies" circuit into his dotage. Petty would boast: "We watched Roy give an incredible concert and kept nudging each other and saying, 'Isn't he great? He's in our band.' We were real happy that night."

The album that would become *Volume One* was recorded quickly from May 8 to 21 (due to Orbison's tour commitments) at the house of Dylan's then producer, Eurythmic Dave Stewart. Writing and recording a song a day, George described the working practice: "We'd assemble after breakfast at about one in the afternoon, and just sit around with acoustic guitars, then someone would have a title or a chord pattern and we'd let it roll . . . it worked because it was so unplanned." Orbison would add, "We all enjoyed it so much. It was so relaxed. There was no ego involved and there was some sort of chemistry going on."

The Wilbury name had actually been invented as a fantasy idea by George and Lynne during the *Cloud Nine* sessions. "We'd start inventing a group that would have all our favourite people," recalled Lynne. The name The Trembling Wilburys was born out of a *Cloud Nine* in-joke referring to studio gremlins. On Dylan's suggestion the super-group was renamed The Traveling Wilburys (with an American spelling – due to the superior number of Yanks in the group).

Masquerading as half-brothers sired by the same father – Charles Truscott Wilbury, Senior – the five appeared under their chosen pseudonyms. Harrison became Nelson Wilbury, alongside Lucky (Dylan), Lefty (Orbison), Otis (Lynne) and Charlie T. Wilbury JR. (Petty).

When the album was released the songs showed that the five Wilburys had primarily come together to have a good time and transcend the high expectations that dogged them as individuals.

Produced by Harrison and Lynne the album the arrangements would be a mixture of the high-tech and the rootsy, a combination that Harrison called "skiffle for the 1990s."

To back the assembled line-up of five guitarists, Harrison rounded up the usual suspects, nicknamed "The Sideburys" for this junket: Jim Keltner, Jim Horn and Ray Cooper, with Ian Wallace (ex of King Crimson) on tom-toms.

The album kicked off with the irresistible lead single "Handle with Care," a song made up of three parts. The song certainly sounds very much like a George song melodically and lyrically that would have sat comfortably on *Cloud Nine*, although I'm not sure George could have reached Orbison's high notes. A wonderful song, with some truly sublime vocals that deserved a higher chart placing than number twenty-one in the U.K.

Although not as strong as "Handle with Care," "Heading for the Light" too sounded like it could have been written for *Cloud Nine*. However, with "Devil's Radio" and "Wreck of the Hesperus" on that album, there was probably not enough room for another hook-filled R 'n' B blitzkrieg, absolutely soaked to the skin with Jim Horn's saxophone playing.

The other "Harrisong" on the album was the upbeat ride-into-the-sunset sing-a-long "End of the Line." Featuring vocal turns by all the Wilburys except Dylan, the Wilburys suitably rehashed the theme of it being alright to play rock 'n' roll into your 1940s and 1950s, "if you got something to say." Having said that, *Volume One* was not really about making serious religious or political statements.

Throughout the feel-good jamboree Harrison sounded great and he also sounded happy, thrilled no doubt to be playing in the same band as Dylan. George fans must have been overjoyed to hear their idol making such harmlessly tongue in cheek music, preoccupied as he had been throughout his solo career with weightier issues.

Of the other tracks Lynne and Petty would get one solo number each. Lynne's was "Rattled," a retro-sounding rockabilly number, while Petty would tackle the ersatz reggae track "Last Night," a song redeemed only by Orbison's vocal on the middle eight. Alongside the semi-instrumental filler "Margarita," these songs would represent the album's low points.

One of the highlights on *Volume One* was the obligatory "lonely romantic" Orbison ballad, "Not Alone Any More." Assisted by some wonderful backing vocals from Harrison and Lynne, the song proved that Orbison had lost none of his operatic vocal prowess after years of creative oblivion.

Most reviewers seemed more interested in Dylan's Springsteen pastiche, "Tweeter and the Monkey Man," a song that managed to parody virtually all of Bruce's lyrical tics. "Tweeter" is crammed with Springsteen song titles and themes that often crop up in Bruce's lyrics, such as Vietnam and nobody giving a damn, highways and running out of gas, young marriages, car crashes, guns, prison, and oddly named misfits. Perhaps Dylan was hoping to show Springsteen who really was The Boss.

Of the other two Dylan tracks "Congratulations" was a throwaway dirge, but "Dirty World" showed the Wilburys' collaboration at its best, with Dylan's effective vocals echoed by the others taking it in turns to throw in automobile-related nonsense lyrics at the end. A wonderful piece of work.

The overall result was a light-hearted album filled with songs that retained the spirit of not taking themselves too seriously. The Wilburys had not shot for the moon but had stuck to what they knew best: catchy country-tinged pop tunes performed with complete confidence. Even with one arm tied behind their backs, *Volume One* ended up sounding a good deal better than most of their contemporaries did around 1988. *Rolling Stone* magazine called the album "one large, big fat throwaway – but that's what makes it charming." Following on from the platinum sales chalked up by *Cloud Nine* in the U.S.A., *Volume One* would go one better by breaking the multi-platinum barrier. These sales effectively meant that Harrison ended the 1980s as the most commercially successful ex-Beatle.

Tragically, Orbison wouldn't be able to enjoy the sustained sales and plaudits – dying of a massive heart attack on December 6, 1988. He was fifty-two. The promo video for the album's second single, "End of the Line" would see a guitar symbolically placed on a rocking chair in place of the man they called "The Big O."

For George fans there was one down side to his involvement with The Traveling Wilburys. The super-group meant that George's solo career was once again put on deep freeze, cryogenically, as it transpired.

It was strange that George chose not to capitalise on the success of *Volume One* in the same way as the other Wilburys, who all released albums around this time, with Harrison guesting on all of them. Appearances on Orbison's *Mystery Girl* and Petty's *Full Moon Fever* in 1989 were followed by cameos on Lynne's *Armchair Theatre* and Dylan's *Under the Red Sky* in 1990.

Instead, Harrison seemed to be pinning his career hopes on another Wilbury collaboration. "I hope there will be another Traveling Wilburys album," he would say in an interview with *The Daily Express* newspaper on July 29. "It was one of the most enjoyable things I've done. I was doing it with people I admired and respected and it turned out the public liked it too. I just have to wait for all the other Wilburys to finish being solo artists . . . I don't really have any desire to be a solo artist. It's much more fun being in The Wilburys."

While George wouldn't release a fully-fledged studio album, he would instead release, in 1989, a second "best of" compilation – this time covering the Dark Horse years from 1976 to 1989. The LP was not a greatest hits: only "Blow Away," "When We Was Fab," "All Those Years Ago," "Got My Mind Set on You" had been transatlantic hits, although "Wake Up My Love" and "Crackerbox Palace" had also charted in America.

The album's song selection seemed to be based more on personal choice as opposed to released singles and as a result both "This Song" and "This Is Love" were missing. Unfortunately, personal choice did not stretch to including "Shanghai Surprise" which would have been a perfect choice for a record of this kind.

The Best of Dark Horse did, however, include three new Harrison songs: "Cheer Down" (which also appeared on the *Lethal Weapon 2* soundtrack), "Poor Little Girl," and "Cockamamie Business."

"Cheer Down" (co-written with Tom Petty) is a great song, both lyrically and melodically, and contains some blistering slide guitar-work and chordal twists. Sadly, it turned out to be Harrison's last single during his lifetime.

The inspiration for the title was George's wife Olivia as Tom Petty explained: "Olivia would say that to George when he got a little too happy. He would get a burst of enthusiasm, and she'd say, 'Okay, cheer down, big fellow.'"

In Britain the "Cheer Down" seven-inch was ably backed by "Poor Little Girl." With its brooding verses, optimistic chorus and excellent guitar playing throughout, "Poor Little Girl," was, all in all, a pretty good effort.

Sadly, the same could not be said for "Cockamamie Business," a candidate perhaps for the worst ever Harrisong! With its pedestrian arrangement and inane lyrics, the track was another song dealing with the headaches of the pop music industry, written by someone who didn't like the fame game. "Cockamamie Business" was something of a valediction to the business, inasmuch as George would never release another new solo song on Dark Horse Records during his lifetime.

Still, with three new songs it was hard to complain too much about a compilation which hopefully served to remind people that George had written some excellent stuff since 1976. Unfortunately not many people bought the album – which peaked at a very lowly 132 in the U.S. album charts.

Though Harrison was probably correct not to translate the three new songs into the spine of a new studio album, he *was* writing songs around this time, but rather than recording them himself he would give them away. Two of these compositions would see the light of day: "Run So Far" and "That

Kind of Woman." "Run So Far" (later to be released on Harrison's *Brainwashed* LP) would appear on Eric Clapton's aptly-titled *Journeyman* album in November 1989, while "That Kind of Woman" would find a home on Gary Moore's *Still Got the Blues* LP in March 1990, and Harrison would play on both.

Both were throwaways. "Run So Far" in Clapton's hands was a pleasant if insubstantial country ballad, while "That Kind of Woman" sounded as though George had written it with Moore in mind. As a result, the song is appropriately formulaic, with cornball lyrics and tired blues riffs.

In actual fact "Run So Far," "That Kind of Woman," and, more incongruously, "Cheer Down," were all originally submitted for Clapton's *Journeyman* LP. Though one would think Clapton was wise to reject "That Kind of Woman," he did record a version of his own, donating it to George's next project, *The Romanian Angel Appeal* compilation.

Several years after his help to the people of Bangladesh, George would once again play the role of saviour, this time helping children of Romania, a country torn by the despotic regime of Nicholai Ceaucescu and his wife Elena.

From 1965 to 1989 Romania had been subject to arguably the worst tyranny within the Soviet bloc. The Ceaucescus destroyed villages and buildings and stole basically everything of value from their own people. During a violent revolution in December 1989 the Ceaucescus were overthrown and executed, leaving behind them a country decimated by their rule.

The initial charity scheme had been Olivia's brainchild. With help from the other Beatle wives – Barbara Bach, Yoko Ono and Linda McCartney – she had founded the Romanian Angel Appeal in April 1990, "to develop a committed long-term programme of aid for the thousands of orphans in Romania who suffer varying degrees of deprivation."

While visiting the insufferable living conditions these orphans were subjected to, Olivia had been overcome with emotion. "Even the best conditions I found heartbreaking," she would explain, pointing out that the number of children affected could have been upwards of 120,000.

To that end Olivia hoped her appeal would marshal public opinion, influence policies and raise direct financial aid for the Romanian children. Olivia would explain that the money would go towards funding "a major scheme to provide basic necessities to make their lives more tolerable. The programme includes the provision of new plumbing and sanitation, installing sinks, toilets and washing machines along with the volunteers to install them; the provision of clothing, toys, care, medical aid and food supplies to protect and fortify their health along with the staff to administer them." "Each orphanage will be carefully selected," Olivia continued, "and a full team of carers, builders and medical staff will accompany each project to complete the work and care for the children."

The main weapon in the battle to raise funds was the *Nobody's Child: Romanian Angel Appeal* album that George put together with a little help from his friends.

Released in July 1990, the compilation featured contributions from The Bee Gees, Stevie Wonder, Van Morrison, Guns 'N' Roses and Elton John, among others.

Harrison's own presence was all over the album. Aside from writing and playing guitar on the aforementioned "That Kind of Woman" he also persuaded Duane Eddy to submit "The Trembler," a song Harrison produced for Eddy's eponymous 1987 comeback album.

There were also two "new" George tracks on the album to make it worth buying. First, there a Traveling Wilburys cover version of "Nobody's Child" (a track the Beatles had recorded thirty years earlier with Tony Sheridan), with one new verse written by George to reflect the Romanian situation. The other was "Homeward Bound," the gorgeous duet Harrison had recorded with Paul Simon on their 1976 appearance on *Saturday Night Live*. George's finger-picking and delightful harmonies made alone the compilation album a worthy purchase.

Thanks to the Harrison's prolonged support (George and Olivia met Romanian representatives of the RAA to check on progress as recently as September 2000), the Romanian Angel organisation was able to attain long-term independence and was still going as a stand-alone organisation twelve years later.

With the Wilburys now back in harness, the sessions for the "Nobody's Child" single would also coincide with the recording (at a private studio in Bel Air, California) of the Traveling Wilburys' second album, *Volume Three*.

After the sudden and tragic death of Roy Orbison, the four remaining Wilburys decided against replacing him and his vocal presence was very much missed. Dylan and Tom Petty would be much more centre stage on *Volume Three*. Furthermore, Orbison's loss also seemed to have inadvertently robbed the quasi-band of a little bit of the first volume's spontaneity and there was arguably nothing as good as "Handle with Care" on the sequel, although *Volume Three* was a more cohesive whole.

"With the first album," George would say, "we were all a bit nervous of each other, but this time no one even thought about it. We rented a house in LA and I was just hanging around the first morning and all of a sudden I heard acoustic guitars start up. I went down and Jeff and Tom were there and I picked up a guitar. Bob walked in and said, 'Hello mate, how are yer?' Within an hour we'd got the first song, 'Inside Out.' We did two that day. We just banged 'em out like that, Monday to Friday and we had ten songs by the end of it. Lyrics were added later . . . "

Released in October 1990, the album was cryptically entitled *Volume Three* (presumably as a result of Harrison's "Python-esque" sense of humour) and was again produced by Harrison and Lynne. The LP sounded as though they'd spent more time on it this time around and had actually come prepared with songs written in advance. Everyone seems to be trying a bit harder second time around and of course the novelty factor had worn off. The album is less rootsy than their début with Lynne's production techniques more intrusive. The foursome also changed their pseudonyms for *Volume Three:* George became Spike, Tom became Muddy, Bob became Boo and Jeff became Clayton.

The bad news was that George did not sing a complete lead vocal on any of the album's eleven tracks, although his unmistakable brogue could be heard (in impressive form) on the middle-eights of "She's My Baby" and "Inside Out," on the bridge of "Where Were You Last Night" and on one verse in both "Wilbury Twist" and "The Devil's Been Busy" (to which Harrison also added a sitar-sounding guitar solo).

Harrison can also distinctively be heard contributing (with Lynne) to the almost girl-group feel of the vocals on "New Blue Moon" that, along with "You Took My Breath Away," didn't sound a million miles away from Harrison's "Cloud Nine" style.

Unfortunately, Jeff Lynne would sing lead on "You Took My Breath Away," as he would on "Runaway" (the Del Shannon cover that appeared on the "She's My Baby" twelve-inch single), both with rather faceless results.

The vocals on the rest of the songs were taken by Dylan and Petty. Most critics felt that Dylan and Petty had taken over the Wilbury project to which George answered, "I let them take over!" Dylan, in fairness, did deliver some fantastic vocal takes, particularly on "Where Were You Last Night" and "If You Belonged to Me," on which he wheezes his heart out.

The album even included a couple of pseudo-hard rockers rather than the tried and tested formula of country-tinged shuffles. The album's opener and lead single "She's My Baby" even came with an overblown Gary Moore guitar solo.

If the album sounded a bit more contrived and conventional the band seemed to have lost none of the sense of humour and fun that permeated *Volume One*. This was especially noticeable on the goofy "Wilbury Twist," a song that gives the directions on how to do the most difficult dance in the world – a cross between doing "The Mash Potato" and playing twister.

Rolling Stone magazine nonetheless would venture that *Volume Three* "lacks the element of surprise that made *Volume One* such a fresh pleasure, and the soaring strains of the late, irreplaceable Roy Orbison are missed." They would qualify this by saying the album "finds famous folks enjoying themselves and one another, refusing to take their reputations as seriously as some of their fans do."

It wouldn't be too long before both Wilbury records were out of print making them almost impossible to find, even in second hand record shops. The only possible reason for this is that those who bought them have kept them, which is always a good sign.

Perversely, I actually prefer the second album. *Volume Three* seems more complete and contains nothing as utterly throwaway as "Marguerita" and mercifully does not have the ersatz reggae served up by Petty on "Last Night." Unfortunately second time around the public was not as impressed – where *Volume One* had gone multi-platinum and climbed to number three in the American album charts *Volume Three* would stall at number eleven.

Although Harrison would not sing a completely solo lead vocal on any of the album's eleven tracks, Harrison did proffer one "solo" cut for inclusion – "Maxine" – a rambling picaresque that told the story of a girl George had met in a market somewhere. Despite the strong lyrics, the composition's lack of hooks make it, in fairness, not too difficult to see why the demo was rejected.

It's strange that The Wilburys never recorded a third album, especially when you consider how much the individuals involved professed to enjoy the collaboration. For Dylan, tossing a handful of songs to The Wilburys every two or three years would not have been beyond his prolific song-writing abilities and it goes without saying that Lynne and Petty's careers would have always welcomed the boost presented by close proximity to Harrison and Dylan. For Harrison, meanwhile, the Wilburys seemed an ideal project: the group recorded quickly, required hardly any promotional duties and there was no pressure to tour. And, best of all, it was successful.

Nonetheless, the stumbling block did indeed appear to have been George's lack of interest in pursuing the project, that he had by and large instigated and owned the rights to, via his deal with Warner Brothers. Jim Keltner (the group's drummer) added weight to this theory when he said, "I think it really all comes down to George. When I talk to the other guys, Tom or Jeff or Bob, they all sound like they're into it. George wants to sometimes, and other times he gets busy on other things."

And it was evidently Harrison who put the kibosh on any thoughts of a lucrative Wilbury tour. "I kept getting down on my knees in front of George," Tom Petty pleaded, "saying, "Please! It's so much money." [But] like George says, 'I can't see waking up in a hotel in Philadelphia and having to do a Wilburys sound check.'"

Rumours did, however, later surface that three songs were recorded with Del Shannon as the fifth Wilbury, a project prevented from being taken further by Shannon's suicide.

It was also rumoured, in June 1999, that Carl Perkins would be joining the band. The only snag being that, at the time of these rumours, like Orbison and Shannon, the rockabilly superstar was dead.

Apparently Harrison contacted Perkins' son Stan in order to gain access to some unreleased songs by Perkins, who had passed away in January 1998. Stan offered the group four tracks from his dad's vault, including "You Can't Run Away from the Blues" and "One of these Days." According to unsubstantiated rumours, The Wilburys planned to incorporate these tracks into a new album, using a process not unlike the one George, Paul and Ringo would use on John Lennon's tapes for *The Beatles Anthology*. It seems likely that work on this exciting project was never even scheduled, and in the eyes of the public, Harrison seemed content to while away his time on vacation throughout most of the 1990s.

One such holiday, in March 1991, found Harrison secretly attending the Annual George Formby fan convention at the Winter Gardens in Blackpool, on the condition that none of those gathered told the media. (For those unfamiliar with the work of the gap-toothed, ukulele-strumming Lancastrian, George Formby was unarguably the most successful British entertainer of the 1940s.) After some coaxing, George hopped on to the stage with his ukulele, and his son Dhani, to perform Formby's "In My Little Snapshot Album" – George once again proving that he was not your average, decadent rock star.

CHAPTER THIRTEEN

1991-1994

*Well, obviously I haven't really played live. It's
very difficult. I mean, I do enjoy it. Once you get
to do it, it's really enjoyable. There's nothing
nicer than being in a band when it's all rocking.*

George Harrison, 1991

In late 1991 George did the unthinkable and went on tour
. . . in Japan! Whichever way you slice the cake this was
extremely bizarre behaviour from a man who seemed for all
the world to have a morbid fear of touring, especially after all
his bad experiences as a Beatle and the critical annihilation
he'd received on his Dark Horse tour.

What's more there seemed very little reason for him to
tour – what was the impetus? There was no new album to
promote and he had shown absolutely no interest in touring
since 1974, even when it might have done his career and
record sales some good. Besides, he surely had nothing left to
prove, even to himself. More than anything, he was nearly
forty-nine years old!

Nevertheless, it was great to see George back on stage
and Harrison fans have his "husband-in-law," Eric Clapton,
to thank for persuading him to do the tour. While "Slow-
hand" had been touring in South America, interviewers had
repeatedly asked him about the "reclusive" Beatle and an idea
began to take shape in his mind. Eric called George and asked
him if he wanted to join him "on the road." After his sour
experiences of 1974, George quite naturally demurred. Eric
persisted, explaining to George that he had "the world's best
band" (his words), a lighting rig and a great crew all ready to
roll. All George had to do was turn up on stage with his gui-

tar and Clapton, and his touring ensemble would take care of the rest.

George reportedly changed his mind about five times before finally agreeing to the twelve-date tour of Japan beginning on December 1, 1991.

It was Clapton's belief that Japan would be a perfect place for George to tour – an environment that would not present the intense critical scrutiny of Britain or the U.S.A. Though Clapton's attitude was patronising, Japanese audiences would undoubtedly go ape for any ex-Beatle without condition, and would even listen to the songs, something that Harrison had probably not experienced since Hamburg. It was a no-lose situation for George. With the back catalogue arsenal available to the pair, how could their show be anything but entertaining?

Rehearsals for the tour commenced on November 1, 1991, at Bray Studio, Windsor, and continued until November 24, where according to one onlooker there was "a friendly but highly organised" structure with Clapton orchestrating things.

Keyboardist Chuck Leavell kept a journal of the rehearsals and had this to say: "I don't think George was very comfortable being in charge, and he was never one to say, 'OK, we're going to learn this or that.' He would say things like: 'Do you think we should try this song?,' or, 'That one isn't really worth doing, is it?' He would never say, 'I want you to play this part,' or, 'Do it like this' which was somewhat endearing, because it made you feel more involved with the process, as though you were part of a band rather than being a sideman."

"Several interesting people dropped in to rehearsals to see how things were going," Leavell continued. "I recall that early on Ringo came along and sent some flowers, and Phil Collins also came in. As rehearsals were coming to a close, there was some discussion about performing a show before we left for Japan. We thought it would be good to play the set in a small theatre somewhere, to see how people reacted. That didn't come about but an obvious alternative was to invite an audience to the last day of rehearsals. It was by special invitation only and the phone was ringing off the hook for requests to see it . . . We had never played the set before to anyone, really, and between us we knew just about everybody in the audience and we all felt a bit nervous. Afterwards Eric said it was really hard and that it was like playing for your parents, which is exactly how it was."

The audience of musicians evidently liked the show, which must have set George's mind at ease. Leavell would say: "We had some really positive comments and suggestions afterwards as to how we might improve the show, and I remember Steve Winwood came up with the idea of ending, 'Isn't It a Pity' by letting the band carry on playing while George walked off stage."

When George and Eric arrived in Japan at the New Tokyo International Airport on November 28 they were mobbed like Beatles. Such was the furore, that, though George was initially only scheduled to play seven concerts, tickets sold so well that five more dates had to be added.

During the next day's Tokyo press conference Clapton would pay tribute to his friend: "I've always thought that he's a great songwriter, a great musician, a very unique man, and he gave up smoking. I have to respect him for that. I think he's very brave to come here because he hasn't worked on the stage for a long time and it can be a very frightening experience, but I think it will be rewarding. But I always thought of George as being a little like an older brother I never had, and I respect his judgement and his values and I think he's a wonderful man. I like the way he bends the strings, too. He's a great slide player, most of all he's a fantastic slide player."

In Tokyo George explained his decision to tour in more detail: "Well, the reason why I came to Japan was because Eric suggested to me that this time of year would be good if I wanted to do a concert tour. He was not working and he and his band were available to become my band. That was one reason why I thought about working, because Eric asked me. And the reason we came to Japan was, he likes Japan and he suggested we come here. That was the first question. To convey to my fans, really, just whatever the meaning of the songs are, if they have some meaning for the fans of Japan."

Entitled "The Rock Legends Tour," the band included Clapton and Andy Fairweather-Low on guitars, drummer Steve Ferrone, bassist Nathan East, backing singers Tessa Niles and Katie Kisson, keyboardists Chuck Leavell and Greg Phillanganes and Ray Cooper on percussion. Admittedly, on paper it hardly looks like the Harlem Globetrotters of the world's top bands!

George looked great and from the sounds of the *Live in Japan* album was in extrovert form vocally, which was surprising after such a lengthy absence from regular singing. On the album, Harrison comes across as the most live element of the show, in stark contrast to his backing band's perfunctory professionalism, although they did provide a solid backing.

The set list would initially run to twenty-five songs, although "Love Comes to Everyone" would be dropped after the first show on December 1 and the ragged-sounding "Fish on the Sand" would be jettisoned after the following night. For the remainder of the tour Harrison selected ten solo classics, "Roll Over Beethoven" (during the encore) and eight Harrisong Beatle tunes: "While My Guitar Gently Weeps," "Something," "Here Comes the Sun," "If I Needed Someone," "Old Brown Shoe," "Piggies," "I Want to Tell You" and "Taxman," the latter four being performed in public for the first time.

The "Roll Over Beethoven" encore, seemed to go down especially well with Japanese journalists and fans alike. At a press conference for the tour the first question was, "Mr. Harrison, are you going to play 'Roll Over Beethoven' in concert?" When George replied in the affirmative, the whole hall stood up and applauded! According to George "It was such a such a big thing for them, which seemed so funny. Then I realised they must still think I wrote it."

In the middle of George's show, Clapton was allotted four songs, "Pretending," "Old Love," "Badge" (the Cream song he and George had written in 1969), and "Wonderful Tonight."

With Phillanganes and Leavell faithfully reproducing all of the string and horn parts on keyboards, sacrosanct Beatles' arrangements were not defiled. Clapton's solos were invariably the only things to deviate from the script, even adding a solo to "I Want to Tell You" that wasn't originally there.

Though one couldn't fail to be impressed by Phillanganes and Leavell's keyboard skills, the overall sound of the band on both the shows and the *Live in Japan* album was a tad too slick. Thus the shows missed a golden opportunity to take a few liberties with Beatles arrangements.

Things *were* twisted slightly to accommodate the female backing singers and George did change a few lyrics: slightly altering the words to "Piggies" to reflect modern times, and having the girls sing the name "Boris Yeltsin" and "Mr. Bush" in place of messers Wilson and Heath on "Taxman."

As Clapton had correctly predicted, the shows were ecstatically received by the Japanese audiences, and according to Chuck Leavell, "All the shows went well and to me there were always two songs that got a tremendous reaction from the audience. The first was "Isn't It aPity." The lyrics are just a great comment, anyway; but in performance the song had a wonderful way of building throughout its course, culminating in the crescendo at the end. At this point I always looked out at the audience to see their faces and could see how visibly moved they were by that song in particular. The other was "While My Guitar Gently Weeps," where Eric was just tearing up the guitar with his solos."

"Dark Horse" and "My Sweet Lord" were the other big plusses from the shows and the subsequent live album. Unencumbered by problems with his throat, the catchiness of "Dark Horse" positively shines through. "My Sweet Lord," meanwhile, was performed in a more relaxed, stripped-down manner, emphasising the song's contemplativeness rather than its energy, although George still sang the song with the same conviction as he had thirty years ago.

With George performing "Something" and Clapton doing "Wonderful Tonight," it couldn't have escaped anybody's attention that the two men were singing about the same woman, which must have been rather surreal.

Whether this had anything to do with the alleged backstage tensions is difficult to say. Certain Clapton biographers suggest that "Slowhand" grew to resent George picking up the plaudits and all the attention for what was effectively a tour with his band. Surely anyone with a scintilla of objectivity would have realised that that was inevitable.

One Clapton biographer even claimed that Eric had justification for this jealously because he was manifestly the bigger star. This is unempirical hagiography: on what planet is Eric Clapton the bigger star!?

Rumours also flew around that some members of the touring party couldn't wait to get home and perhaps there was some truth to this because any plans to bring the tour to the U.K. or U.S.A. were certainly aborted, even though the Japanese tour grossed an estimated $19 million. With the conspicuous exception of Clapton, Harrison, however, did use pretty much the same band at his Albert Hall gig four months later, so no one could have had too many bad memories.

It is more likely that the tension theories were nothing more than idle rumour, because Chuck Leavell had nothing but hyperbole to describe working with George on the tour. "I learned something about George that I hadn't expected," Leavell genuflected. "I have worked with a lot of people, but not with many others who have made me feel at ease so quickly. It wasn't long before we were invited to his home, to get to know the family and himself a little better. During the course of the tour he was always calling up after the show and saying, 'We've got a bit of food – would you like to come and share it with me?' or 'How about coming up for a glass of nice wine?' even though he wasn't drinking at all. It was all very genuine and it makes you want to work much harder for someone who treats you like that. He has that kind of personality where there is nothing to hide and he is very open and honest, which can be a refreshing thing in this business."

When it was released in July 1992 the *Live in Japan* album was slightly overproduced, taking away some of the live feeling. Some of the songs might just as well have been studio recordings, which is the problem I always have with live albums generally: original versions of Beatles songs, in particular, are rarely improved upon.

Luckily I didn't have to rely on this obligatory tour souvenir for my memories of George on stage, because in 1992, I finally got to see him in concert.

On April 6, 1992, George finally got around to doing his first fully-fledged U.K. show since leaving the Beatles, and what a show it was. I heard about the concert almost by accident. My friend heard the announcement on the radio while I was at school. He then phoned me and said did I want to go and see George Harrison. Well, dur! I recall my friend using his mum's credit card (with her permission) to get tickets from The Royal Albert Hall, the only appropriate venue for an event of this magnitude.

With a general election on the horizon, George announced that he was staging the concert in aid of The Natural Law Party, a Bedfordshire-based political party, whose manifesto promoted Transcendental Meditation and a spiritual lifestyle. If I thought my friend was playing a belated April Fool's Day joke, by now I was convinced.

One thing that certainly was an April Fool's gag was George's interview with the BBC the day before the gig, during which he announced that he would be "recording a new studio album in the summer and will be touring with it upon its release." Naturally, neither "prediction" came true.

George would also explain his reasons for supporting the Natural Law Party during this interview: "I will vote for the Natural Law Party because I want a total change and not just a choice between left and right. The system we have now is obsolete and is not fulfilling the needs of the people. Times have changed and we need a new approach. I believe this party offers the only option to get out our problems and create the beautiful nation we would all like to have. The General Election should be a celebration of democracy and our right to vote. The Natural Law Party is turning this election into a wonderful national celebration and I am with them all the way." Or at least with them all the way until they unsurprisingly gained not one single seat in Westminster.

Still, they got George on stage, so I too was with them all the way – at least from the time Harrison got on stage until the time he left it.

When the big night arrived, punters had to sit through the interminable sets of Joe Walsh and Gary Moore, who were acting as support acts. Thankfully I was able to sleep through Walsh, but I was not as lucky with Moore. Moore played blues for what seemed like the average time-span of puberty, blissfully unaware, as he bled every last ersatz blues hammer-on, that few people in the audience even remotely knew who he was.

After these two has-beens it was almost time for the main event. After NLP spokesman Geoffrey Clements had given a mercifully brief political spiel, on walked George, looking sharp in his black suit, white shirt and moustache ensemble. Amusingly, Clements did not look *that* unlike George, and it's interesting to opine that the doppelganger had been sent on as a gauge of the audiences' reaction.

Not that Harrison needed to worry. When he walked on stage the audience went crazy, with decibel levels reaching Shea Stadium levels, to which George, looking a little nervous, reacted with genuine surprise.

With the bulk of the band from the Japanese tour (Andy Fairweather-Low, Tessa Niles, Greg Phillanganes, Katie Kissoon, Steve Ferrone, Chuck Leavell and Ray Cooper), plus Will Lee on bass and Mike Campbell on guitar, George would perform a 105-minute set, only slightly pared down from the Japanese tour version.

His set that memorable night was "I Want to Tell You," "Old Brown Shoe," "Taxman," "Give Me Love," "Something," "What Is Life," "Piggies," "Got My Mind Set on You," "Cloud Nine," "Here Comes the Sun," "My Sweet Lord," "All Those Years Ago," "Cheer Down," "Isn't It Pity," and "Devil's Radio," his confidence improving with each song.

With the crowd on their feet demanding more, George came back on stage for the encore and announced a couple of old friends lurking in the wings. If the night couldn't get any better, the old friends turned out to be Ringo . . . and Gary Moore! Ringo had said in the papers that while he would be attending the concert, he had no intentions of appearing. What lured him on stage: the grease paint or the green room? Ringo would later say that he went to see the show with his ex-wife Maureen and their children and to see his son Zak play with Joe Walsh.

"I was there just to watch," Ringo would later recount. "The show went so well, George was just groovin'. He should have taken it on the road. I told him that. He should be doing what God wants him to do: perform. So then Joe sauntered off-stage and said, 'George wondered whether you wanted to come on.' It didn't take much coaxing."

With Ringo behind the drum stool the audience resembled bedlam as the reinforced band launched into "While My Guitar Gently Weeps" with Moore in the Clapton role. After that Ringo remained on stage and sparked off a completely uncalled-for five minute drum jam with Ray Cooper and Steve Ferrone, not that I knew anything about it because by this time I was in the street, running to catch my train home. Unfortunately that meant I missed George's final encore of "Roll Over Beethoven" accompanied by Joe Walsh and his thirteen year-old son Dhani (who had also joined his father on a couple of encores during the tour of Japan).

Still, I never thought I'd see George performing "Taxman" and "Something" in the flesh, and it remains one of the most memorable nights of my life. I seem to recall that the highlight was "Isn't It a Pity," on which Ray Cooper really shone on the tubular bells.

The post-show party looked like a truly Beatle affair with Mary McCartney and Julian Lennon representing their absent fathers, at least on the syndicated photographs.

George had obviously rediscovered his taste for performing because a few months later he was at it again when he appeared at The Bob Dylan Thirtieth Anniversary Concert on October 16, 1992, at Madison Square Garden. The concert was sponsored by Columbia Records to mark the Pearl anniversary of Bob Dylan's career in the business that is show, and in the best traditions of the Friar's Club Roast, many artists mercilessly crucified Dylan's songs.

Harrison was, inevitably, one of the exceptions. Looking relaxed, resplendent and sounding great, George (aided by a visible but presumably unnecessary autocue) performed energetic versions of "If Not for You" and "Absolutely Sweet Marie" (although the 1993 souvenir album of the concert would only feature the latter) and also pitched in with guitar and backing vocals on "My Back Pages" and "Knockin' on Heaven's Door."

There would be several more interesting stage and television appearances throughout 1992, which kept Harrison's profile quite high for a man oft-described as a recluse.

June found George appearing with Carl Perkins at London's Hard Rock Café, while in October, he would twice join Gary Moore on stage – first during the encore of the bluesman's own Albert Hall show on October 5, and then on the 25, the two friends would jam at The Crooked Billet pub in Henley.

On December 14, George would also perform onstage with Eddie Van Halen during a benefit concert in Los Angeles for the family of ex-Toto member Jeff Porcaro, who had recently died.

In June 1992 George would also crop up (on British TV) on Channel 4's *Mister Roadrunner* which included a 1991 film of him nonchalantly playing the ukulele while singing the old Harold Arlen number, "Between the Devil And the Deep Blue Sea." Accompanied by Jools Holland on piano, Joe Brown on guitar, Herbie Flowers on tuba and Ray Cooper on drums, the track would be released, in slightly pared-down form, on 2002's *Brainwashed*.

After the *Live in Japan* live album, and Dylan concert album, the rest of the 1990s would be a long decade of non-activity for George as a solo recording artist, with only one *new* song released bearing his name. If George fans were still clinging to the hope *Cloud Nine* would herald return to regular album releases, they were to be disappointed.

The summer of 1992 would see the release of *Songs by George Harrison Volume Two,* which included a further fifty-nine lyrics, beautifully illustrated by Keith West and published by Genesis. Again the print run was limited to 2,500 individually numbered copies, each one hand-bound in a beautiful black three-quarter leather binding, and personally autographed by George and Keith.

As with the first volume, the second edition came with another four-track EP of previously unreleased material: "Tears of the World" (the last outtake to be released from the rejected *Somewhere in England* LP), a demo version of "Life Itself," "Hottest Gong in Town" (from the *Shanghai Surprise* soundtrack), and a live version of "Hari's on Tour (Express)" from the 1974 Dark Horse Tour.

Though not radically different from the version on *Somewhere in England,* the demo version of "Life Itself" did provide a rare chance to hear one of Harrison's songs in its embryo form, with all instruments played by George himself. A charming insight.

Though the book was, once again, an instantly collectible thing of beauty, it still cost a pricy $510 U.S.!

Perhaps it would have been nicer if the two *Songs by George Harrison* discs had been used to form the spine of a nice little album – alongside the three new songs from *The Best of Dark Horse,"* the *Shanghai Surprise* tracks or even further tracks from his 1974 tour.

Instead, the only new song that George's common or garden fans could buy in 1992 was "Ride Rajbun," a song about an Indian rabbit called Rajbun. The song had been written with and for David English, the producer of *The Bunbury Tales,* a television cartoon series about cricket-playing rabbits screened on Britain's Channel 4. Unfortunately, though an accompanying soundtrack album was released, it was withdrawn shortly afterwards and those who watched the show, or bought the equally hard-to-find home video to hear "Ride Rajbun," would have been disappointed to find they couldn't hear the song because of the narration over the top. This was a shame because the song is excellent, with a delightful melody, earnest vocals and some great sitar work by Ravi Shankar, all conspiring to make this another truly great "lost" Harrison gem.

George was clearly in no mood to consider mainstream releases. What was the reason for this? On the one hand, there was no need for George to work. How much more success was left for him to achieve? In 1994 when American radio airplay figures were announced "Something" had surpassed the four million mark, while "Here Comes the Sun" had been played over two million times. Furthermore, since his Harrisongs company had published both songs, the rights were not owned by Michael Jackson, who had paid $47 million for the Northern Songs catalogue in August 1985, much to McCartney's chagrin. That portfolio did, however, include most of George's compositions written for the Beatles albums up to, but not including, *The White Album*.

In fairness to Harrison, his music-making activities had not really abated from the *Shanghai Surprise* in 1986 soundtrack to The Traveling Wilburys' *Volume Three,* a full-time involvement that had been extended by his tour of Japan in 1991. Perhaps it was just time for another rest after a hectic five years.

Or perhaps Harrison felt that there was no need to release music simply for the sake of it; he didn't need the money and he clearly never shared McCartney's workaholism. If there was nothing he wanted to say, why make music that was no longer sincere? Besides, as one of the richest men in the world, why would he want to spend all his time in the studio making pop songs?

Not that this prevented Harrison from winning the first ever Annual Billboard Magazine Century Award for his outstanding artistic accomplishments to the music industry in December 1992. Admittedly the award was just another trinket, but it was good to see George getting some recognition for his solo career. ·

Another possible reason for George's lack of musical output was the painful distraction of having to sue his former business partner and financial manager, Denis O'Brien, alleging breach of contract, breach of fiduciary duty and mismanagement of both Harrison's and HandMade's assets.

And although O'Brien contended, in his defence, that he had helped Harrison make millions, Harrison countered by saying he had also *lost* millions due to O'Brien's mismanagement. "O'Brien made secret decisions, concealed and misrepresented the facts and took actions contrary to Harrison's wishes and directions," Harrison's lawyers alleged, "and through his improper and inept management, caused the film organisation to lose huge sums of money."

The case came to trial in 1995, and in January 1996, George won. Harrison was awarded $10.9 million in compensatory damages, to be delivered within a year of filing the suit. A spokesman for Harrison said, although the ex-Beatle was pleased with the decision, "Winning's one thing, collecting's another." It is unclear whether George ever saw a penny of this money.

The problems surrounding the court case had given the impression to the press that George was facing bankruptcy. Some journalists even speculated that if George lost the case against O'Brien he might lose his beloved Friar Park mansion.

Though this couldn't possibly have been true of a man

with a quarter stake in the never-ending sluice of Beatles royalties, any further tabloid talk of insolvency was banished by *The Beatles Anthology* hoopla that lay in wait just around the corner.

CHAPTER FOURTEEN

1994-1996

It was interesting to actually get back together. For Ringo and Paul and I, we've had the opportunity to let all the turbulent times go down the river and under the bridge, and get together in a new light.

George Harrison, 1994

Let's face it, George didn't need a solo career to get him into the charts when his former band was still doing such brisk business. Everything the Beatles touched during the 1990s turned to gold.

From 1994 onwards EMI would release a string of Beatles products that would earn the group yet more millions and keep them at the top of world-wide charts for virtually the rest of the 1990s. Who needs solo albums when nobody else can even compete with your past! *The Beatles Anthology* project alone would bring more success than virtually every other artist could ever see in a lifetime.

The project started in earnest at the start of 1994. McCartney claimed that the timing of *The Anthology* was when the business problems were *finally* resolved.

According to McCartney: "The first thing we started talking about after the dust had settled was maybe we could do something together, maybe we don't have to live our lives completely separately from here on in." Paul would have meant this sincerely and it was obvious that he was the most excited to be back in the Beatles, a group he had never really wanted to have to leave in the first place.

At the start of March 1994, when *The New York Times* newspaper reported that the trio were "adding new vocal and instrumental lines" to an unissued composing tape, made by John Lennon in the late 1970s, it precipitated a world-wide orgasm. After all, waiting for the Beatles to reform had been an international pastime for twenty-five years. For Beatles fans it was almost like the planets had aligned.

It was George and Neil Aspinall who had initially started the ball rolling by approaching Yoko Ono with the idea to add new instrumentation and vocals to some John Lennon demos. Then, in January 1994, when Paul went over to New York to induct John into the Rock Hall of Fame, Yoko personally handed over the tapes.

Maybe Ono saw a certain symmetry in coughing up the demos that got the Beatles back into the studio, albeit a member short. "I did not break up the Beatles," she stated, "but I was there at the time, you know? Now I'm in a position where I could bring them back together and I would not want to hinder that. It was kind of a situation given to me by fate."

Paul asked Yoko "not to impose too many conditions on us, it's really difficult to do this, spiritually. We don't know, we may hate each other after two hours in the studio and just walk out. So don't put any conditions, it's tough enough. If it doesn't work out, you can veto it. When I told George and Ringo I'd agreed to that they were going, 'What? What if we love it?' It didn't come to that, luckily."

Was there a likelihood that this would happen? On January 31, 1994, when a *Newsweek* magazine article announced the remaining Beatles' plans to record again, Paul admitted that he and George "occasionally get on each other's nerves." Hardly the best start to proceedings!

The reunion had been scheduled for January but Ringo decided he'd rather go skiing with his wife Barbara than make history. As it was, Paul, George and Ringo, or the "The Threetles" (as the press dubbed them) instead first met up to begin recording in February.

Paul told Ringo to have his hanky ready as they took their first stabs at "Free As a Bird," "Real Love," and "Grow Old With Me," at McCartney's remote Mill Studio in Sussex.

Reforming or recording without vital original members was also not unheard of; in fact, it was positively *de rigeur*. The Who had continued without Keith Moon, The Stones without Brian Jones and Bill Wyman, Pink Floyd without Syd Barrett and Roger Waters. The Byrds had reformed for their own retrospective box-set without Gene Clark and Michael Clarke, and the Beach Boys continue to tour with only one original member left on deck. The only problem was that this was the Beatles and therefore sacrosanct. Paul had even posed the question, "Does the world really need a three-quarter Beatle record?"

The initial plan to write new incidental music for the *Anthology* series was jettisoned. About writing new music Ringo would say, "We always hit the wall, and OK, Paul had a song, or George had a song, or I had a song, well that's the three of us, why don't the three of us go in and do this? And we kept hitting that wall because this is the Beatles; it's not Paul, George, and Ringo."

George concurred, iterating that the Threetles "weren't going to get kind of Roger Waters and go out as the Beatles," because, in his view "the only other person who could be in it was John." As long ago as November 28, 1989, Harrison had issued the now famous and much imitated quote: "As far as I'm concerned, there won't be a Beatles reunion as long as John Lennon remains dead."

Using the same exacting standards when it came to choosing those who would be involved in the project, Harrison insisted on Jeff Lynne as producer. Paul's choice had been Sir George Martin, and indeed thought it might be a bit insulting not to ask the venerable knight. George, meanwhile, lobbied for the more contemporary ears of Lynne, although on what basis he considered Lynne "contemporary" in 1994 is beyond my ken. Paul was clearly worried there might be "a bit of a wedge," as he called it, with Lynne coming to the project with a Harrison slant on things.

In fairness to Harrison it is possible that Sir George Martin would not have been *au fait* with the technological problems presented by Lennon's demo tapes (recorded on primitive home equipment) that needed to be ironed out, particularly on "Real Love."

George Martin was frequently questioned why he didn't produce "Free as a Bird," to which he diplomatically replied, "The Beatles are very good record producers and they don't need me anymore. They wanted to keep this project to themselves as much as possible. I knew about it, I knew it was happening and there was no rancour about it. What they did with John's tape is exceptionally clever and very good. Jeff Lynne has done a brilliant job, and having heard it now, I wish I had produced it. I've been working on *Anthology* all year, and if I had to choose between working on the single or the album, I'd have chosen *Anthology*, because it's the bigger one." It's a shame that Martin hadn't been chosen to produce because Jeff Lynne's production would make the Beatles sound more like his own records, much to the commercial detriment of the two new records.

The whole experience, however, couldn't have been too much of an anathema to Paul, considering he engaged Lynne's services on *Flaming Pie* (his first post-*Anthology* solo album) and Lynne obviously did a great job painstakingly cleaning up the tapes before recording could even begin, removing tape hiss, clicks and other abnormalities.

The first three songs tackled had already been heard by the public in some form: "Real Love" and "Grow Old With Me" had already been officially released posthumously on Lennon albums, on the 1988 *Imagine: John Lennon* soundtrack and the 1984 *Milk and Honey* respectively. "Free as a Bird" had been broadcast on the U.S. radio series, *The Lost Lennon Tapes.*

The Beatles focused their initial attentions on "Free as a Bird," a late 1977 piano demo, that Lennon had written for "The Ballad of John and Yoko," a musical that he and Yoko, were collaborating on shortly before his death.

To get everyone psychologically prepared, McCartney suggested they play make-believe: "When we did 'Sgt. Pepper' we pretended we were other people, so we pretended that John had just rung us up and said, 'I'm going on holiday in Spain. There's this one little song that I like. Finish it up for me. I trust you.' Those were kind of the crucial words: 'I trust you.'"

The mood in the studio that day was mostly upbeat. "It's the only session I've ever done where the talk in between is so good that I didn't even want to start recording," beamed Jeff Lynne.

Engineer Geoff Emerick, brought over from his home in America to work on the *Anthology,* agreed with Lynne: "Whenever they are in a room together there's just an energy there, and I guess that's really the only word I can use to explain that." When Harrison, McCartney and Starr started work on "Free as a Bird," Emerick would say, "We hadn't been in the same room together for twenty-five years, and it was just like it had been a week ago. We just carried on recording."

Ringo kick-started the song off with two beats on his snare followed by George's bluesy slide-guitar riff. The demo was further augmented with George and Paul's acoustic guitars, Paul's bass guitar and piano (doubling with John's original) and the familiar sound of Paul and George harmonies behind John's ghostly lead.

Half of Lennon's demo was merely vocalising and repetitions of the title phrase, which meant that Paul and George would have to complete the song with new words. The fact that the song had been unfinished was, according to Paul, "One of the reasons for choosing the song; it allowed us some input . . . George and I were vying for best lyric."

George would explain that they also made changes to John's demo musically: "If you hear the original version you know that John plays very different chord changes in it as well. Historically, what we'd say would be: 'Well, hang on, I'm not too sure about that chord there, why don't we try this chord here?' So we took the liberty of doing that, of beefing the song up a bit with some different chord changes and different arrangements."

With George and Paul competing for best lyric there was a spot of creative tension although this apparently diffused quickly. "I had a couple of ideas that he didn't like and he was right," Paul would admit, "I'm the first one to accept that, so that was OK."

For "Free as a Bird" Paul originally heard it as a big, orchestral, 1940s Gershwin thing, but instead the Threetles decided to do it very simply. It's perhaps a shame that they didn't go with McCartney's initial instincts. In Paul and Ringo you have arguably popular music's finest ever rhythm section but on "Free as a Bird" their trademark styles are suppressed to root notes and a perfunctory backbeat.

McCartney would defend this, explaining, "What I liked was I played very, very normal bass, really out of the way, because I didn't want to 'feature.'" Paul did let loose a little bit on the faux psychedelic segment at the end, but it would have been nice to have heard his melodic, rubbery bass playing given more of a chance to shine in the main body of the song.

George certainly had no such qualms about featuring his slide guitar chops, a factor that had perturbed McCartney: "I was worried because it was going to be George on slide. When Jeff suggested slide guitar I thought, it's 'My Sweet Lord' again, it's George's trademark. John might have vetoed that. But in fact he got a much more bluesy attitude, very cool, very minimal, and I think he plays a blinder." And so did most commentators who felt that it was Harrison who brought the most to the table to improve Lennon's low-fidelity demo.

When Ringo heard "Free as a Bird" in the control room, excitement got the better of him as he exclaimed, "It sounds like the bloody Beatles!"

With so much slide guitar on it, the minimal rhythm track and Jeff Lynne's production it's hard to agree with Ringo. Certainly George's verdict was a bit more restrained: "'Free as a Bird' does sound like the Beatles, only a more modern version. But we went through a lot of changes musically in the 1960s so it's hard to actually put your finger on what was the Beatles sound. When you say it sounds like the Beatles, people may expect it to sound like '65 or '68. It's very similar in some respects to *Abbey Road* because it has the voicing, the backing voices like 'Because.' But the whole technical thing that has taken place between 1969 and 1995 is such that, you know, it sounds a lot more like now."

McCartney seemed to have bent over backwards to accommodate Harrison during the sessions, even down to the ukulele solo and use of George Formby's "turned out nice again" catchphrase in the coda of "Free as a Bird!" and reluctantly allowing Jeff Lynne to sing backing vocals.

Being allowed to sing on the record was possibly the reason why Lynne seemed to be the one enjoying himself the most. "Although a long time has passed since they last recorded as one unit," Lynne would recall, "they worked terribly well together. Being in the control room watching and listening to them interact with each other was fascinating. Paul and

George would strike up the backing vocals and all of a sudden it's the Beatles again. They were having fun with each other and reminding each other of the old times. I'd be waiting to record but I was too busy laughing and smiling at everything they were talking about. It was a lovely, magical time."

Paul couldn't stop telling people how pleased he was with the results. "I am quite proud of it," he would say at the time. "I think it worked great, it's actually a Beatles record. It's spooky to hear John singing lead, but it's beautiful. People said beforehand we shouldn't do it, but that kind of focused us up a bit. I thought, f*** you! We'll f***ing show you! It's fatal if they come out in the papers and say we shouldn't do it, because I want to do it even more. It was a joyful experience, it was magic, it was a really good laugh to be making music together again."

Ringo too was satisfied, "Oh, I was shocked, it just blew me away . . . Doing this project has brought us together. Once we get the bullshit behind us, we all end up doing what we do best, which is making music."

All three Beatles seemed happy to brag about how well they still worked together. Paul would describe his feelings: "Not having done it for so long, you become an 'ex-Beatle.' But of course getting back in the band and working on this *Anthology*, you're in the band again. There's no two ways about it. And it was good, it was good being them again for a little while. We work well together, that's the truth of it; we just work well together. And that's a very special thing. When you find someone you can talk to, it's a special thing. But if you find someone you can play music with, it's really something, y'know."

George was also enthusiastic, "It was interesting to actually get back together," he insisted. "For Ringo, Paul, and I, we've had the opportunity to let all the past turbulent times go down the river and under the bridge and to get together again in a new light. I think that has been a good thing, it's like going full circle, and I feel sorry that John wasn't able to do that, because I know he would have really enjoyed that opportunity to be with us again."

Things went so well that the reunion sessions were extended from a week to almost a month, although further recording sessions were delayed due to George's sale of HandMade Films to Canada's Paragon Entertainment Corporation for a paltry $8.5 million, in May 1994. What Paragon got for their money was HandMade's library of twenty-plus films and various distribution rights.

Speciously, the press seemed to interpret the HandMade sale as further evidence that Harrison was broke, suggesting that his very involvement in the *Anthology* was motivated purely by an apocryphally precarious financial situation. Luckily Derek Taylor was on hand to dismiss the speculation but added, "now it may be the case that they all would like the money, because once you've got a lot of money you do like to have more."

Harrison rejoined his confrères in June, again at Paul's Mill Studio, to rehearse for the following day's filming at Friar Park. There, accompanied by their respective wives, Paul, George and Ringo had arranged to perform a symbolic version of "Let It Be." Unfortunately, John's absence was so overwhelming that, after a long discussion the idea was abandoned and the Fab Three turned their hands instead to jamming on oldies and rock 'n' roll classics.

With George and Paul on acoustic guitars and Ringo on brushes the trio were filmed running through a number of oldies, including "Thinking of Linking" (an early Lennon-McCartney effort), "Raunchy," (the song that had won George his place in The Beatles all those years ago) and "Blue Moon of Kentucky." All three performances would eventually be included on the 5-DVD "Anthology"-set put out at the end of March 2003, alongside ukulele versions of "Ain't She Sweet" and "Baby, What You Want Me to Do" performed on the grass of George's garden.

One thing that certainly did see the light of day, in November 1994, was the *Live at the BBC* compilation. EMI had used the album as a completely unnecessary road-test of fan base fealty. They needn't have worried, the two-disc set became one of the fastest selling albums of the year – entering the charts at number three in the U.S.A. and number one in Britain (the thirteenth to do so in the U.K.).

Recorded live at the BBC between March and June 1965, the tracks were then digitally remastered by George Martin for the compilation – no easy task due to the fact that the BBC no longer had the master tapes for several of the performances and, although copies of the missing programs did exist, the quality, in many cases was extremely poor.

Although the songs were mainly cover versions of early rock, pop and country tunes, there were thirteen Lennon-McCartney songs, including the otherwise unrecorded "I'll Be on My Way," with the well-honed John-Paul-George harmonies in full three-pronged attack.

In April 1995 "Baby It's You" was released as the only single from the album and climbed as high as number seven on the British charts.

Live at the BBC also annihilated all the other BBC session albums that have been released by other artists, before or since. For George fans there was the previously unreleased "Crying, Waiting, Hoping," "I Forgot to Remember to Forget," "Glad All Over," and, best of all, the energetic and timelessly fine "Young Blood" and "Nothin' Shakin."

While it was great to see EMI succumbing to public demand by releasing these gems officially, there were some who regarded the album as a wasted opportunity. The set offered only fifty-six of the eighty-eight individual songs recorded at the BBC, and only thirty of the thirty-six tracks that were never recorded at Abbey Road. Among those missing were "Beautiful Dreamer," "A Picture of You," "Lend Me Your Comb," and the excellent "Dream Baby" with Pete Best on drums.

Nit-picking aside, the fifty-six tracks that *were* included on the compilation made *Live at the BBC* an indispensable addition to any Beatle fan's collection, and a timely reminder that the Beatles, when all was said and done, were a great little four-piece band.

In February 1995 the Beatles reunited again to tackle "Real Love" and "Now and Then." Having decided to focus their attention on the gentle acoustic ballad "Real Love," for Jeff Lynne, there were further unwelcome technical problems.

Though John's voice was stronger and clearer on "Real Love," the tape sounded like a third generation copy, smothered with a thick veneer of hiss, mains hum and clicks throughout the song. Lynne would claim that "putting fresh music to it was the easy part!"

The Beatles sped up John's demo recording, so that their new version was a semi-tone higher than the original. To give the song a timeless Beatles feel to the track many of the groups old instruments were used, many of which Paul had in his collection, including the celeste that Lennon had played on "Because" and the harmonium that John had used on "We Can Work It Out" (both played by on "Real Love" by Paul). This approach was further enhanced by George playing his psychedelic *Magical Mystery Tour* Stratocaster, and of course Ringo's Ludwig drum kit.

While McCartney was not as effusive about "Real Love," saying, "I don't quite like it as much as "Free as a Bird" because I think "Free as a Bird" is more powerful," he did acknowledge that it was "catchier." "There was one real nice moment when were doing 'Real Love,'" McCartney added, "and I was trying to learn the piano bit, and Ringo sat down on the drums, jamming along. It was like none of us had ever been away."

Unlike McCartney, Harrison seemed to prefer "Real Love," which moved him to joke, "I hope somebody does this to all my crap demos when I'm dead, make them into hit songs."

Ringo, meanwhile, would sum up his feelings as follows: "Recording the new songs didn't feel contrived at all, it felt very natural and it was a lot of fun, but emotional too at times. But it's the end of the line, really. There's nothing more we can do as the Beatles."

But Ringo was wrong – there was more they could do as the Beatles. As mentioned earlier, another piano-based Lennon demo from the 1970s, "Now and Then" was also tackled during the February 1995 sessions. The song had a chorus but was totally lacking in verses and much work needed doing on it. As a result the song was not completed. Jeff Lynne explained how much work had gone into "Now and Then": "We did the backing track, a rough go that we didn't really finish. It was a bluesy sort of ballad, I suppose, in A minor. It was a very sweet song. I like it a lot and I wish we could have finished it."

According to Paul the song "would have needed a lot of rewriting and people would have had to be very patient with us. We'd have to do a hatchet job on it." Its non-completion was a real tragedy because once you've had two new Beatles songs, you get greedy!

Sensing the fact that there wouldn't be too many more Beatles recording dates, the February 1995 sessions were also discreetly filmed (by Geoff Wonfor and Kevin Godley), for inclusion in the promo video that accompanied the "Real Love" single.

Undoubtedly the most interesting fly on the wall snapshot was the moment when McCartney gives Harrison an awkward hug. A moment to cherish for Beatle fans everywhere!

The Threetles would get together again in May, but "Real Love" would be the last thing to be released. During the sessions in May the trio worked on "All for Love," a brand new song written by George and Paul. Allegedly, "All for Love" was completed, but Lennon's absence made it hard to present the song as a Beatles recording, and it was therefore shelved.

The non-release of "All for Love" was perplexing and somewhat contradictory since the *Anthology* volumes were released, at least to some extent, because fans were desperate for access to the treasure trove of previously unreleased material. Even if some recordings didn't meet the exacting standards of their 1960s heyday, that was missing the point. The massive sales that greeted the *Anthology* albums were testament to how much Beatles fans were prepared to pay for historically important recordings, irrespective of quality.

Explaining his objections to the release of "All for Love" Harrison would say, "We always said the Beatles was us four and if ever one of us wasn't in it then it's not the Beatles, and the idea of having John as the singer on the record, it works, it is the Beatles. There was talk about us doing stuff on our own but I have no desire really to do a threesome." So why write and record the song in the first place? It's non-release was criminal.

Joining "All for Love" and "Now and Then" on the shelves were further tasty morsels, such as, footage of the three Beatles and Sir George Martin together again at Abbey Road.

"It was March 31, a day I shall never forget," recalled Allan Rouse, Abbey Road's Beatles Co-ordinator. "I was in Studio Two control room at the time, playing back some more archive recordings to George Martin. At any other time, this would have been par for the course, but on this occasion we were joined by Paul, George and Ringo. This was the first time all four had been in that studio since 1969, and quite honestly the atmosphere can only be described as sheer magic. They were all totally at ease in each others company, taking photographs and videos and obviously enjoying the unique occasion as much as everyone else."

The visit to Sir George Martin at Abbey Road (footage of which was also included on the bonus disc of the *Anthology* DVD set) wasn't purely nostalgic. Martin had decamped to Abbey Road to begin compiling and mixing unreleased Beatles material for the *Anthology* albums immediately after *Live at the BBC* had been completed. Due to the fact that archived Beatles tapes are never allowed outside the Abbey Road building, all the listening and subsequent mixing sessions were held at the studio's penthouse suite.

Of the *Anthology* albums Martin would say, "I am trying to tell the story of the Beatles lives in music, from the moment they met to the moment they split up in 1970. I have listened to everything we ever recorded together. Every take of every song, every track of every take, virtually everything that was ever committed to tape and labelled 'Beatles.' I've heard about 600 separate items in all. I didn't start any serious listening until early this year, when I got Paul, George and Ringo to come in occasionally and listen with me. Of course they couldn't sit through all the sessions, so I would tend to have them come in about once a week."

Paul McCartney would describe sitting in Abbey Road Studio Two, where they always worked, as "like being archaeologists. We're actually finding tracks that we didn't remember recording, that we didn't want, or thought, 'No, that's not too good.' Now of course, after thirty years, they don't look too bad at all. There were obvious reasons why a lot of the stuff didn't make it into the shops, but we're not looking at it from a recording quality point of view. It's history, and what we've been putting together is an historical document."

When it was released on November 21, 1995, *The Beatles Anthology 1* featured a sixty-track mother-lode of previously unreleased studio outtakes, live recordings, TV appearances and the Beatles' own private tapes covering the period 1958 to August 1964. When first day sales broke all previous records, Apple Press Officer, Derek Taylor was moved to say, "It's a new strain of Beatlemania. My phone should have stopped ringing in 1970, but I've never been so busy."

Of *The Beatles Anthology 1* Harrison would say, "it goes into our Hamburg material. We recorded a couple of songs there for Polydor. Then it goes through to the Decca audition." Of their rejection by Decca, Paul would deprecate, "You can kind of see why," though he would add, "You can see our development. You can see it happening on the CDs."

At last fans got to hear The Quarry Men's spirited cover of Buddy Holly's "That'll Be the Day," and an edited version of the country-flavoured "In Spite of All the Danger" (credited to Harrison-McCartney), recorded at a home studio in Liverpool in 1958.

Alongside these two tracks there were also three recordings, "Hallelujah, I Love Her So," "You'll Be Mine," and "Cayenne," from a 1960 rehearsal at McCartney's boyhood home, featuring Stuart Sutcliffe on bass.

And while on the subject of forgotten Beatles, ten tracks on *The Beatles Anthology 1* would feature the drumming of Pete Best. Pete seemed happy that he was "now being recognised for my contribution to the band," and even went so far as to review the album for *The Sun* newspaper in Britain, calling it "The Beatles' greatest ever album, and not just because I'm on it! Frankly, I'm bloody proud and believe they really stand the test of time." Unfortunately, his drumming had *not* withstood the test of time, explaining as it did more satisfactorily why he was sacked from the band. A fact no doubt softened by the alleged seven-figure royalty cheque he would receive for his contributions.

His drumming on the EMI audition version of "Love Me Do" was especially interesting to hear. While the charitable would call his performance adequate, those of a more honest bent would describe it as pedestrian, or maybe even sloppy. The Pete Best recordings demonstrated once and for all how essential Ringo Starr's drumming was, to both the sound and energy of the Beatles success.

Anthology 1 also contained excellent live performances from the 1963 Royal Command and their legendary first appearance on *The Ed Sullivan Show* in New York City on February 9, 1964. Arguably the album's standout track, however, was "Leave My Kitten Alone," a scintillating cover of the R 'n' B classic originally recorded by Little Willie John.

For the George fan, the undoubted highlight of *Anthology 1* was the first ever release of "You Know What to Do," Harrison's second ever composition submitted to the Beatles. Its appearance was a remarkable discovery given that it seemed to have emerged from nowhere. Though fans had been vaguely aware of the song title, it had never even turned up on bootlegs before.

Of "You Know What to Do" McCartney would recount, "There was a song of George's that the engineer Allan Rouse discovered. EMI didn't know they had it. When they called in anything anyone had in Abbey Road, or EMI world-wide, with 'Beatles' on the box, this arrived. They thought it was lost. I do believe there will be a bunch of people interested in hearing the George Harrison song from thirty years ago that no one to this day had heard. It's not the greatest thing that George ever wrote, but it's an undiscovered nugget. If you find a little Egyptian pot, it doesn't have to be the greatest Egyptian pot. The fact that it is Egyptian is enough."

"You Know What to Do" had actually been recorded as a demo late one evening after a *Beatles for Sale* session in 1964, but never finished as a composition. In the last verse George changes the verse melody slightly, suggesting that he wasn't quite sure which way to take it.

McCartney's generous praise does not necessarily mean the song is a lost classic, although the song was evidence of George's evolution as a songwriter, and it's a shame the Beatles couldn't have attempted to beef it up and include it on a B-side or slipped it onto an EP.

The Beatles Anthology 1 entered the U.K. charts at number two, setting a world record for the biggest double album sales in a week. By mid-December, EMI reported that the album had qualified for double-platinum in the U.K. and that seven million copies had been shifted world-wide. In the U.S.A. nearly one million copies were bought in the first week alone. As Macca himself gloated, "Thirty years on, the Beatles are selling as if it's the new thing."

The release of the "Free as a Bird" single on December 4 also featured a four minute edit of "Christmastime Is Here Again" that had not been included on the *Anthology* albums. However, even this wasn't enough to push "Free as a Bird," the first new Beatles single in twenty-five years, to number one. McCartney was believed to be particularly upset by this result, especially since it was his nemesis Michael Jackson's "Earth Song" that had stood in the way. Unfortunately, the Beatles and Apple had themselves to blame – its release date, a fortnight after the album had hardly helped sales.

Further indignation in Britain was to come when "Real Love" was released in March and the BBC scandalously refused to include the single on their Radio 1 play-list, on the grounds that it was "not of sufficient merit."

Radio 1's dismissal of "Real Love" caused an uproar in the press and even elicited comments from two Members of Parliament. Apple was not at all happy either, spokesman Geoff Baker would describe the Beatles' reaction as "indignation, shock and surprise. We carried out research after the *Anthology* was launched and this revealed that 41% of the buyers were teenagers."

"Real Love" still jumped into the charts at number four, selling 50,000 copies in its first week. But, despite Paul's impassioned efforts, "Real Love" only spent seven weeks on the U.K. chart. As a result, "Real Love" had the distinction of being the poorest chart performer of any "new" Beatles single in Britain, trailing behind the previous shortest runner, "Lady Madonna," which only lasted eight weeks on the charts in 1968.

Nonetheless, "Free as a Bird" and "Real Love" both went on to become gold singles, giving the Beatles their twenty-first and twenty-second such awards, the most for any group in history.

Shortly after the release of "Real Love" came *The Beatles Anthology 2,* a 45-song body of work covering the peak period between February 1965 and February 1968.

Alongside a clutch of unreleased songs (such as "If You've Got Trouble," "That Means a Lot," and "12-Bar Original") *Anthology 2* allowed fans a glimpse into the band's studio world. Some of the highlights included "I'm Looking Through You" in its prototype form, an excellent rock trio version of "Good Morning, Good Morning," and a fascinating new edit of "A Day in the Life." There was an also a fascinating alternate take of "And Your Bird Can Sing," which showed Harrison in especially impressive form with a radically different guitar part, albeit one obscured by an uncontrollable fit of Lennon and McCartney giggling.

While the unadorned takes of "Across the Universe" and

"I Am the Walrus" (sans overdubs) must have been treats for Lennon fans, George acolytes were treated to "Only a Northern Song" with alternate lyrics, a version of "Taxman" (with different answering phrases from John and Paul), and an instrumental version of "Within You, Without You" that underlined the song's melodic complexity and beauty.

The majority of reviews for *The Beatles Anthology 2* were positively ecstatic. *Q* magazine in Britain described it as "magnificent" and fawned that the "talent of Macca glows like a nuclear accident." The film magazine, *Empire*, glowed "even in rehearsal the Beatles shook the world." Again the album entered the chart at number one on both sides of the Atlantic.

The third and final chapter of the *Anthology* collection comprised the period 1968-1970. Press reviews, were slightly less effusive about the third collection.

The NME in Britain called *The Beatles Anthology 3* "an enthralling glimpse between the shutters of a band in chaos," while *Melody Maker* described it thus: "If *Anthology 2* was the parallel Beatles, stacked with portmanteau mixes which would never have existed otherwise, then *3* is the Beatles Unplugged. Naked genius, no less."

Highlights of the album included the chance to hear the demos of *The White Album* tracks the Beatles recorded at George's house in Esher in 1968 that included a run-through of Harrison's "Piggies." Also delightful were George's acoustic demos of "Something," "All Things Must Pass," "Old Brown Shoe," and "While My Guitar Gently Weeps."

In the spirit of Glasnost, McCartney even listed the "While My Guitar Gently Weeps" demo as one his favourites from the album, describing it as "just George on acoustic and nothing else, no Beatles, no Clapton playing the lead." Certainly the demo had always been regarded by many as the Koh-I-Noor of Abbey Road's vaults.

Anthology 3 would also finally see the official release of "Not Guilty" (rejected from *The White Album*), "I Me Mine" (the last song ever recorded by the Beatles), and a Twickenham rehearsal of "For You Blue." With eight songs on *Anthology 3*, George would finally get a healthy chunk of the song-writing royalties from an *Anthology* album.

Sales of *Anthology 3* were again phenomenal. When the album entered the U.S. album charts at number one, to become their eighteenth chart topping album and their third consecutive US. number one in a year, they achieved a feat they'd not even accomplished during the 1960s.

In America, the combined sales of all three *Anthology* packages, plus the group's back catalogue, ensured that the Beatles were the top selling album act of 1996, thirty-two years after they had first achieved this status. Official *Stateside* figures showed that the group sold more albums in 1996 than they had in any year since the 1960s.

According to Neil Aspinall, "The Beatles didn't hold anything back from the three *Anthology* CDs. Everything they thought was worth releasing is on those three CDs . . . They haven't left stuff there, thinking, 'We can put that out later,' or 'If we do a box set of *Anthology* in a couple of years time then we can have a few bonus tracks on there.' The bonus tracks are already on there."

This is slightly disingenuous, given that many other songs were considered for inclusion. Ultimately vetoed, were further tracks from the Decca audition, live performances from Hamburg, and several demos of songs that had been written and given away to other artists, such as Paul's rendition of "Goodbye" and John's "Bad to Me." Live versions of "She's a Woman" and "Nowhere Man" were also considered alongside vocal-only renditions of "Think for Yourself," "Love You To" and "Paperback Writer," and the mythical 27-minute version of "Helter Skelter."

Alternate takes of "From Me to You," "Getting Better," "Magical Mystery Tour," and "Yer Blues" had all been slated for the *Anthology* CDs, only to be rejected. McCartney's "Carnival of Light" (his 1967 avant-garde experiment) was also discarded, vetoed by George, Ringo and Yoko who felt that it had never been intended for the Beatles.

Apple was also believed to have acquired an acetate of Paul singing an acoustic version of "Love of the Loved," while EMI purchased at auction a live Quarrymen tape with John singing "Putting on the Style" and "Baby Let's Play House." Similarly nixed was a recording from the afternoon Lennon met McCartney due to the appalling sound quality.

There was also of course "All for Love" and "Now and Then." Paul confirmed that work on "Now and Then" had been stopped by George. "I actually wanted to do it on *Anthology 3*," Paul would complain, "but we didn't all agree . . . There was only one of us who didn't want to do it . . . But things change and the thing is that it might not go away." Had the reaction to "Free as a Bird" and "Real Love" been more positive, or had either gone to number one then maybe the Threetles would have had no choice but to complete the third song. Who knows, one day the world might get to hear these last two Beatles songs, and it's interesting, though craven, to speculate whether Harrison's death makes this more likely or less so.

It was revealed that their bank balances could have been further swelled had they accepted the inevitable tour proposals that found their way to Apple's letterbox. Allegedly the Fab Three were offered $100 million to play ten concerts but McCartney insisted there would be too big a hole where Lennon should be. "I really feel strongly that it would be a mistake for the three of us to go on tour," Paul would demure, though he did acknowledge that the money was good.

The cash they missed out on by not touring was compensated by the syndication of the *Anthology* TV series and video sales. The six-hour documentary (extended to ten-hours on video) would be seen in ninety-four different countries. It was reported that Apple received $75 million from the *Anthology* television broadcasts.

For North America alone ABC-TV paid $20 million for the broadcast rights, a figure recouped when the network sold 80 percent of the series' commercial slots in less than three weeks at premium prices, with thirty-second spots commanding fees over $300,000.

Discussing the series Harrison would contend, "It's difficult when four people are telling a story 'cause it's actually four different stories. I mean, you must realise it's got to be somewhat of a compromise when four people are involved. But we're trying to just say how it felt to us."

Originally entitled *The Long and Winding Road,* the documentary project had been hanging over them since the break-up. As long ago as 1970, Paul McCartney had instructed Neil Aspinall to collect all past TV newsreels about the Beatles from around the world. Recalls Neil, "So I started to do that, got in touch with all the TV stations around the world . . . got news footage in . . . we edited something together." With all the business wrangles of the 1970s the project was shelved, only to be revived in the mid-1980s when Apple showed Steven Spielberg a rough edit during a failed search for a director, after which the documentary was shelved again.

Interestingly, Lennon had legally supported the project in one of his last acts of business before his death. On November 28, 1980, as part of a deposition for Apple against the producers of the "Beatlemania" stage show, Lennon had stated, "I and the three other former Beatles have plans to stage a reunion concert, an event to be filmed and included as the finale to *The Long and Winding Road,* an official Beatles produced documentary to be released in the mid-1980s."

In 1989, when Apple won a reported $80 million settlement from Capitol, all parties agreed to play happy families and suddenly the documentary was revived again and renamed *Anthology* upon George's insistence, because he didn't want the project to be associated so closely with a McCartney song.

Paul, George and Ringo granted hundreds of interviews for the documentary over the course of three years and each approved every frame of footage as the work-in-progress was screened for them.

Harrison was said to have dreaded the idea of sitting through all the old Beatlemania footage – the hysterical girls at the airport, the kooky press conferences, the frenzied chase scenes from *A Hard Day's Night,* etc. Eventually his pride kicked in, gloating to series director Geoff Wonfor one day in the editing room, "If U2 thinks they're a big and popular band, then they should sit through this shit and they can see how popular a real band can be."

The filmmakers worked with the constant dread that the band members would kill the project. As Derek Taylor puts it, "we were all prepared for them to say, 'Oh, f*** it, who needs all this?'" To add to the pressure, when the press learned of the *Anthology* they began bombarding Apple for updates. As a result Apple took to calling the project "T.T.T.F.O," a mneumonic for "Tell Them to F*** Off" should a journalist phone.

The Beatles and Yoko Ono had absolute control over the *Anthology* documentary, meaning there weren't any shocking revelations or renegade voices. Ono herself declined to appear in the documentary, denying the series some fascinating insights, particularly in regard to the break-up.

The documentary was made without a narrator, probably

because Ono and the Beatles would have clashed over the text. "There would have been untold horrors," confided a source close to the project.

The documentary series contained as fascinating a collection of films as the CDs had contained music. These included outtakes from the *Let It Be* and *Magical Mystery Tour* films, the "Strawberry Fields Forever" and "Penny Lane" promotional videos, a long-overdue colourised version of the "All You Need Is Love" from the *Our World* satellite broadcast, and home movies from holidays in Greece and India, some of which had never even been developed.

"I quite enjoyed telling the story," Harrison was quoted as saying, surprising everybody, "the upside of the Beatles was really always far bigger than the downside, and it was good to remember that."

Charmingly, the documentary series showed how the band-mates' memories had undergone the inevitable slippage over the years. But the filmmakers turned that slippage to their advantage, and made a documentary that revels in conflicting memories and emotions.

To be fair, at least they'd finally given a reunion a shot, and perhaps it was unreasonable to ask the three of them to have given any more. For the *Anthology* Paul, George and Ringo had emptied not only their personal archives but also their Pandora's Box of resentments. In light of George's death, I'll bet Paul and Ringo are glad that they'd had that closure and public reconciliation, and I'm sure George was glad too.

Certainly they must have felt mightily relieved to have put an end to forever having to field questions about reunions, although those questions will probably never go away until they're *all* dead. The anthology showed that, although their relationships could still be complex, it was also obvious that there was still a bedrock of real love for each other.

When Harrison was asked by a journalist whether he still hugged or shook hands with McCartney and Starr, he faxed back: "Yes!"

When asked: "Is the *Anthology* a new beginning, or is it simply the end?" Paul replied, "Ends are beginnings and beginnings are ends," while Ringo added, "This is the end of the beginning." George's take was, "Well, it's always the end of the beginning isn't it? Play the game existence till the end of the beginning."

Apple Corps had the final word when they released the following statement in November 1996: "The end has finally arrived. The Beatles are no more. The official word is that Paul McCartney, George Harrison and Ringo Starr will never play together as a group."

And of course they never did.

CHAPTER FIFTEEN

1997-1999

I'm not going to die on you folks just yet.
George Harrison

The phenomenal success of the *Anthology* albums presented on a silver platter to each of the surviving Beatles the most propitious time for releasing solo records since 1970. While both Paul and Ringo took advantage of these favourable conditions to release *Flaming Pie* and *Vertical Man* respectively, George would instead occupy himself with producing Ravi Shankar's *Chants of India* album. Released in May 1997 in the U.S.A. and in September in the U.K., the LP had been recorded throughout 1996 in London, Madras and Harrison's own Friar Park Studios.

Harrison was all over the album: providing backing vocals, bass, glockenspiel vibraphone, autoharp, marimba, and guitar to several of the songs.

Ravi would praise George's work on the album very highly: "I have never before worked so closely with George in recording, overdubbing, balancing, mixing and editing and I have been highly impressed by his expertise and sensitivity. My estimation of him as a musician has reached a very high level."

For his part Harrison would say, "I like producing Ravi's music, because for me it's educational as well as a joy to work with. It's actually soothing to your soul, and it helps you to focus or transcend."

George put a lot of effort into not only producing *Chants of India* but would also edit and introduce Ravi's lavish autobiography, *Raga Mala*, published in 1997 by Genesis, who had published George's *I Me Mine* in 1979.

To promote these two projects Harrison would appear with Ravi on American television's *Good Morning* in June, followed in July by a mythical appearance on a VH-1 special, entitled *George and Ravi Shankar: Yin and Yang.*

Coaxed by VH-1 presenter John Fugelsang, Harrison proceeded to treat listeners to an impromptu mini-concert. From audio recordings of the show Fugelsang can be heard to ask: "Wanna try one of the Beatles' tunes? Wanna try 'Something'? A Bob song, a Carl Perkins song? I'll take a Rick Astley song, George. I'll take a Spice Girls medley, George."

Instead, Harrison would hesitantly busk his way through a version of "All Things Must Pass," altering the vocal melody slightly. Someone at VH-1 made the decision to drench Harrison's voice in reverb, which added to the ghostly poignancy of this lovely rendition.

Similarly haunting was George, Ravi and Ravi's wife Sukanya's performance of "Prabhujee," a track from the *Chants of India* album, with Harrison's distinctive voice very much to the fore. Though "Prabhujee" was an enjoyable mantra, it was not surprising that Fugelsang was more interested in getting George to sing some of his own songs, practically begging George to do some more.

Harrison obliged with the Traveling Wilburys' song "If You Belonged to Me" (originally sung by Bob Dylan on *Volume Three*), and, best of all, at Sukanya's suggestion, the hitherto unreleased song, "Any Road." Sukanya's request obviously took George by surprise because he seemed to have trouble remembering his own composition. Although the song was a relatively straightforward folk tune, the rhyming-couplet lyrics were full of wit, and it was great just to hear a new George track. "Any Road" would, of course, be officially released five years later on *Brainwashed.*

The whole VH-1 show was affecting and full of charm and it's a shame that it didn't last longer than twenty-two minutes, because sadly, these twenty-two minutes would represent Harrison's last ever live, public performance.

On the *Good Morning* show Harrison had said of the spiritual music on *Chants of India:* "It's something that I believe in, and I think it's a benefit for people during the day, you know everybody gets stressed out, and this music is particularly inclined to calm you down. It's an antidote to stress."

If ever George needed an antidote to stress it was in July 1997, when he discovered a lump in his neck while gardening at Friar Park. By early August it was revealed that George had undergone tests for cancer. It was to be the start of a long and ultimately unsuccessful battle.

At first there seemed no reason for excessive worry, and to quell the worst fears of the public, Apple Records spokesman Geoff Baker released the following statement: "George is absolutely fine. There is no reason why he shouldn't be. He had a quick operation for a small lump outside of his neck. He doesn't think he has cancer and is totally cool about it. As far as he is concerned it is no big deal."

George was, nonetheless, admitted to a private hospital in Windsor, west of London for surgery. During the ten-minute operation, doctors removed lymph tissue, which was later sent to a lab to be analysed.

The tabloids described George's lump as a benign one. Geoff Baker, however, would again quash such melodramatics saying it couldn't be called benign because it was never biopsied. "That was a complete invention of the British press," Baker announced, "and after they invented the tests, they invented the results." Baker said that George was only hospitalised for twenty-four hours and the lump had been successfully removed. "He's fine," came the official line. "There's been no cancer scare."

In an interview printed in Britain's *News of the World*

newspaper Harrison would add a trademark dash of black humour to the proceedings saying: "I'm not going to die on you folks just yet."

Acknowledging that there had been cause for concern, George would blame the whole worrying episode on cigarettes: "I gave up cigarettes many years ago but had started again for a while and stopped in 1997. Luckily for me, they found that this nodule was more of a warning than anything else."

Despite Baker's emollient palliatives, deeper investigation of Harrison's health seemed to suggest that the scare had been more serious, or was at least taken more seriously than George would have had the world believe.

In June 1998, Ringo was asked by U.S "shock jock" Howard Stern, "Did you see that in the paper that George has cancer?," to which Ringo replied, "No, he had a problem with cancer, he's had it removed."

Backed into a corner by Starr's candour, George would confirm to the *News of the World* on June 27, 1998, that the lump had contained cancerous cells.

George revealed that he had undergone two successful radiation courses at England's leading cancer centre, the Royal Marsden Hospital and had also been checked out by the famous Mayo Clinic in Rochester, Minnesota in January. There he was told that the cancer had not resurfaced, a diagnosis that was reiterated during a return trip in May.

"I went back and was given the final all-clear, a clean bill of health," George reassured everyone. "Sometimes, if you say the word 'cancer,' everybody automatically thinks it will end in misery, but it's not always the case. I was very lucky because it didn't go anywhere, all it was was a little red mark on my neck. There are many different types of cancerous cells, and this was a very basic type."

George added that his battle with the disease has made

him confront his own mortality and how tenuous life can be. "It reminds you that anything can happen," he said, comparing life to "a raindrop on a lotus leaf."

Indeed, anything *could* happen, and Harrison's playing down of the whole affair might have been as a sign of respect for Linda McCartney, who was battling cancer herself around this time, a battle she too would tragically lose.

Another who would lose the fight was George's friend, collaborator and long-time Beatles publicist Derek Taylor, who died in September 1997, peacefully in his sleep after a lengthy battle with throat cancer. He was sixty-five. McCartney issued the statement, "He was a beautiful man. It is time for tears and words may follow later." George was no doubt too upset to comment.

Taylor's association with the Beatles had gone back as far as 1963 and of all the Beatles, Taylor had been closest to George, ghost-writing Harrison's early 1960s column for *The Daily Express* newspaper. In 1964 Taylor he became the band's official press officer, a title he would hold on and off for the next thirty years.

George – alongside Neil Aspinall – was the only Beatle to attend the funeral. Wisely, George would attend regular cancer therapy himself until nothing more could be done.

If Derek Taylor's death had been hard to take, George was dealt another body blow when his dear friend Carl Perkins died at the start of 1998. George had long credited Perkins with being his primary influence as a guitar player, and it was the rockabilly star's HBO Special that had brought George out of semi-retirement in 1985.

As recently as June 1996 George had produced "Distance Makes No Difference With Love" for his old friend at his Friar Park Studio, a track that would appear on Perkins' "Go Cat, Go!" album released in October of the same year. The album featured Carl's last recordings before his death and was an all-star affair, with contributions from Bono, Johnny Cash, John Fogerty, Willie Nelson, Tom Petty, and Paul Simon, not to mention Paul McCartney and Ringo Starr, who Perkins regarded as "The royalty of the musical world."

"Distance Makes No Difference With Love" was the album's undisputed standout, a stately latter-day Perkins original with George on slide guitar and bass and Jim Capaldi on drums. Though Carl took the lead vocal, George's backing vocals and harmonies would feature so prominently that the song is almost a duet.

Harrison's subtle production and exquisite solo on this aching ballad was invested with such love and respect that it was clearly the work of a pupil repaying his mentor and guitar muse. An indispensable track for fans of both men.

George would attend Carl's funeral at the Lambuth University auditorium in Jackson, Tennessee. There George would pay his respects by serenading the other celebrity mourners, including Garth Brooks and Jerry Lee Lewis, with a version of the Perkins' tune "Your True Love," accompanied by his own acoustic guitar.

Although there were no new releases from George, his music could be heard on the soundtrack of the 1998 film *Everest,* a cinematic documentary of a climbing expedition to the Himalayan zenith directed by David Breashears and Greg MacGillivray. The film premiered at the Boston Science Museum on March 4, 1998, followed by the release of the soundtrack shortly after.

The film's composers Steve Wood and Daniel May chose to include reworkings of "All Things Must Pass," "Life Itself," "This Is Love," "Give Me Love," and the *Live in Japan* version of "Here Comes the Sun." All five compositions appeared prominently as thematic threads within the soundtrack, blending Harrison's melodies with the instruments and sounds of Tibetan folk music and traditional Buddhist chants. MacGillivray chose Harrison for his music's spiritual quality and his ties to eastern religion.

George would have reason to call upon his famous spiritual beliefs a month later, in April 1998, when Paul's wife Linda died after a brave fight against breast cancer. She was fifty-six.

George issued the following statement: "Linda will be missed not only by Paul, her children and brother John, but by all of us who knew and loved her. She was a dear person with a passionate love of nature and its creatures and, in her passing, has earned the peace she sought in life. May God bless her."

As a result of McCartney's bereavement, the buck was passed to Harrison to handle the publicity chores for the September 1999 release of the *Yellow Submarine* song-track album, overseen by the three surviving Beatles to coincide with the reissue of the restored cartoon film. For the technical face-lift, United Artists lavished on the original print a frame-by-frame refurbishment, and replaced its mono soundtrack with a meticulously reconstructed stereo mix that allegedly improved upon the original album versions – hence the release of the song-track LP.

Described by Apple records as "the trippiest Beatles album ever" – the re-mastered *Yellow Submarine* included all the Beatle songs included in the film.

George seemed pleased to be lending his time to the project, possibly due to the fact that four of the album's fifteen tracks were his compositions, his highest percentage on a Beatle album ever, although Michael Jackson owned the publishing rights to all four. Alongside "It's All too Much" (which George helped remix) and "Only a Northern Song" from the original album, "Love You To" and "Think for Yourself" were also included on the mark II version.

Although this was yet another excuse to repackage material people already had, it was a worthwhile and representative soundtrack to the film, as opposed to the original release which contained George Martin's orchestrations, filling up the entire Side One.

To discuss the new releases George granted a lengthy interview to Timothy White of *Billboard* magazine in June, in which he expounded on a range of subjects. George told White that he and the other Beatles had purchased the American Beatle cartoons: "We bought them all a few years ago, just so we had control over them for the future. I always kind of liked them – they were so bad or silly they were good, if you know what I mean. And I think the passage of time might make them more fun now, in terms of being more watchable than they really were back then. But we don't have any plans for them at the moment."

George would also openly talk about how his "Only a Northern Song" was a bitter commentary on the deal he signed with Dick James. George would explain that the song was written "at the point that I realised Dick James had conned me out of the copyrights for my own songs by offering to become my publisher. As an eighteen or nineteen year-old kid, I thought, 'Great, somebody's gonna publish my songs!' But he never said, 'And incidentally, when you sign this document here, you're assigning me the ownership of the songs,' which is what it is. It was just a blatant theft. By the time I realised what had happened, when they were going public and making all this money out of this catalogue, I wrote 'Only a Northern Song' as what we call a 'piss-take,' just to have a joke about it."

George would also humorously reflect that the Blue Meanies from the film "have got a bigger stranglehold on the planet right now than they even had back in 1967! And it looks like there's no musical group coming along to break the bubble of greyness, because even the music industry has turned grey and is dominated by Blue Meanies."

To publicise the *Submarine* re-releases a promo video of "Hey Bulldog" was also released into the public domain. "What it was is that when we were in the studio recording 'Bulldog,'" Harrison would explain, "apparently it was at a time when they needed some footage for something else, some other record ['Lady Madonna'], and a film crew came along and filmed us. Then they cut up the footage and used some of the shots for something else. But it was Neil Aspinall who found out that when you watched and listened to what the original thing was, we were recording 'Bulldog!' This was apparently the only time we were actually filmed recording something, so what Neil did was, he put [the unused footage] all back together again and put the 'Bulldog' soundtrack onto it, and there it was!"

In the interview, George also gallantly paid tribute to Aspinall's role in the Beatles story. "Having lasted 40 years with the Beatles, Neil is the only person who's ever really been able to keep in contact with the four of us at the same time through all the various conflicts and whatever. And I met him when I was like thirteen years old, smoking behind the air-raid shelters at the Liverpool Institute high school."

Of course Beatles re-issues were all very well, but the big question on White's lips was when was George going to release a new *solo* record?

During the *Billboard* Q&A Harrison had announced that he was in the final stages of recording a new solo album, as well as preparing a multi-CD retrospective of his solo demos, outtakes, and previously unreleased material.

Since the ownership of his Dark Horse/Warner Brothers catalogue (which included the two Traveling Wilburys albums) had reverted back to him in June 1999, George also signalled his intention to re-release all of his currently out-of-print CDs.

In March 1999, while in Australia, *The Melbourne Herald Sun* newspaper also asked him when he would finally release a new album, George replied "Maybe next month, maybe not. Maybe sometime, maybe not. I'm saving them up for when I kick the bucket. Some people will really want it then and I will sell more copies!"

I guess we'll never know whether he was joking, or grimly forecasting the future.

CHAPTER SIXTEEN

2000

*I could feel blood entering my lungs. I could feel
my chest deflate. I felt blood in my mouth and air
exhale from my chest. I believed I had been fatally stabbed.*

George Harrison, 2000.

Christmas 1999 saw Harrison receive the ultimate flattery
any celebrity can ever wish for, when he got his first official
stalker. Two days before Christmas Day 1999, a twenty-seven
year-old girl by the name of Cristin Keleher was discovered
in the main house of the Harrison estate on Lower Nahiku
Road in Maui.

Unfortunately Cristin wasn't the only fruitcake on the
loose and by the end of the week George would have another unwelcome visitor, although this time he wouldn't be so
lucky as to be on a different continent.

Keleher, who believed she had a "psychic connection" to
George, allegedly entered the former Beatle's home through
an open sliding glass door. Once inside, she did her laundry,
telephoned her mother in New Jersey, and helped herself to
a can of root beer and a DiGiorno frozen pizza – showing
that stalkers want the same guarantee of quality as the rest of
us when it comes to their frozen foods of choice. The brand
of root beer, however, was not established at the pre-trial
hearing.

Luckily George was not in Hawaii to share the smorgas-
bord. Keleher was found by his sister-in-law, Linda Tuckfield,
who alerted the caretaker, who called the police who then
arrested the confused, unemployed twenty-seven year old.

When Keleher appeared in a Maui courtroom in the new

year she pleaded not guilty to first-degree burglary and fourth-degree theft, which is bizarre logic when you consider she was caught red-handed with her fingers covered in melted cheese.

"She was there without permission," a police spokesperson told *The Honolulu Star-Bulletin* newspaper. It came to light that Keleher was born in New Jersey and had been a Maui resident for the previous three years.

Judge Shackley Raffetto ordered Keleher's bail to be set at $10,000 and set a pre-trial conference for April 6. The Associated Press reported that if convicted, Keleher faced up to ten years in prison and a $10,000 fine. Her bail was later reduced to $1,500 when her legal representative explained that though she was homeless, she did have a place to stay if released. For the meanwhile Keleher was remanded to custody.

Proving that stalkers are a lot like busses (you wait around for ages and then two come at once), further tragedy was to strike a mere seven days later. As the rest of the world prepared for their millennium celebrations, horror of the most awful kind almost befell another Beatle. It's almost too much to bear the thought of two Beatles killed by insane fans, just for being in a pop group.

George's worst nightmare happened at about 3:00 a.m. Thursday, December 30, 1999, when a thirty-three-year-old man named Michael Abram from Liverpool broke into Friar Park, using a statue of George and the Dragon he'd ripped up from the garden to smash a window.

Asleep in their upstairs bedroom, George and Olivia were awakened by the sound of the breaking glass. Olivia woke up first, thinking a chandelier had crashed to the floor before realising that there was an intruder downstairs. While Olivia alerted staff on an intercom, George fearlessly went to investigate.

From the top of the stairs, Harrison spotted a man's figure illuminated in the kitchen area. George would recount, "He stopped and looked towards me. He started shouting and screaming. He was hysterical and frightening. He said words to the effect of, 'You get down here, you know what it is.' I could see a knife in one hand and the spear from part of the statue in the other."

Harrison called out and was lunged at by the man. Due to the accent, George was immediately able to identify that the man was a scouser, and George made the split second decision to tackle the man, aware that he was the last line of defence between the madman and his family.

"Armed only with the element of surprise, I ran at him," George detailed. "My first thought was to grab the knife and knock him off balance. He thrust the knife at me. I was fending off the blows with my hands and arms. He was stabbing down towards my upper body."

Upon hearing her husband's screams for help, Olivia ran downstairs. Seeing Olivia on the landing, Abram stepped over George's body and moved toward her.

In a desperate attempt to subdue her assailant, Olivia struck Abram first with a poker, and then with a table lamp with a heavy brass base, smashing Abram across the side of his head, stunning him. Abram then staggered up to the landing where he collapsed.

After the attack, Tom Petty sent George a fax joking, "Aren't you glad you married a Mexican girl?" – a reference to how, in Petty's words, Olivia "really kicked ass."

"I had to," Olivia would later tell Katie Couric in 2002. "George was coaching me, I have to say. And George was very brave and people don't know that. Because he had already been injured and he had to jump up and bring him down to stop him from attacking me. You know, he saved my life too."

"I was aware of my wife approaching and striking him about the head with a brass poker," Harrison stated in his court deposition. "It appeared to have little effect. He stood up and chased my wife. I feared greatly for her safety and hauled myself up to tackle him. I placed my hands around the blade. He again got the better of me and got on top of me. I felt exhausted and could feel the strength draining from me. My arms dropped to my sides and I vividly remember a deliberate thrust of the knife down into my chest. I could feel blood entering my lungs. I could feel my chest deflate. I felt blood in my mouth and air exhale from my chest. I believed I had been fatally stabbed. My wife struck the man with the vase and he slumped down. I encouraged my wife to keep on hitting him."

During the ten-minute altercation Olivia sustained minor cuts to her forehead and wrists. George was not so lucky. During the scuffle, George was stabbed at least ten times as he bravely tried to protect his family. The struggle would leave him with a punctured right lung, and a trail of blood through three rooms.

After overpowering Abram, George and Olivia somewhere found the strength to hold him down until police arrived at 3:30 a.m., after being called by a member of staff. When the police did arrive at the scene they found George lying on the floor, holding a towel to his chest, and Olivia kneeling beside him trying to comfort him.

Abram was treated for injuries at John Radcliffe Hospital before being taken into police custody where the Thames Valley Police booked him for breaking and entering and attempted murder charges.

Initially, Abram's motives appeared unclear. Was he merely a chancer trying to nick a few baubles or an obsessed fan intent on killing a Beatle? Police spokesman Guy Bailey told Reuters, "Taste in music is pretty far down the questions police initially ask a suspected murderer . . . The intruder has head injuries so there was a serious struggle put up by Harrison and his wife."

Paramedics initially rushed George and Olivia to the Royal Berkshire Hospital in nearby Reading to be treated for their injuries. Since no major organs had been injured, George was then transferred to Harefield Hospital in northwest London, where he was listed in stable condition. A statement issued by the hospital said the transfer was precautionary, since Harefield had a chest surgeon on duty and Royal Berkshire did not. Olivia was treated for a laceration to the skull, scrapes and bruises, but thankfully her injuries were not serious enough to warrant admission to Harefield, though she remained at her husband's side. Dhani had also been at Friar Park, but was sleeping in another wing at the time of the attack and therefore remained unharmed by Abram's bloodlust.

Detective Chief Inspector Euan Read, the officer leading the investigation described the attack as "vicious," and relayed the fact that Harrison had credited his wife with saving his life. The knife blade, deflected by a rib, had actually missed his heart by less than an inch, which of course meant that George had only narrowly escaped death. Chest surgeon William Fountain at Harefield Hospital told reporters George's injuries were "not life-threatening but that is mainly by chance."

George did not need to undergo surgery, though the main stab wound required six stitches to close and a chest drain was fitted to remove excess fluid and air from his partially collapsed lung.

George had also suffered cuts to his left hand from trying to take the knife away from Abram during the attack. Although stitches were also needed on his thumb and fingers, George was thankfully reassured that he would regain full use of his hand. The hospital would also say that George was "in excellent spirits and he certainly hasn't lost his sense of humour."

George was certainly well enough to make the short statement from his hospital bed saying that the man "wasn't a burglar and he certainly wasn't auditioning for the Traveling Wilburys." Thankfully this gave hope that Harrison's condition was not similar to Lennon's.

Within hours, many fans sent flowers, cards and gifts to the Apple Offices and Friar Park. No doubt breathing a communal sigh of relief that Harrison's injuries were not fatal as at first feared.

After a night's sleep the next day tests and X-rays showed that a full recovery was expected within three weeks, with a small scar being the only physical reminder of this nightmare. "I can see the headlines already," Harrison joked, "George has had a hard day's night."

Paul and Ringo (who were warned to be on the alert for copycat attacks by Thames Valley Police) each made public statements. Paul would say, "Thank God that both George and Olivia are all right. I send them all my love." Ringo added, "Both Barbara and I are deeply shocked that this incident has occurred. We send George and Olivia all our love and wish George a speedy recovery."

Yoko was also notified, and an "insider" would later say that Yoko was understandably "spooked" by the attack on George. Yoko sent her sympathies stating, "My heart goes out to George, Olivia and Dhani, and I hope he will recover quickly."

More touchingly, Bangladesh's State Minister for Foreign Affairs, Abul Hasan Chowdhury, expressed his deep regret at the attack and wished him an early recovery. In a statement Chowdhury recalled George's support during the Liberation War "that drew the attention of the world community to the sufferings of our people." "The people of Bangladesh are indebted to him," Chowdhury would say on behalf of his country, showing that they had never forgotten George's efforts nearly thirty years previously.

Early in the morning of New Year's Eve, Abram appeared before Oxford magistrates' court where he was formally charged with breaking and entering, aggravated assault and attempted murder. Harrison would spend his New Year's Eve drowsy from painkillers in his hospital suite at Harefield hospital, instead of enjoying the Millennium Eve party he and Olivia had planned, at Friar Park.

Sporting a black eye and battered face from the shellacking George had meted out, and flanked by three policemen, Abram spoke only to confirm his name and address during the 45-minute hearing. Abram was bailed by magistrates until February 11, and sent to the medium security Scott Clinic in Merseyside, to receive psychiatric treatment. Magistrates ordered him to be held at Scott Clinic until his trial in November 2000.

With the man's identity common knowledge, the newspapers dug up everything they could about Abram's past. It came to light that Abram was an unemployed father of two, known locally as "Mad Mick," and not because of his completely off-the-wall sense of humour. Regarded as a danger to himself, Abram had been first diagnosed as a paranoid psychotic in 1990, and had spent two weeks in the psychiatric ward in Merseyside's Whiston Hospital. It was here that doctors failed to properly identify his schizophrenia, and sent him home after he assaulted a nurse.

It also transpired that "Mad Mick" had been a heroin addict for fifteen years, and, reportedly, had been taking methadone until six or seven months prior to the attack. Abram would walk around Liverpool for hours, wearing a Walkman and screaming pop lyrics at the top of his lungs. He often stood on the tenth-floor balcony of his flat, sometimes naked, screaming and throwing empty beer cans at children.

Both Mad Mick's ex-girlfriend Jeanette and his own mother Lydia would sell him down the river for chump change by telling the tabloids that Abram was a religious fanatic, who over the two weeks leading up to the attack had become dangerously obsessed with the Beatles. His ex-girlfriend would reveal that Abram "thought John Lennon was a prophet and Paul McCartney was the Devil," and that "he identified with George Harrison because of the song 'My Sweet Lord.'"

Jeanette would also say that, on Christmas Eve, Abram had boasted, "I am going to be famous one day soon, Jeanette, just you wait and see."

Michael Abram's mother, Lydia, would try to rationalise her son's mental health problems thus: "He takes all music literally. It is the Beatles at the moment but a few weeks ago it was Oasis. He has been running in pubs shouting about the Beatles. He hates them and even believes they are witches and takes their lyrics seriously. He started to wear a Walkman to play music to stop the voices in his head. I could not believe what he had done because he has never been violent. He shouts and likes to shock but has never been violent."

"He hears voices in his head and sees things coming out of the walls," Lydia Abram continued. "He has been off drugs completely since May. He is on absolutely nothing, and if you ask me, that is when you need the help. He was on heroin. Now he is not on methadone. He does not even smoke pot. I was told he has got drugs psychosis. He was told if he stops taking the drugs the psychosis will go."

Forensic experts set about examining the crime scene. A dark blue holdall of the type favoured by serial killers was found in the garden of a house directly opposite the main entrance to Friar Park. The police shrewdly believed this to belong to Abram and security cameras in Liverpool later confirmed that Abram had been sighted with the same bag on Wednesday, the day before the attack.

The long pilgrimage by a deranged fan to carry out a vicious attack once more revived chilling memories of the 1980 killing of John Lennon. Detective Chief Inspector Euan Read said, "We are doing a painstaking forensic examination of the house at the moment to put in place details of where blood is and so on to try to piece together a picture of precisely what happened." Merseyside police searched Abram's squalid, unfurnished flat in Liverpool and left with four bags of evidence.

Questions remain as to how Abram penetrated Friar Park's intense state of the art security system, known by neighbours as Fort Knox. "There's an awful lot of security on the house. You'd be doing pretty well to get through the gates," wagered Daniel Andrews, who lives across the road from Harrison's home.

The police believed Abram had climbed over the twelve-foot main gates that have no razor wire on top. Another theory was that Abram had simply walked through the gates when they were opened briefly for a truck delivering champagne and party trays for a New Year's Eve celebration.

Harrison was discharged from Harefield Hospital on Saturday evening January 1, 2000, after being examined by a chest specialist, who reassured him that he wouldn't suffer long-term consequences from his wound.

George had intended to recuperate at his home in Maui, but cancelled those plans when he found out about the arrest of Cristin Keleher. Instead, he had to be satisfied with Friar Park and its increased security, and to this end, two ex-SAS soldiers and dogs were instantly hired to patrol the perimeter of the mansion. The *Sun* newspaper in Britain reported that while George's ex-SAS guards did not carry any firearms, they were trained to kill with their bare hands.

First to visit George was his good friend Eric Idle, which must have lifted his spirits. Idle would tell journalists that George was feeling much better. Visiting "Mad Mick" at the psychiatric unit at Scott Clinic was the slightly less famous Lydia Abram who told reporters that her son knew what he had done but didn't realise the magnitude of his actions.

The suspect's mother claimed that the health system let him down: "The system is totally useless. If they had listened to me and listened to Michael, this would never have happened."

Acting Chief Executive of St Helens and Knowsley NHS Health Authority, Dr. Martin Murphy, did acknowledge that an error of judgement had been made regarding Abram in the following statement: "In view of the serious nature of the incident and the possibility that further lessons could be learned, the health authority has instigated an external health inquiry into the case."

Speaking to *The Henley Standard* newspaper on January 7, Harrison "praised police for their prompt response" after the attack, while Sergeant Ali Driver of the Thames Valley Police commended George and Olivia's bravery.

In his first public statement after the attack George would thank fans and friends for their support: "Olivia and I are overwhelmed by the concern expressed by so many people. We thank everyone for their prayers and kindness." He also issued a photo of himself and Olivia looking healthy, taken on holiday in Ireland on January 15, a mere two weeks after his release from hospital.

A spokesman for the Harrisons had said, "We do not foresee him leaving home for a long while yet," when he had returned to Friar Park to rest and recuperate. Instead, George and Olivia had gone to Ireland and then to Barbados on January 25, with Dhani, Joe Brown and three ex-

SAS guards, underlining their resilience. Tabloid snoopers reported that George was taking long walks and eating well and was "getting better all the time." In February, the Harrisons *et al* were joined by Rod Stewart and his girlfriend Penny Lancaster.

Contrary to logical prediction, the dubious honour of having two stalkers did not deter Harrison from making public appearances.

It was not that long before he was performing his duties as Joe Brown's best man where, by all accounts, George made a witty wedding speech. He certainly looked in good shape, judging from the photographs that appeared in the society magazines.

In May 2000, Harrison was spotted jamming with Donovan and Shane MacGowan at a series of small concerts in Smithfield, Ireland. There, it was reported the trio played a surreal version of "Dirty Ol' Town" and a beautiful version of "Raglan Road."

It was also reported in *The Daily Express* newspaper in August that George played at a fancy dress fortieth birthday party for Damon Hill, at the retired Formula One racing driver's mansion in Hambildon, Surrey. The impromptu performance featured George and Damon on guitars, Ringo Starr on drums, and the diminutive Leo Sayer on vocals. "The two former Beatles were brilliant," said an observer, "they did a series of old hits by the Who."

In June, when Abram appeared in court, he pleaded not guilty to accusations of attempted murder and denied charges of grievous bodily harm, malicious wounding and aggravated burglary, after which he was sent back into custody pending the trial scheduled for November.

But what of Cristin Keleher, the scrofulous Maui stalker, who had dined so sumptuously on George's prized DiGiorno pizzas a week before the stabbing?

You may remember that Keleher had been remanded to custody with bail set at $1,500. When this was posted Keleher had been released from custody. However, her time outside of jail lasted only two months. Keleher was arrested again for violating one of the conditions of her bail that forbade her to go to Hana or Nahiku. Jeffrey Hunt, the police officer who arrested her for breaking into Harrison's home, arrested the confused young woman again as she rode on the back of a motorcycle through Hana on April 28. To make matters worse for Keleher, she kicked and injured the police officer while he was taking her into custody. After this altercation, Keleher was confined at Maui Community Correctional Centre where she stayed for four months.

At the trial on August 25, 2000, Deputy Public Defender Susan Arnett said Keleher had not been burglarising the Harrison residence in December 1999, and nor had she been stalking the former Beatle. Incredulously, Arnett claimed her client had been in Nahiku to visit a friend in the area, but the friend wasn't home. Since it was raining, the ill and disoriented Keleher just happened to seek shelter at Harrison's home. Arnett pointed out that there was no forced entry at the residence, after all Keleher did get in through an unlocked door. Deputy Prosecuting Attorney J.W. Hupp disagreed, saying Keleher's presence in George's house had not been an accident or a coincidence. He affirmed that Keleher was looking for Harrison and knew where he lived, because she had visited the Harrison residence a month or two before her arrest to inquire about the former Beatle. It was during this visit that she had told a bemused estate caretaker that she had a "psychic connection" with Harrison.

Keleher acknowledged being a fan of George, but told Circuit Judge Artemio Baxa that she meant him no harm when she illegally entered his home. Keleher entered a no-contest plea to first-degree criminal trespass and fourth-degree theft.

The no-contest plea agreement with George's lawyers provided for Keleher to get a year's probation and called for her to move to New Jersey to live with her parents while serving her parole.

Prosecuting Attorney Hupp said that he was happy Keleher was going to be under her family's care and commented that George had been upset about the Maui incident, "He has definite security concerns. He was very alarmed that someone was found in his house."

When it came to her turn to speak, Keleher apologised for her actions, telling Baxa she learned a "very big lesson," and that she was able to get through her four months confinement at the correctional centre because of her faith in Jesus Christ. "I thank God George did not press charges," she simpered, "I did not go to his house to cause any problem."

One man who could not say the same was "Mad Mick" Abram. When his two-day trial came to Oxford Crown court on November 14, Abram admitted breaking into Friar Park but denied the counts of attempted murder by reason of insanity.

The jury was told there was no dispute over whether Abram committed the offences. As Harrison's prosecuting lawyer Simon Mayo began, "His objective was to kill Mr. Harrison. There will be no dispute about his objective. The central issue to resolve in the case is whether at the time of the incident, the defendant was sane or insane."

Although George did not have to testify and therefore stayed away, Olivia and Dhani did attend the court proceedings. George's testimony was entered as a written statement, in which he reaffirmed his belief that he "had been fatally stabbed."

When it came to her turn to be questioned Olivia choked back tears as she described how she became as frenzied as Abram while trying to fend him off, grabbing his testicles and striking him repeatedly across the head with a poker.

"There was blood on the walls, blood on my hands," Olivia stammered, "and I realised that we were going to be murdered and this man was succeeding in murdering us and there was absolutely nobody else there to help."

The jury was told in traumatic detail how Abram had beaten and stabbed George and how Olivia had helped her husband.

Giving evidence, psychiatrist Dr. Phillip Joseph believed that at the time of the attack the defendant was clearly mentally ill, and to demonstrate Abram's paranoia and schizophrenia the court was told how Abram liked to listen to rock music while sitting on an upturned flowerpot!

The court learnt how, prior to the attack, Abram had walked into a local church and had asked, "Can you tell me where the squire lives?" The vicar, David Buskill, at first thought Abram was seeking God, but his wishful thinking was shattered when he realised Abram meant Harrison.

Dr. Joseph said he believed that when Abram was stabbing Harrison "he was suffering from such a defect of reason that he did not believe it was wrong. He believed his actions were justified. The actions were ordained by God, justified by the Bible and he needed to kill George Harrison because he was possessed by George Harrison."

"His life was falling apart, he was living in squalor," Dr. Joseph continued. "He was looking for a meaning to his life, but he was preoccupied by his mental illness."

Joseph said Abram's mental health had worsened after 1999 total eclipse of the sun. "He thought George Harrison was the alien from hell. He thought the Beatles were witches flying on broomsticks from hell."

The court was told that Abram had been seen by a psychiatrist only weeks before the attack, but the consultant failed to diagnose his illness. Psychiatrist Dr. Nigel Eastman told the jury: "Clearly this was a very severe illness which had been missed by various professionals. His mental state was such that in relation to the alleged offences he was legally insane."

Eastman would go on to say "Mad Mick" had been driven by his psychosis and delusions (fed by reading Exodus in the Bible) to carry out the attack. Eastman told jurors Abram thought all the Beatles were practitioners of black magic, and that he believed he had been sent on a mission from God to kill Harrison, whom Abram described as the "phantom menace," a figure from the writings of Nostradamus.

Harrison had said he tried to disorient Abram by chanting "Hare Krishna, Hare Krishna!" Dr. Philip Joseph testified that Abram had told him he would have stopped the attack "if George Harrison had talked normally to him," but Harrison had "cursed him in a devil's tongue and spoken backward to him." This psychobabble was enough to convince Judge Astill to instruct jurors to find the defendant innocent by reason of insanity.

Abram was sentenced to be detained in a secure mental hospital for psychiatric treatment "without time restriction," and must gain the approval of a mental health tribunal if he seeks release. Judge Astill, saying that would be a matter only for medical experts, turned down the Harrisons' request that they be notified of any application for Abram's release. This was clearly a cause of concern to George and his family who criticised the "ancient lunatic law" that allows acquittal on mental grounds.

On behalf of the Harrison family, Dhani read out a statement to reporters after the trial: "It is a tragic occurrence that anyone should suffer such a mental breakdown, but we can never forget he was full of hate and violence when he came into our home." The statement went on to say, "We will ask the Home Secretary to notify us of any attempt to release him. The prospect of him being released back into society is abhorrent to us. We hope the authorities will act with the utmost responsibility in avoiding it in future and allow us to be consulted before reaching a conclusion. We firmly believe that the victims of crimes of violence should have the right to be heard at all appropriate times."

Abram himself would apologise in a statement read by his attorney, also after the trial's conclusion: "I wished to say how sorry I am for the alarm, distress, and injury that I have caused when I was ill. I have seen many doctors prior to the attack and I was never told that I was suffering with schizophrenia or any mental illness. I thought my delusions were real and everything that I was experiencing was some kind of witchcraft. I know that Mr. and Mrs. Harrison fought for their lives . . . and that they must have been terrified by the lunatic in their house." However, Jack Straw, then the British Home Secretary, overruled the judge and did promise to tell George and his family if Abram was ever released.

When Abram was conditionally released from Liverpool's Scott Clinic on July 4, 2002, that promise was reneged.

Understandably, Olivia and Dhani reacted angrily to this *fait accompli* saying George would have been "dismayed" by the decision, and released a statement to that effect: "No one had the courtesy to tell us in advance there had been an application for his discharge, let alone a date for a hearing. We were thus given no opportunity whatsoever to have our say, or to review the medical evidence and instruct our own expert. We can never forget how brutally close Abram came to killing dear George and myself, nor the trauma inflicted on our son and family . . . We certainly wish Mr. Abram no ill, but to be presented with this as a fact after the event is deeply upsetting and insulting, and we feel again completely let down by the system . . . It remains the case in this country that the victim simply has no voice. The law must be changed."

After the Abram court case George would be given the

best medicine a man can have: several more millions of pounds in royalties courtesy of yet more Beatles product.

Just in time for the gift-giving season came *The Beatles Anthology Book,* a lavish hard-backed tome running to 368 pages, 340,000 words, and 1,300 photos.

The Beatles Anthology Book was written with the aim of publishing the definitive account of life in the Beatles, presenting for the first time, in print, the well-told and over-familiar story in their own words, in effect, the Beatles' autobiography.

The initial idea for the book came from Neil Aspinall, though McCartney was the driving force behind the project, and it was he who helped convince Harrison and Starr of its merits.

McCartney told Harrison and Starr: "It will dispel some of the myths and put the record straight, as every Tom, Dick and uncle of a friend of the milkman has been writing books on the Beatles since 1963."

Genesis Publications began work compiling *The Beatles Anthology Book* in 1995. Paul, George and Ringo sat for extensive new interviews specifically for the book, while other comments and observations were culled from the transcripts of the interviews conducted for the *Anthology* documentary by Jools Holland. Friends of the trio say they met "dozens of times" to compare notes. John, meanwhile, was fully represented by quotes drawn from a multitude of magazine and broadcast interviews.

To provide additional depth and objectivity there were also reminiscences from George Martin, Neil Aspinall, Derek Taylor their late publicist and friend, Yoko, and their long-deceased roadie Mal Evans. Aspinall's recollections were among the highlights of the book and made one yearn for an autobiography he will never write.

The book cost £35, which newspapers speculated would

yield sales figures of about £1billion. This speculation lay in the fact that the initial press run of two million copies in the U.S.A. and the U.K. was sure to sell out and that there were plans to translate the book into dozens of languages. The money would be split equally between the three Beatles and Yoko Ono, even though she was not actively involved in the project.

The Beatles also opened their personal archives specifically for this project, allowing the unprecedented release of photographs, as well as fascinating documents and memorabilia. These included John's letter to the Queen returning his MBE, and the letter that John and George sent Paul telling him that they had just met with EMI behind his back to order the delay of *McCartney*.

Of great interest were the snapshots from their family collections most of which had not been seen before, and the opening four chapters in which each Beatle told the story of their early life in Liverpool. The remainder of the book was arranged into chronological year-by-year sections.

The revelations were few and relatively modest, but this was always likely to be the case considering how thoroughly the Beatles have been studied – everything that happened during their lifetime is more or less common knowledge to even the uninitiated. *The Beatles Anthology Book*, however, did flesh out the events that led to the break-up.

McCartney would describe putting the book together as therapeutic: "We had a good time doing it, and it brought us closer. In truth, we had healed the wounds already when we decided we wanted to do the book."

With each Beatle having their say on each subject the text was for the most part warm, and a tone of forgiveness; celebration and friendship resonates throughout. Not that the book is about them sitting around patting each other on the back and congratulating each other.

Though one can understand their reluctance to open up old wounds that McCartney claimed had healed, there was a nagging feeling that the book could have been improved by a little dirt.

Many reviewers felt that, while the book faithfully re-told the story, the Beatles were holding back the harsh truths and that McCartney, Harrison and Starr spoke with the caution of people who feel they *still* have something to protect.

McCartney's anecdotes had been told and Chinese-whispered so many times that recycling them seemed redundant. Not that Paul covers things up or only let's people hear what he wants them to hear, it's just that Paul has the sunniest disposition of all the Beatles. This is especially noticeable when he's playing the press, where he seems to live in a bubble of happiness, especially when it comes to John Lennon. Ringo's spectacles seemed to be the most rose-tinted, whereas George unsurprisingly, seemed the least starry-eyed by their shared roller-coaster ride.

As a character George was easily the most forthright of the three, the one who suffered fools the least gladly, and since he so rarely gave interviews during his last years, his insights came across as the most fresh and direct.

George, for instance, did not seem averse to throwing in a couple of light digs at Paul and vestiges of past acrimony occasionally surface in *The Beatles Anthology Book*. Similarly, past jealousies and rivalries also bubbled to the top, particularly in relation to Lennon, where George and Paul seem to compete over who was closest to him.

Most reviewers rated Harrison's quotes as the most interesting throughout the book. Indeed, for the prurient, the highlight of the book was certainly George's revelation that he lost his virginity in Hamburg, with Paul and John and Pete Best all watching!

Not that the overall lack of bombshells stopped the book

from heading straight to the top of the best-seller lists with people seemingly not batting an eyelid at the price tag.

Hot on the heels of *The Beatles Anthology* in November came *The Beatles 1,* a collection of all twenty-seven number one hits the group had on both sides of the Atlantic. Sir George Martin would say of the album: "It barely took eight years to cover this collection – 'Love Me Do' to 'The Long and Winding Road' – but it was a lifetime in the world of rock and roll."

Backed by an unnecessarily intense publicity campaign *The Beatles 1* shot straight to the top in its first week of release to become the group's fifteenth U.K. number one LP. The album actually sold more units in its first week than any other U.K. release that year, making retail mincemeat of Oasis, Robbie Williams, Westlife, and all the other flavours of the month vying for stocking filler space.

A spokesman for Tower Records in Britain stated, "Teen bands seem to knock each other off the charts week after week . . . They don't seem to have staying power, but the Beatles certainly do." Paul, George and Ringo were reportedly "dead chuffed" that thirty years after their break-up, the Beatles still had the same chart-topping prowess as they did in their prime.

George would say that he was amazed by the success of the compilation: "I thought it would do well, but not that well . . . It is like a new Beatlemania. I suddenly noticed that everyone had the album, even the six- and seven-year-olds. They act as if I belonged to a boy band." Harrison would go on to say, "When people see me they see a Beatle. But for me it was all such a long time ago. Sometimes I ask myself if I was really there or whether it was all a dream."

Reuters news agency revealed that by the end of the third week of its release the album had gone to number one in twenty-eight different countries. Sales of twelve million copies within those first three weeks made it the fastest sell-ing album ever!

Back, to some extent, in the public eye, Harrison would again tantalise his fans with vague promises of a new album. In late December 2000, George announced that he had "enough material for three albums but none of the songs are really complete so I have to work on all of them."

Surprisingly, he also revealed that he would not be work-ing with Jeff Lynne on this next studio offering. "I have stopped working with Jeff because I did not want him to make ELO albums out of my songs." Harrison would pre-sumably joke, "On this album you can hear guitar, bass and drums and no computers." Continuing his rant George would say, "Anyone can make music using computers today. But the worst thing for me is the drum machine. They are like a disease which spreads more and more over the entire world. I hate it and it makes me sick."

Nevertheless, Harrison remained friends with Lynne until the end, playing on Lynne's 2001 ELO comeback album, *Zoom,* and working with him on the as-yet-unre-leased Traveling Wilburys anthology, tentatively entitled *Maximum Traveling.* And despite Harrison's forewarning, Lynne *did* ultimately co-produce Harrison's posthumous album.

Regardless of who sat in the producer's chair, George was as defiant as ever about his music. "I don't listen to any-thing, and I don't read the papers, and I don't watch TV, and I don't go to concerts," he would tell *Rolling Stone* magazine. "And so my music, it doesn't matter if I did it twenty years ago or if I did it tomorrow. It doesn't go with trends. My trousers don't get wider and tighter every six months. My music just stays what it is, and that's the way I like it."

CHAPTER SEVENTEEN

2001

Thirty years is a hell of a long time, but it just flies by.

George Harrison, 2000

With *The Beatles 1* still at its rightful place at number one, the good news would continue into 2001 with the long overdue re-issue of *All Things Must Pass*. To say the good news wouldn't last is, of course, the understatement of all understatements.

Basking in the success of the greatest hits collection George would tell *Billboard* magazine, "It's amazing, I thought I'd cash in on the craze and put out all my old tracks!"

Released on January 23, 2001, the re-issue of *All Things Must Pass* marked the thirtieth anniversary of its original release and symbolically brought Harrison's solo career full cycle.

"Thirty years is a hell of a long time, but it just flies by," George would lament, acknowledging that the timing couldn't have been better. "It's like Beatlemania is happening again," he was quoted as saying during a break in recording a guitar solo on a cover of "Love Letters" for Bill Wyman's *Double Bill* album.

To publicise the re-issue Harrison quickly found himself back in the tabloids, expressing his timeworn views on his junior status within the Beatles. In an interview printed in Britain's *Daily Mirror* newspaper, George whinged that "Paul and John were obviously talented and they were a great duo, but they also had a massive ego which left little room for others. I felt ignored and undervalued for years. Not all the songs released back then were good, far from it. Since the split, I have written songs which are just as good if not better than the best of the Beatles. The difference is that the Beatles' songs would go to the top of the chart in a matter of days."

Since he has expressed these sentiments many times before – perhaps it was time George let go of this bitterness that *The Beatles Anthology Book* had purportedly exorcised. Or maybe he was just giving good copy to plug his album.

The re-issue would be a digitally remastered affair with five bonus tracks: three alternate mixes ("Beware of Darkness," "Let It Down," and "What Is Life"), the previously unissued "I Live for You" and a newly recorded version of "My Sweet Lord."

The album was also resequenced – on the original album the all-star "Apple Jam" did not follow the actual order of the original recordings due to the time limitations of the vinyl. George restored the now less muddied jams to their true sequence, so that the 11-minute "Out of the Blue" became the fifth and closing track instead of the first.

As with the original, the re-issue was beautifully packaged, and its design was overseen by George personally. The front cover featured a new colourised version of "George & the Gnomes" with roads and urban development added to symbolise Harrison's view that the world is being concreted over.

The re-issue also came with a 20-page booklet, which contained new Harrison-penned liner notes, rare photos and lyrics to all the songs. The album's enhanced credits also meant that Eric Clapton could now be given his due after thirty years of omission without fear of contractual reprisal. Another person officially credited at last was Phil Collins, for his conga playing on "The Art of Dying."

It must be stressed that the album was not a remix but a remastering, overseen by Jon Astley (Pete Townshend's brother-in-law), who had done such an excellent job on the

Who's back catalogue in 1990s. The remastering got rid of the hiss but left George's vocals where they were in the original mix. Harrison revealed that he had been sorely tempted to remix the album, but feared that it might tamper with the feel of the original, even though at the time of the re-release Harrison announced that he felt that the Spector "Wall of Sound" now seemed dated.

Nonetheless, the sound and balance of all the instruments was much improved, allowing the listener to hear more of the backing vocals and instruments up front and clear.

The real plum, however, was the previously unreleased "I Live for You," a haunting ballad with some beautiful pedal steel guitar from Pete Drake. Lyrically the song sounds like another paean to God, and George's vocals are appropriately tender and humble. The track would have made an excellent addition to the country and western flavour of Side Two on the original album, but Harrison obviously did not feel that the song was up to sufficient scratch.

When asked why "I Live for You" had been left out of the original line-up, George replied "I didn't think that we had got a good enough take on it. Except for Pete Drake, the pedal steel guitar player. At that time, I had so many other tracks as well, so we just left it off. It did need patching up in the drum department."

The new version of "My Sweet Lord" was an interesting variation on the original. George added a new guitar intro and solo, and also laid down a new lead vocal. George's son Dhani was also on hand to beef up the new arrangement with some additional guitar work, as was Sam Brown (taking the stead of her late mother Vicki, who had accompanied George so effectively on "Shanghai Surprise") on backing vocals. If anything George's vocal was more gospel inflected on the new version, on which he at times reaches for a falsetto register. Harrison certainly sings it as sincerely as he ever did and you could tell he still meant it, probably even more so given his deteriorating health. While a doubt remained as to whether the original could have been improved upon, "My Sweet Lord (2000)" revealed the George of the new millennium, and how his voice had subtly aged.

Of the new version George said, "I just like the idea and the opportunity to freshen it up, because the point of 'My Sweet Lord' is just to try and remind myself basically that there's more to life than the material world . . . At the time, the song was so popular and also so controversial that the most important thing about it for me was that it, in its small way, conjured up a touch of spirituality, something we are very short of."

During his interview with the German news agency DPA, George talked about playing with his son on the track, praising Dhani's "beautiful voice," but bemoaned the expectations placed on the children of famous artists, citing Julian Lennon as an obvious example. Either way there are no signs that Dhani has any plans to follow his old man into the music business.

Of the other bonus tracks, "Beware of Darkness" was an alternate take from the one included on the original album; a naked demo of "Let It Down" which George described as "the original guitar and vocal from the same tape as 'Beware of Darkness' with a little overdubbing circa 2000." "What Is Life," meanwhile, was a rough, horns-heavy mix of the backing track.

The album sold like hot cakes, a success that surprised EMI and Capitol who so underestimated its demand that there was a rumoured back order of 20,000 units in the U.S.A. alone! This underestimation was baffling in light of the recent success of *The Beatles Anthology Book* and *The Beatles 1* and the fact that *All Things Must Pass* had long been considered the best Beatles solo album.

Critical reception of the album was wholehearted and any negative comments were only really nit-picking. Most people just seemed genuinely glad that George was temporarily back in the public eye with a "new" record. It's good to know that George lived to see his solo masterpiece regain its rightful place in the hall of fame of classic albums.

George threw himself wholeheartedly into the promotion of the album, even if he did conduct most of his publicity from the safety of his telephone. Still, it was amazing that he even bothered to do that!

During his publicity spree George stated that the *All Things Must Pass* re-issue was a prelude to his plan to revitalise his entire catalogue "and get it back on the shelves." Particularly mouth-watering was the prospect that his 1976-1992 Dark Horse back catalogue would be re-issued, much of which had never been released on CD, and the two Traveling Wilburys albums, the rights to which had reverted back to him in 1999.

George would hint that each of solo albums would be remastered, like *All Things Must Pass,* and would all include outtakes and bonus tracks. In light of his death, it's likely that these will be in the shops sooner rather than on the pearl anniversaries of their original release.

While it will be good to see those albums back in the High Street, that, even in mid-2002, is still a Sahara of George product. What will happen to Harrison's plan to release a box set of all his unreleased material? A Harrison solo anthology, if you will.

Harrison had originally predicted that the boxed set of unreleased songs, demos and outtakes would follow eighteen months after the release of his next album. "I'm trying to get everything that has ever been done out there," he would promise, "it'll just take a little time."

To promote the album Harrison embraced modern technology by taking part in a couple of on-line web chats, for MSN Live! and Yahoo. For the latter George sat for the questions live from the Capitol Tower in Hollywood, with the answers then typed by Yahoo in another locale.

Naturally the questions relating to the Beatles were of most intrigue. Answering a question about a Threetles reunion tour, Harrison teased, "Stranger things have happened," as a pig flew by the Capitol Tower.

George was also asked, "Does Paul still piss you off (tell us the truth)," to which George replied: "I'm sure there's enough about me that pisses him off, but I think we have now grown old enough to realise that we're both pretty damn cute!"

During the web chats George confirmed yet again that he was still working on a new studio album and claimed to have "many songs in various states of completion. Possibly thirty-five songs that I have been working on over the years."

Aside from the songs that did appear on *Brainwashed*, rumours also surfaced that George's vaults contained a cover of Bob Dylan's "Every Grain of Sand," the Ry Cooder song "How Can a Poor Man Stand Such Times and Live," and the Harrisong title, "Valentine." Another who ventured further information about song titles was George's friend and former Traffic drummer, Jim Capaldi. In an interview with Brazilian newspaper, *Folha de Sao Paulo*, Capaldi mentioned that he had lately recorded two songs with George: the co-written "Love's Got a Hold on Me" and the curiously-named "Doing the Bonzo Dog." According to Capaldi, neither were completed. It remains to be seen whether any of these titles will see the light of day.

Before settling on *Brainwashed*, the new album's title had also been a rich source of speculation, although the witty, Python-esque suggestion, *Portrait of a Leg End*, was sadly jettisoned at an early stage.

Another title Harrison jokingly mentioned for consideration was *Your Planet Is Doomed – Volume One* because of his concern over the all-too-rapid development of technology. "The world is just going mental as far as I'm concerned," he told Reuters. "It's speeding up with the whole technology and everything that's happening. Basically I think the planet is doomed, and it's my attempt to try to put a bit of a spin on the spiritual side, a reminder for myself and for anybody who's interested."

Of course, George could be forgiven for being pessimistic, though he did add that, while downbeat about the environment, he was positive about "my place in creation . . . and I don't have any worries whatsoever about that."

During the syndicated interview, Harrison also revealed that he had played the bulk of the instruments himself on the "new album" and that meant no computers. "My music doesn't seem to belong to any particular period," he would say, "I just make it the same way as we made it back in the '60s, which is analogue tapes, microphones and guitars, bass, drums, pianos." The new tracks, Harrison confirmed, would also feature contributions from his son Dhani and legendary drummer Jim Keltner.

After George's death, Keltner would add, "It was fantastic to be in the studio with him again. Some of the songs are very poignant concerning his life in the past few years. It will be obvious when you hear them what they are about."

George had also speculated that he might bring in an outsider for some finishing touches. Could this outsider have been none other than Sir Paul McCartney? In fact, George actually said, misleadingly as it turned out, that it was "likely" that Paul would be "helping out" with a few numbers, citing "recent incidents" and "life changes" that had helped him reconcile his past reluctance to work closely with his ex-band-mate. "I must say I look forward to Paul's input. I hear he's had a few hits," Harrison joked.

George's relationship with Paul seemed to be as healthy as it had ever been. When asked, "What is your relationship like with Paul and Ringo, lately?" George would answer "They're a part of my life. We've known each other since we were teenagers and it's fun to go to a birthday party at Ringo's and see how old we've gotten. Paul and I are different. But I think that destiny has brought us together. It was written that we'd find each other."

It's comforting to know that in the last year of George's life, the waters were serene in Beatleland, and that George was fully reconciled with the man he had known since he was a teenager. Considering all they'd been through, good and bad, it was amazing that they even gave each other the time of day, as they both approached sixty. The fact that they still occasionally saw each other is testament to the strength of the Beatles' bond.

George also commented that he still believed in the power of music "to inspire, give comfort or another outlook" on "all the terrible things we're doing to ourselves and each other these days."

Of course everyone hoped that the music he was working on in the new millennium would reaffirm the inspirational power of his own music, and that the overwhelmingly ironic November 2001 release date he'd pencilled in for his new album would be the start of a renewed period of music making.

Cruelly, George himself had seemed optimistic as he promoted *All Things Must Pass* at the start of the year that this would be the case, telling *Billboard* magazine that his next album was "not going to be the end – it's going to be one of lots of records. Then I'll go on holiday again."

CHAPTER EIGHTEEN

2001

Life is fragile, like a raindrop on a lotus leaf, and you better believe it!"

George Harrison, 2001

The first signs that time was running out came on May 4, 2001, when it was announced, by his solicitors, that George had again undergone surgery at the Mayo Clinic in Rochester, Minnesota, this time for cancer of the lung.

"Because of his previous health problems," his legal representatives stated, "he is checked regularly to ensure that if there are any problems they can be discovered immediately. Thankfully after one of these checks they discovered the very small tumour. A tiny part of his lung was removed along with a very small cancerous tumour. They also checked his throat to see if the cancer had returned there, but thankfully it hadn't. The operation was a complete success and he is now recuperating with his wife. He has made a very good recovery and is fit and well, all things considering. He is now enjoying a holiday in Tuscany."

There, a contented looking George posed for photographs with his cryogenically beautiful wife Olivia who looked as though she hadn't aged in twenty years.

While in Tuscany it was reported that the couple had been paid a visit by Paul, no doubt keen to hear from the dark horse's mouth how George was bearing up. An unnamed source reported: "Paul really wanted to see how George was and thought it was an ideal opportunity to get together because they were both in Italy at the same time. It was quite a moving meeting for both of them."

But things looked bleaker when, in July, Harrison was

forced to embark on a *new* course of treatment at the San Giovanni Oncology Institute in Bellinzona, Switzerland, for a brain tumour.

To be near the institute, George and Olivia purchased an £8 million 14-room villa in Montagnola. Harrison told villagers that he planned to make the villa his permanent home and pay taxes in Switzerland, suggesting George had finally turned his back on the bad vibes at Friar Park. The property was found by George and Olivia with the help of Pietro Balerna, the local parish clerk. "He seemed peaceful and almost jolly," Balerna would later elegise, "he was full of hope."

During May and June, under the care of Dr. Franco Cavalli, one of Switzerland's leading cancer experts, George paid regular visits to the clinic in the Italian-speaking canton of Ticino, where he underwent cobalt ray radiation therapy.

On July 10, Dr. Cavalli told the Associated Press: "Mr. Harrison was referred to the hospital to undergo a course of radiotherapy. He successfully completed this course more than a month ago and we foresee no need for further treatment here." As a result there seemed every reason to believe that George would emerge from these trials with a clean bill of health.

To further allay fears George's *All Things Must Pass* website posted a splash message that read: "Dear Friends and Fans, George Harrison would like it to be known that he is feeling fine, is not in the hospital and is sorry for any disturbance the press may have caused. Please do not worry."

But there was every reason to worry. Soon George was checking into the Staten Island University Hospital, which houses a world-famous cancer facility, where he was treated by Doctor Gil Lederman, the hospital's director of radiation oncology. Lederman had pioneered an experimental and controversial procedure known as stereotactic radiosurgery, a process that uses radiation to target large and advanced tumours by delivering high doses of radiation to the diseased tissue without damaging the surrounding area. Though this treatment has been criticised by some medical experts, Lederman claimed the procedure could double the survival rate of patients with inoperable tumours.

Since none of this medical mumbo-jumbo was familiar to the majority of George fans at this stage, all reports relating to Harrison's health and whereabouts were interpreted as perfectly prudent precautionary tactics rather than last-ditch attempts to save his life.

While the newspapers speculated, there was evidence that George was on the mend when it was announced November 2001 would see the release of his first brand new song in a very, very long time.

The new track (written by George and his son Dhani) was called "Horse to the Water" and appeared on *Small World, Big Band*, the new album from Jools Holland, British television personality and leader of his ersatz Rhythm and Blues Orchestra.

Though *Small World, Big Band* also featured collaborations with such legendary figures as Sting, Van Morrison, John Cale, Eric Clapton and David Gilmour, Harrison's snaky, swaggering "Horse to the Water" was inevitably the album's focal point.

"I was thrilled and delighted that George was part of the album," Holland told *Billboard* magazine's website. "Not only is he one of the most important musicians of the twentieth century, he was the lead guitarist in an incredibly popular group, and he was also of course in the Beatles! I was so honoured, when I was looking for people to do this record with me, that he agreed."

George overdubbed his lead vocals for "Horse to the Water" (on to Holland's backing track) on October 1, at his home in Switzerland in just two takes. *Billboard* described the song as showing "Harrison in fine voice and strong writing form, on a brassy uptempo song with a narrative style reminiscent of his sometime Traveling Wilburys band-mate Bob Dylan." One of Holland's flunkies described the song as a cross between 1960s Bob Dylan and early 1970s John Lennon.

I take issue with the easy pigeonholing of George's style as a cross between Dylan and Lennon. Melodically the song is pure George, with a blistering guitar solo that reminded everyone just how good he could be and, with its appropriately meaningful lyrics, "Horse to the Water" can be interpreted as a poignant reflection of Harrison's struggle with cancer. The libretto also found Harrison playing the tut-tutting sage one last time – pleading with people to reject drugs and drink in favour of wisdom and God realisation.

Not that Harrison exempted himself, lyrically acknowledging both the dangers of smoking and the fact that he ignored the evidence. If he was addressing himself perhaps he should have called the song "*Dark* Horse to the Water."

Given the circumstances, it is obvious Harrison had intended "Horse to the Water" as a final message, and, prophetically, the song was published by "R.I.P. Ltd. 2001" which proves that while George did indeed know he would not see the new year, he did at least pass away with his own unique sense of humour still in tact.

Returning to "Horse to the Water," I'm reminded of the old Hollywood maxim that you're only as good as your last film. If this adage is applied to music then George bowed out on a high.

CHAPTER NINETEEN

R.I.P. 1943-2001

There are celebrities whose deaths inspire in the general public an impression of personal bereavement. Particularly since the death of John Lennon, the odds seemed stacked against Harrison ever belonging in that category – he'd appeared in public too infrequently, released too few records. He was an almost invisible celebrity, and although this was of his own choosing, it left him devoid of that indefinable something that turns famous men and women into "national treasures," or global ones for that matter.

But George Harrison had been in the Beatles, and that is tantamount to sainthood for millions world-wide. When the tributes poured in one could detect a genuine melancholy, a real sense that the world had lost one of its favourite sons.

I was in the car when I heard the news on Friday, November 30, 2001. As someone who rarely watches morning television, the only thing telling me that something was wrong was a strange feeling in my stomach. The reason for this intuition, the radio announced, was that the Beatles' baby was no more, a rather cryptic way (I felt) of saying that George Harrison had finally lost his battle with cancer. George had passed away the previous day on a bedroom chaise longue covered in a yellow silk blanket strewn with rose petals, with Olivia and Dhani at his side. Though the location remained a closely guarded secret even after his death, it was thought to be at a private address rented for him by his friend Gavin de Becker somewhere in Southern California. ("They still don't know where George died, and they never will," de Becker proudly stated later, "which proves that even a very famous man can lead a private life and have a peaceful, private death"). The official time of death was 1:20 p.m., Pacific Standard Time. He was fifty-eight.

Annette Lloyd, a funeral director at Hollywood Forever said her staff was called out just twenty minutes after Harrison's passing, without knowing on whom they were attending. "Before the body was taken from the home to the doctor's office, the family, our staff and the security staff joined hands and said a prayer around him." George's body was cremated shortly afterwards without a ceremony and then the tragic news was leaked to the world.

Via de Becker, the Harrison family then issued the following statement: "He left this world as he lived in it, conscious of God, fearless of death, and at peace, surrounded by family and friends. He often said, 'Everything else can wait but the search for God cannot wait, and love one another.'"

It was revealed that during his last weeks Harrison had checked himself out of the Staten Island Hospital (where he was undergoing radiation therapy), and flown to UCLA's Medical Centre for last ditch attempts to save his life. George had fought against death as bravely and as desperately as he had when repelling the psychotic knife attack at his Friar Park home two years before. Unfortunately, with cancer rumoured to be affecting every organ in his body, this was a bout with fate he could not win.

Having naively believed for so long that the imminence of Harrison's death was merely the stuff of tabloid exaggeration, and the "days to live" headlines mere guesswork, I had refused to accept that behind that locked door, George was indeed dying.

In hindsight, the fact that Paul and Ringo had visited him at the Staten Island University Hospital two weeks prior to November 29, and that Paul left in tears was *not* a promising sign. I'm sure both Paul and Ringo were grateful that they were able to say a proper goodbye, an opportunity Mark

Chapman's bullets had deprived them of when John Lennon died.

Back in England, after George's death had become public knowledge, it was McCartney who impressively handled his quasi-official duties as "Spokesman for Planet Beatle." Talking at length, Sir Paul, chose his words beautifully, skilfully avoiding any repeat of his misunderstood "it's a drag" gaffe almost twenty-one years earlier.

Paying tribute to the man he described as his "baby brother," McCartney repeatedly described Harrison's courage and bravery throughout his long battle.

"I am devastated and very, very sad," McCartney eulogised. "He was a lovely guy and a very brave man and had a wonderful sense of humour. He is really just my baby brother. I've known George forever and he's a really beautiful guy who I love dearly."

McCartney said that although he knew George had been ill for quite some time, he said that he had been praying for some kind of miracle. It was clear from the sheer volume of eulogies that McCartney's prayers had not been a lonely vigil.

"He had a long battle with his cancer," McCartney continued, "and I saw him a few weeks ago and he was full of fun and he always was a lovely guy who is full of humour as I was saying. When I saw him last time he was obviously very unwell but he was cracking jokes like he always was and he'll be sorely missed. He's a beautiful man. The world will miss him."

McCartney also revealed that he had been in contact with Olivia Harrison and was reassured to hear that George had died peacefully. "I understand from his wife," McCartney added, "that he went peacefully which is a great blessing and it was a very peaceful golden moment apparently . . . He was a very lovely man who didn't suffer fools gladly and didn't like interferences in his private life. He was a great man, a loving man, and I would like to ask people, particularly the media, to be very kind to Olivia and Dhani at the moment and to try and support them this time, because they need support."

Ringo paid his own tribute to George saying he had lost "a best friend." Speaking from a friend's house in Vancouver, Canada, Starr said: "George was a best friend of mine. I loved him very much and I will miss him greatly. Both Barbara and I send our love and light to Olivia and Dhani. We will miss George for his sense of love, his sense of music and his sense of laughter."

And then there were two.

With the flags flying at half-mast in Liverpool, I'm sure up in heaven George and John were enjoying a warm reunion and a good old laugh.

As the condolences poured in, tearful Beatles fans pilgrimaged to their nearest personal Stonehenge to lay flowers and messages. Soon Friar Park, Abbey Road, the Cavern and the Strawberry Fields monument in Central Park (across the road from where John had lived), were awash with grieving fans. Touchingly, at Abbey Road, Allan Rouse (the studio's official Beatles co-ordinator), supervised the moving of a huge speaker into the doorway of the studio so *All Things Must Pass* could play to those outside. The studios had done the same when John died.

The blanket media coverage, though, was a pleasant surprise. Sure Harrison had been one quarter of the Beatles and that alone guaranteed the personal sympathies sent by various heads of state, but to see every C-list climbing over each other to add their two-penn'orth about a man most of them had almost certainly never met was strangely gratifying.

Acknowledging Harrison's status as a hugely popular and much loved world figure, the Queen of England and President George W. Bush were both reported to have been saddened by the news, the latter saying he considered the Beatles "one of the greatest groups of any time in music." Prime Minister Tony Blair's tribute, meanwhile, was delivered in a specially arranged press conference with the Irish Taoiseach Bertie Aherne.

A solemn looking Blair said: "A generation, including myself, grew up with the Beatles. Their music, the band and the personalities of the band were the background to our lives. I think people will be very sad at his death." Blair added that he wasn't just "a great musician and artist, but he did an immense amount for charity. He will be very, very sadly missed by people right around the world."

I can't envisage another musician (with the obvious exception of Paul and Ringo) eliciting personal responses from the two leaders of the free world and a reigning monarch of the Commonwealth.

It was the fact that all the eulogies mentioned Harrison's less well-known but nonetheless equally impressive achievements that made his passing such a body blow to so many people. While the plaudits justly celebrated Harrison's pivotal and influential contributions to the Fab Four, George also finally received sufficient praise for his solo career. Furthermore, Harrison received his due for resuscitating an ailing British film industry via HandMade Films, and for his influential role in bringing Indian culture to the attention of the west and indirectly creating the "world music" market in the process. It's just a crying shame that such fulsome praise had to be bestowed posthumously.

Likewise, Harrison was also given credit for being rock music's first avatar, thanks to his Concert for Bangladesh, a fact that I'm sure most people had overlooked. Naturally the people of Bangladesh had never forgotten his efforts and they were quick to offer their empathy. Bangladesh President Badruddoza Chowdhury was quoted as saying, "The people of Bangladesh consider Harrison as their beloved man, who felt for them in 1971 during their days of agony and distress," while Bangladesh Prime Minister Khaleda Zia added, "George Harrison will be remembered forever by the people of Bangladesh."

Further accolades poured forth from everyone from Sir Bob Geldof to Allen Williams (the Beatles' first manager), to Jeff Lynne, who said: "You always knew where you stood with George, he was totally honest. I feel blessed to have been so close to him. He was a great friend. He wrote brilliantly original songs, played the greatest slide guitar and had the most amazing sense of humour. He really had the 'Inner Light,' and always will be. Some of the happiest days of my life were spent in the studio with George."

Allen Williams' tribute included the line, "It is an honour to talk about such a great person," and that seemed to be the tenor of most people's summaries. Behind all the tinselly mourning, you got a real sense that what people would miss most was not the Beatle or the musician but George Harrison the man, a gentleman, coupled with a respect for his lack of disingenuousness and artifice, his courage and his integrity, a man who never sold out.

In an age when, literally, every cheap jack wants to be famous for fifteen minutes without the talent to achieve any longevity beyond this quarter hour, it was only fitting that there should have been genuine respect for a man of iron integrity who mocked such ephemera and looked for a deeper, more edifying and more spiritual meaning to life. A star in very sense of the word.

Recognising that it was hard to live up to what the Beatles had achieved, Bob Geldof (who had consulted George when organising Live Aid) reminded everyone that George "did it very well and with great grace and dignity. George never let anyone down. He was never disappointing. I can't think of a naff thing he did. That's pretty amazing."

Bizarrely it was the words of Oasis mainman Noel Gallagher that touched me the most, saying, "It's very, very sad I hope he found what he spent his life searching for." I believe George *did* find what he was searching for and went to the grave safe in the knowledge that his God existed.

Certainly Olivia and Dhani Harrison were positive that this was so in their statement thanking everyone for their kindness, "We are deeply touched by the outpouring of love and compassion from people around the world. The profound beauty of the moment of George's passing – of his awakening from this dream – was no surprise to those of us who knew how he longed to be with God. In that pursuit, he was relentless."

Perhaps the most compelling evidence that God exists is that George Harrison had also existed, and that he was born in the same city within roughly the same age group as John Lennon, Paul McCartney and Richard Starkey.

As a fitting memorial, Olivia and Dhani invited all those who cared about George to join them in a minute of meditation in honour of his journey, on the Monday after his death.

Not surprisingly, George left the bulk of his £99 million estate to his wife and son, as well as allegedly donating a sizeable amount to various charities while he was still alive. Olivia and Dhani announced that George's ashes would be scattered in India, near Allahabad where the Ganges and Yamuna Rivers converge. This, however, turned out to be Harrison's final joke, a red herring to misdirect the hundreds of gawkers who George correctly predicted would camp out for days on these river banks to witness the ceremony.

Instead, his remains were scattered in the beautiful home he'd purchased in Switzerland near to the San Giovanni Oncology Institute in Bellinzona where he had undergone radiotherapy. Even in death Harrison had been determined to shield his family from the intrusion of paparazzi and Beatlemaniacs.

While I find it difficult to put into words a fitting epitaph to a great man, I did come across a review of *The Concert for Bangladesh* from *Rolling Stone* magazine (which, I think, perfectly sums up the way George Harrison was perceived, how he lived his life and how he faced death), describing George as a man, "with a sense of his own worth, his own role in the place of things, and as a man prepared to face reality openly and with a judgement and maturity with few parallels among his peers."

POSTSCRIPT

2002

> *Unreleased material? I've got more stuff than Jim Reeves ever dreamed of. It's all lying there in the attic. It's all the stuff that no one ever wanted because it wasn't commercial or it said things that no one wanted to hear . . . But, anyway, I've got loads of it.*
>
> George Harrison, 1988

Three days short of the thirty-first anniversary of its initial release, "My Sweet Lord" was at number one in the British charts for the second time. Its instant rise to the top spot was not only a testimonial to the enduring power of the record, but also a testament of the abiding popularity of George Harrison, the man.

But while seeing George at number one again was gratifying, it was the prospect of a new solo album that his fans yearned for.

In a personal and heartfelt foreword to *Harrison* (a commemorative publication put together by the editors of *Rolling Stone* magazine), Olivia Harrison wrote, "The silence of George's absence in our lives is deafening." For his fans that deafening silence was at least partially broken on November 19, 2002, when, ten days before the first anniversary of his death was marked by a star-studded tribute concert at the Royal Albert Hall (featuring Joe Brown, Eric Clapton, Jools Holland, Jim Keltner, Jeff Lynne, various Monty Python alumnae, Tom Petty, Billy Preston, Ravi Shankar, and, of course, Ringo and Paul), the new George Harrison studio album, *Brainwashed,* finally hit the shelves.

Though a first glance at the line-up for the twelve-track

legacy suggested a posthumous "odds-and-sods" collection, George had actually started work on the album in 1999, assisted and encouraged by his son Dhani.

Several of the tracks on *Brainwashed* had been lying around in Harrison's vaults for some years in demo form, and Harrison aficionados would have been familiar with five of the titles, which was something of a surprise. Since Harrison himself had repeatedly bragged about "thirty-five songs in various stages of completion," it was nonetheless a pleasant surprise to see the inclusion of "P2 Vatican Blues" (a fifteen year-old *Cloud Nine* outtake), "Between the Devil and Deep Blue Sea" (originally recorded for Channel 4's *Mister Roadrunner,* screened in 1992), "Any Road" (originally performed by George on his and Ravi Shankar's VH1 special in 1997), "Rocking Chair in Hawaii" ("based" on the 1970 demo, "Down to the River"), and "Run So Far" (the Harrisong donated to Eric Clapton's *Journeyman* album). All of which proved, if nothing else, that Harrison was never one to waste a good tune.

Reportedly, Harrison and son worked on the songs in a variety of different locations, including Los Angeles, Australia and Switzerland. "We'd be by ourselves a lot of the time and it was like a cottage industry," Dhani would say, while handling the album's promotion in his father's stead, "I'd be pressing the play and stop buttons. I did it because he needed a buddy and we were friends. He was just playing around. But when my dad played around he was very serious."

Work continued on the record right up until the end when Harrison made his last trip from Switzerland to America, where he died, at a venue unknown. Prevented from finishing the album himself, the production baton was thus bequeathed to Dhani and Jeff Lynne.

If left to his own devices, George might have felt that the work was its own reward, and an official release unnecessary, if only to avoid those abhorrent publicity chores, but after his father died, Dhani felt compelled to complete the record: "I don't think my dad cared if he released it. But I cared because in my opinion the record was so good. He never said I should finish it but I always knew I'd have to eventually."

To some extent Lynne's involvement was surprising. After all, had George not stated, in 2000, that he would not be working with the bearded Wilbury on his next studio offering because he "did not want him to make ELO albums out of my songs."

However, with George no longer around, Lynne was the obvious choice to reproduce the wonder of *Cloud Nine*. Besides, George had been sharing his new songs with Lynne throughout the recording process. "George would come round my house and he'd always have a new song with him," Lynne explained. "He would strum them on a guitar or ukulele. The songs just knocked me out."

George also left the duo with specific instructions about final arrangements, presumably to avoid his musical legacy being mixed in a way that sounded uber-produced, "ELO-style."

Dhani and Lynne worked on the album in Los Angeles, spending several months in the studio putting the finishing touches to what Dhani described as his father's "posh demos." "We worked through it methodically and filled in where needed," Dhani detailed. "But we never committed fraud on the recordings. It was all my dad and we worked according to his rules and values. It just took us a bit longer because he wasn't there to ask if it was right or not."

"George constantly talked about how he wanted the album to sound," Jeff concurred. "He told Dhani a lot of things he would like to have done to the songs and left us little clues. There was always that spiritual energy that went into the lyrics as well as the music."

Though George could not be in the studio in person, his son certainly felt his father's "spiritual energy" pervading his and Jeff's working environment. "Little things happened every day that were weird," Dhani explained. "You can hear a crow cawing at the end of 'Rising Sun.' There was this bird sitting on the window outside trying to get in . . . little things like that happened every day and his spirit was very much there. How could it not be? We were evoking him by thinking about him and playing his music all day every day for months. There must be some vibration or presence through that. I'm sure he had an input to the record after he died."

And certainly the templates that Dhani and Jeff had to work from were no scratchy Dictaphone affairs like Lennon's "Free as a Bird" and "Real Love." Harrison's demos were almost fully realised, if the liner notes are anything to go by, with George contributing electric and acoustic guitars, dobro, ukulele, bass and keyboards, in addition to lead and backing vocals. The rest of the "band" consisted, for the most part, of Jeff Lynne (bass, piano, guitars, keyboards and backing vocals), Dhani Harrison (electric and acoustic guitars, Wurlizter and backing vocals) and the ever-faithful Jim Keltner on drums for eight of the tracks.

The album opens with the Wilbury-esque, "Any Road," a breezy chugalug, heralded by Harrison's control room command: "Give me plenty of that guitar." Though resourceful fans of the Quiet One would already have been familiar with the composition, the version here is a delightful opener with George in particularly scintillating form with his signature bottle-neck. George also sounds in good voice, particularly when he steps up an octave in the coda, and the wry philosophy of the lyrics sets the tone of the album perfectly. Perhaps that was why the track was chosen as the album's lead single, which climbed to number thirty-seven on the British charts in May 2003.

On "P2 Vatican Blues (Last Saturday Night)," Harrison continues the "Wilbury" vibe started by "Any Road." Though I would be tempted to stick with George's initial instinct as far as this song goes (that is, if it wasn't good enough for *Cloud Nine,* why had it suddenly become good enough for *Brainwashed*), it is an enjoyable romp nonetheless, if a little too close to "pub-rock" for my tastes. It was, however, odd to find Lynne here restraining his "kitchen sink," since a bigger sound might have improved the song. The drums sound more like a wet bag of crisps being tapped by a swizzle stick, and double-tracked vocals would certainly have helped.

Much better was "Pisces Fish," described by *Billboard* as "a partially autobiographical rock hymn," and if it's rock hymns you're after, who are you gonna call? With its lilting verses and mournful chorus, structurally "Pisces Fish" is a great example of a late-period Harrison track, that, unlike "Vatican Blues," would have slotted onto *Cloud Nine* quite nicely. That said, a nagging feeling persists that again Lynne might have done so much more with the song: perhaps by adding "some more of that guitar," like his friend had requested at the start of the record, or finding a more convincing way of ending the song rather than simply fading it out. The poetic introspective lyrics are excellent however, a touching self-portrait of their author in repose.

Though I read "Pisces Fish" described as a ballad with a heavy Dylan influence, in countless reviews, I've always disliked this lazy and rather facile comparison, since it suggests that Harrison was in stylistic thrall to his friend, which I regard as patently not true.

"Looking for My Life" was another lyrically strong number, in which Harrison confronts his own mortality. Despite the dark candour of the lyrics, the composition is *Brainwashed*'s bounciest AOR track, as if Harrison was trying to leaven the subject matter. That said, the composition is short-changed somewhat by a thin arrangement and that infernal chorus pedal very much to the fore.

Although "Looking for My Life" was the lyric that most pointedly seemed to deal with his illness, it has to be said that the track was no maudlin testament to his mortality as Dhani was keen to point out: "He was happy and doing his singing. He never felt sorry for himself or went into depression. He was working and doing what he could." In an interview with Katie Couric, to promote the album, Olivia too would remind everyone that her husband faced death with no fear and no regrets and that certainly comes across loud and clear throughout the album.

"Rising Sun" was obviously a stand-out, with its strong Beatles edges, powerful vocal, tasteful slide-guitar careens, stratospheric melody and towering, cinematic arrangement. Happily, for once the production is spot on and the retro strings are splendid (purportedly arranged by George himself), adding that all-important dash of texture that Lynne tends to resist throughout the rest of the LP.

For Dhani Harrison, the track stirred up powerful memories of the recording of the album while his father was still alive: "I remember him during the recording of 'Rising Sun,'" Dhani recalled. "A strong memory: I'm with him in this room, I'm listening to him playing his solo. I remember people looking at him with admiration while he plays. Everything goes round and round in my mind, between sounds and vibes. It's like listening to a radio and trying to reproduce them."

Another track that inspired admiration for the way George played guitar was the elegiac slide-guitar instrumental, "Marwa Blues." Even without a vocal there was no mistaking who was behind it, but then a song as eloquent as this didn't need lyrics. As Harrison himself once sang on 1973's "That Is All": "Silence often says much more than trying to say what's been said before." Instead, the song's articulacy lies in the melancholy of Harrison's exquisite and subtle fret-work. The short quote from "Within You, Without You" in the mix was also a nice touch, though I would again complain that this beautiful requiem is frustratingly faded out.

It is a shame "Stuck Inside a Cloud" wasn't chosen as the album's lead single (instead of "Any Road"), because it was easily a candidate for the *Brainwashed* "best track" award. Described by the mandarins at Capitol Tower as "a classic George record!" was exactly right, since "Stuck Inside a Cloud" is sublime, with contemplative and bittersweet lyrics carried by a perfect melody, and Harrison's appropriately world-weary vocals.

While "Run So Far" was not the best thing George ever wrote, it did pleasantly evoke Harrison's 1979-82 period and would easily have sat comfortably on *Somewhere in England* or *Gone Troppo*. If the song had failed to ignite on Clapton's *Journeyman,* in the hands of its composer it is transformed here into a charming, chiming countrified peach.

Though its title portended to be the album's "big ballad," "Never Get Over You" was closer in style and execution to "Unknown Delight" and "Baby Don't Run Away," than "Something" or "Can't Stop Thinking About You." Perhaps Jeff Lynne again could have nixed the chorus pedal effects on George's guitar, and added a lush string accompaniment and more interesting harmonies, as he had done on "Someplace Else," a song "Never Get Over You" doesn't quite recreate. Nonetheless, "Never Get Over You" was a slow burner that grows on you, helped by a gorgeous middle eight.

The only non-original on the album was the Harold Arlen chestnut "The Devil and the Deep Blue Sea," and one of my favourites. Though the song had long been a staple of Harrison fans' bootleg collections, there is no doubt an offi-cial Dark Horse labelling was deserved and overdue. With

George blissfully crooning and strumming that ubiquitous uke, the band that included Jools Holland (piano), Joe Brown (acoustic guitar), Ray Cooper (drums) and Herbie Flowers (bass & tuba) swing happily in the background. It is, however, a shame Lynne and Dhani tweaked the original template by mixing out the band at the start of the song, though it does showcase Harrison's adroit ukulele playing in isolation.

As someone who has long lauded "Baltimore Oriole" as one of George's most effective recordings, the release of "Devil" affords me one last chance to reiterate my wish that Harrison had done a whole album of these golden mouldies. If only more performances like this existed!

After some pre-release speculation about the song, this author at least was surprised to discover that the dobro-laden "Rocking Chair in Hawaii" was a compositional re-working of the 1970 demo, "Down to the River," albeit slowed down, with the addition of a middle eight, new lyrics except for the first verse and sans the expletives and yodelling. Although a bit of a filler, "Rocking Chair's" mixture of slide and acoustic guitar and its relaxed, bluesy groove brought to mind "For You Blue."

The title and final track was obviously sequenced to be the album's big statement, Harrison's parting shot at society's ills, and though the critics frothed, for me, the lyrical content was more a hectoring, pedagogical misfire. Though the song was described during Harrison's 1999 *Billboard* interview with Timothy White, as "a blistering anthem about social delusions in a world running down," Harrison picks easy targets, and rails against the manipulation perpetrated by the corporate world, the media, and the government, which is hardly a scoop. Since George is, obviously, no longer with us he can be excused for not capturing the zeitgeist, but surely anyone could have worked out the message here for his or herself. As for the inevitable Harrison panacea of religious salvation, surely religion too is a form of brainwashing (as at least one critic pointed out), and often a more pernicious and insidious one at that.

However, the whole piece is performed with verve and conviction, with help from Bikram Ghosh (tabla), Jon Lord (piano), Sam Brown (backing vocals) and Jane Lister (harp), and the song's showboating latter half is breathtaking, with its Indian FX and Vedic chanting. The Eastern vibe is something I had long hoped George would get around to doing seriously on one of his solo albums, and even though he waited until the last song of his last (?) LP, it was nevertheless a worthwhile reminder that "East meets West" was always his patent.

Overall, since I was expecting *Cloud Nine* mark II then perhaps my "anticappointment" with *Brainwashed* was my own fault and harsh, though I would stand by any criticism of the amount of chorus pedal and Lynne's glossy but uninspired production. Furthermore, the perplexing decision not to employ the services of a recognised bass player, for the most part, seemed more perverse with every listen, robbing many of the songs of a convincing bottom end. Perhaps, Harrison should have left the songs in the hands of one Paul McCartney!

The producer was quick to admit that he couldn't resist adding his trademark gloss to the finished product: "I'd been talking to George for the past couple or three years about finishing these songs. He said 'I'd like you to finish them for me.' We talked about it, and he said that he didn't want the album to be posh. What he wanted, really, was kind of like demos. But these songs deserved more than that, because they were great, as far as I was concerned. So, sorry George, I made them a bit posher than you might have wanted. But I felt I was only doing them justice."

Ordinarily Lynne's excuses might have been acceptable,

but the overall effect on *Brainwashed* is a rather polished blandness at the expense of any real aural texture, muscle and variety, and as a result, parts of the album sound a bit samey.

Without doubt matters would have improved had Harrison lived to complete the album himself, his but herein lies the rub. *Brainwashed* might not match the standards of his very best work, but even this eclectic compilation is a gnawing reminder that Harrison's passing is a loss too large to measure. *Brainwashed* is, for all its faults, a collection of solid songs, each imbued with the trademark spirituality and wit that had always defined Harrison's work.

Despite precious little promotion, *Brainwashed* peaked at a highly creditable number eighteen in the American album charts and débuted at the number one spot in Japan. And though its batting average was compromised by its eventual number twenty-nine high in Britain, critics were almost universally kind to the album. *Rolling Stone* applauded it as "a gorgeously understated album," *Q* Magazine in the U.K. described it "as well-rounded and polished as albums get," while *Uncut* magazine said, "these songs are what George wanted to say at the end, and they say it well."

With every passing year since 1987's *Cloud Nine,* it seemed increasingly unlikely that there would ever be another Harrison long-player, a possibility that looked even more implausible when George died in 2001. Dhani and Jeff should be championed for labouring to bring us this very final chapter of Harrison's career, and a stronger sign-off than one had any right to expect, given how ill George had been during his last two or three years.

But will it be the final chapter? After all, Harrison himself had long claimed to have "enough material for three albums" and various "guestimates" put the amount of songs George was working on as anywhere between twenty-five and thirty-five. According to Dhani, "Some are completed somewhere and some that are reported to exist, don't, and there are some that people haven't heard and they exist."

Asked whether a proposed George Harrison Anthology boxed set would see the light of day, Dhani replied, "Yes, it will, but not for a while. I need a holiday first." And who could blame him after the emotionally draining work on his father's life-affirming final album.

"Making this record with my dad included the joy of working together when we started on it," Dhani would lament, "and the sadness of not finishing it together. I am honoured to have played a part, and proud to be able to release this into the world as a gift to those who enjoy my father's music."

Ultimately *Brainwashed* is an affecting and honest good-bye, and it is hard not to be moved by Harrison's poetry, even though the songs were about life, not death, as his widow Olivia Harrison was quick to point out: "You know, George dedicated a lot of his life to attain a good ending. And I don't have any doubt that he was successful."

At the time of going to press it was announced that February 2004 would finally see the CD re-release of the six albums George Harrison released on his own Dark Horse Records between 1976 and 1992: *33 & 1/3*, *George Harrison*, *Somewhere in England*, *Gone Troppo*, *Cloud Nine* and *Live in Japan*). The overdue reissue programme will see the albums digitally re-mastered and bolstered by previously unreleased bonus tracks: "Tears of the World" on *33 & 1/3*, "Here Comes the Moon (Demo Version)" on *George Harrison*, "Save the World (Demo Version)" on *Somewhere in England*, "Mystical One (Demo Version)" on *Gone Troppo* and "Shanghai Surprise" and "Zig Zag" on *Cloud Nine*.

Furthermore, all six CDs would also come housed in a

boxed set entitled *The Dark Horse Years 1976- 1992 along-side an* exclusive 89 minute DVD containing a feature on the history of Dark Horse records, the promo Videos to "This Song," "Crackerbox Palace," "Faster," "Got My Mind Set on You" (Version I), "Got My Mind Set on You" (Version II), "When We Was Fab" and "This Is Love," footage from the 1991 Japanese tour and musical selections from the movie *Shanghai Surprise*.

GEORGE HARRISON SONGS

(All titles written by George Harrison except where noted)

A Bit More of You. *Extra Texture (Read All About It)*
Absolutely Sweet Marie (Live) (Bob Dylan). *The Bob Dylan 30th Anniversary Concert*
All Things Must Pass. *All Things Must Pass*
All Those Years Ago. *Somewhere in England*
All Those Years Ago (Live). *Live in Japan*
Any Road. *Brainwashed*
Apple Scruffs. *All Things Must Pass*
Art of Dying. *All Things Must Pass*
Awaiting on You All. *All Things Must Pass*
Awaiting on You All (Live). *Concert for Bangladesh*
Baby Don't Run Away. *Gone Troppo*
Ballad of Sir Frankie Crisp (Let It Roll). *All Things Must Pass*
Baltimore Oriole (Webster/Carmichael). *Somewhere in England*
Bangla Desh. 7" Single
Bangla Desh (Live). *Concert for Bangladesh*
Be Here Now. *Living in the Material World*
Beautiful Girl. *33 & 1/3*
Behind That Locked Door. *All Things Must Pass*
Between the Devil and the Deep Blue Sea (Arlen/Koehler). *Brainwashed*
Beware of Darkness. *All Things Must Pass*
Beware of Darkness (Demo) .*All Things Must Pass Remastered*
Beware of Darkness (Live). *Concert for Bangladesh*
Blood from a Clone. *Somewhere in England*
Blow Away. *George Harrison*
Brainwashed. *Brainwashed*
Breath Away from Heaven. *Cloud Nine*
Bye Bye, Love (Bryant/Bryant, parody lyrics added by Harrison). *Dark Horse*
Can't Stop Thinking About You. *Extra Texture (Read All About It)*
Cheer Down (George Harrison/Tom Petty). *The Best of Dark Horse 1976-1989*
Cheer Down (Live) (George Harrison/Tom Petty). *Live in Japan*
Circles. *Gone Troppo*
Cloud 9. *Cloud Nine*
Cloud 9 (Live). *Live in Japan*

Cockamamie Business. *The Best of Dark Horse 1976-1989*
Congratulations (The Traveling Wilburys). *The Traveling Wilburys
    Volume One*
Cool Dry Place (The Traveling Wilburys). *The Traveling Wilburys
    Volume Three*
Cowboy Music. *Wonderwall*
Crackerbox Palace. *33 & 1/3*
Crying. *Wonderwall*
Dark Horse. *Dark Horse*
Dark Horse (Live). *Live in Japan*
Dark Sweet Lady. *George Harrison*
Dear One. *33 & 1/3*
Deep Blue. B-side to "Bangla Desh"
Devil's Radio. *Cloud Nine*
Devil's Radio (Live). *Live in Japan*
Ding Dong, Ding Dong. *Dark Horse*
Dirty World (The Traveling Wilburys). *The Traveling Wilburys Vol-
    ume One*
Don't Let Me Wait Too Long. *Living in the Material World*
Dream Away. *Gone Troppo*
Dream Scene. *Wonderwall*
Drilling a Home. *Wonderwall*
End of the Line (The Traveling Wilburys). *The Traveling Wilburys
    Volume One*
Fantasy Sequins. *Wonderwall*
Far East Man (George Harrison/Ronnie Wood). *Dark Horse*
Faster. *George Harrison*
Fish on the Sand. *Cloud Nine*
For You Blue (Live in 1974). *Songs by George Harrison EP*
Flying Hour (George Harrison/Mick Relphs). *Songs by George
    Harrison EP*
Gat Kirwani. *Wonderwall*
Give Me Love (Give Me Peace on Earth). *Living in the Material
    World*
Give Me Love (Give Me Peace on Earth) (Live). *Live in Japan*
Glass Box. *Wonderwall*
Gone Troppo. *Gone Troppo*
Got My Mind Set on You (Rudy Clark). *Cloud Nine*
Got My Mind Set on You (Live) (Rudy Clark). *Live in Japan*
Greasy Legs. *Wonderwall*
Greece. *Gone Troppo*
Grey Cloudy Lies. *Extra Texture (Read All About It)*

Guru Vandana. *Wonderwall*

Handle With Care (The Traveling Wilburys). *The Traveling Wilburys Volume One*

Hari's On Tour (Express). *Dark Horse*

Hari's On Tour (Express) (Live in 1974). *Songs by George Harrison 2 EP*

Heading for the Light (The Traveling Wilburys). *The Traveling Wilburys Volume One*

Hear Me Lord. *All Things Must Pass*

Here Comes the Moon. *George Harrison*

Here Comes the Sun (Live). *Live in Japan*

Here Comes the Sun (Live). *Concert for Bangladesh*

His Name Is Legs (Ladies & Gentlemen). *Extra Texture (Read All About It)*

Homeward Bound (P.Simon) (with Paul Simon). *Nobody's Child: The Romanian Angel Album*

Hong Kong Blues (Hoagy Carmichael). *Somewhere in England*

Horse to the Water (G. Harrison/D. Harrison). *Jools Holland's "Small World, Big Band"*

Hottest Gong in Town. *Songs by George Harrison 2 EP*

I Dig Love. *All Things Must Pass*

I Don't Care Anymore. B-side to "Ding Dong, Ding Dong"

I Don't Want to Do It (Bob Dylan). *Porky's Revenge Soundtrack*

I Live for You. *All Things Must Pass Remastered*

I Really Love You (Leroy Swearingen). *Gone Troppo*

I Remember Jeep. *All Things Must Pass*

I Want to Tell You (Live)   *Live in Japan*

I'd Have You Anytime (George Harrison/Bob Dylan). *All Things Must Pass*

If I Needed Someone (Live). *Live in Japan*

If Not for You (Bob Dylan. *All Things Must Pass*

If You Believe (George Harrison/Gary Wright). *George Harrison*

If You Belonged to Me (The Traveling Wilburys). *The Traveling Wilburys Volume Three*

In the Park. *Wonderwall*

Inside Out (The Traveling Wilburys). *The Traveling Wilburys Volume Three*

Isn't It a Pity (Live). *Live in Japan*

Isn't It a Pity (Version 1). *All Things Must Pass*

Isn't It A Pity (Version 2). *All Things Must Pass*

It Is "He" (Jai Sri Krishna). *Dark Horse*

It's Johnny's Birthday (based upon "Congratulations" by
    Martin/Coulter). *All Things Must Pass*
It's What You Value. *33 & 1/3*
Just for Today. *Cloud Nine*
Last Night (The Traveling Wilburys). *The Traveling Wilburys Vol-
    une One*
Lay His Head. B-side to "Got My Mind Set on You"
Learning How to Love You. *33 & 1/3*
Let It Down. *All Things Must Pass*
Let It Down (Demo). *All Things Must Pass Remastered*
Life Itself. *Somewhere in England*
Life Itself (Demo). *Songs by George Harrison 2 EP*
Living in the Material World. *Living in the Material World*
Looking for My Life. *Brainwashed*
Love Comes to Everyone. *George Harrison*
Love Scene. *Wonderwall*
Margarita (The Traveling Wilburys). *The Traveling Wilburys Vol-
    ume One*
Marwa Blues. *Brainwashed*
Maya Love. *Dark Horse*
Microbes. *Wonderwall*
Miss O'Dell. B-side to "Give Me Love (Give Me Peace on Earth)"
My Sweet Lord. *All Things Must Pass*
My Sweet Lord (2000). *All Things Must Pass Remastered*
My Sweet Lord (Live). *Live in Japan*
My Sweet Lord (Live). *Concert for Bangladesh*
Mystical One. *Gone Troppo*
Never Get Over You. *Brainwashed*
New Blue Moon (The Traveling Wilburys). *The Traveling Wilburys
    Volume Three*
New Blue Moon Instrumental (The Traveling Wilburys). B-side to
    the "She's My Baby" single
No Time or Space. *Electronic Sound*
Nobody's Child (Foree/Coben) (The Traveling Wilburys).
    Nobody's Child
Not Alone Any More (The Traveling Wilburys). *The Traveling
    Wilburys Volume One*
Not Guilty. *George Harrison*
Old Brown Shoe (Live). *Live in Japan*
On the Bed. *Wonderwall*
(Ooh Baby) You Know That I Love You. *Extra Texture (Read All
    About It)*

Out of the Blue. *All Things Must Pass*
P2 Vatican Blues (Last Saturday Night). *Brainwashed*
Party Seacombe. *Wonderwall*
Piggies (Live). *Live in Japan*
Pisces Fish. *Brainwashed*
Plug Me In. *All Things Must Pass*
Poor House (The Traveling Wilburys). *The Traveling Wilburys Volume Three*
Poor Little Girl. *The Best of Dark Horse 1976-1989*
Pure Smokey. *33 & 1/3*
Rattled (The Traveling Wilburys). *The Traveling Wilburys Volume One*
Red Lady Too. *Wonderwall*
Ride Rajbun (George Harrison/David English). *The Bunbury Tales (Original Soundtrack)*
Rising Sun. *Brainwashed*
Rocking Chair in Hawaii. *Brainwashed*
Roll Over Beethoven (Chuck Berry) (Live). *Live in Japan*
Run of the Mill. *All Things Must Pass*
Run So Far. *Brainwashed*
Runaway (Crook/Shannon) (The Traveling Wilburys). B-side to the "She's My Baby" – 12" single
Sat Singing. *Songs by George Harrison EP*
Save the World – Alternative Version. *Greenpeace – The Album*
Save the World. *Somewhere in England*
See Yourself. *33 & 1/3*
Seven Deadly Sins (The Traveling Wilburys). *The Traveling Wilburys Volume Three*
She's My Baby (The Traveling Wilburys). *The Traveling Wilburys Volume Three*
Simply Shady. *Dark Horse*
Singing Om. *Wonderwall*
Ski-ing. *Wonderwall*
So Sad. *Dark Horse*
Soft-Hearted Hana. *George Harrison*
Soft Touch. *George Harrison*
Someplace Else. *Cloud Nine*
Something (Live).*Live in Japan*
Something (Live). *Concert for Bangladesh*
Stuck Inside a Cloud. *Brainwashed*
Sue Me, Sue You Blues. *Living in the Material World*
Tabla And Pakavaj. *Wonderwall*

Taxman (Live). *Live in Japan*

Teardrops. *Somewhere in England*

Tears of the World. *Songs by George Harrison 2 EP*

Thanks for the Pepperoni. *All Things Must Pass*

That Is All. *Living in the Material World*

That Which I Have Lost. *Somewhere in England*

That's the Way It Goes. *Gone Troppo*

That's What It Takes (George Harrison/Jeff Lynne/Gary Wright). *Cloud Nine*

The Answer's at the End. *Extra Texture (Read All About It)*

The Day the World Gets 'Round. *Living in the Material World*

The Devil's Been Busy (The Traveling Wilburys). *The Traveling Wilburys Volume Three*

The Light That Has Lighted the World. *Living in the Material World*

The Lord Loves the One (That Loves the Lord). *Living in the Material World*

This Guitar (Can't Keep from Crying). *Extra Texture (Read All About It)*

This Is Love (George Harrison/Jeff Lynne). *Cloud Nine*

This Song. *33 & 1/3*

Tired of Midnight Blue. *Extra Texture (Read All About It)*

True Love (Cole Porter). *33 & 1/3*

Try Some, Buy Some. *Living in the Material World*

Tweeter and the Monkey Man (The Traveling Wilburys). *The Traveling Wilburys Volume One*

Unconsciousness Rules. *Somewhere in England*

Under the Mersey Wall. *Electronic Sound*

Unknown Delight. *Gone Troppo*

Wah-Wah. *All Things Must Pass*

Wah-Wah (Live). *Concert for Bangladesh*

Wake Up My Love. *Gone Troppo*

What Is Life. *All Things Must Pass*

What Is Life (Backing Track). *All Things Must Pass Remastered*

What Is Life (Live). *Live in Japan*

When We Was Fab (George Harrison/Jeff Lynne). *Cloud Nine*

Where Were You Last Night? (The Traveling Wilburys). *The Traveling Wilburys Volume Three*

While My Guitar Gently Weeps (Live). *Live in Japan*

While My Guitar Gently Weeps (Live). *Concert for Bangladesh*

Who Can See It. *Living in the Material World*

Wilbury Twist (The Traveling Wilburys). *The Traveling Wilburys Volume Three*

Woman Don't You Cry for Me. *33 & 1/3*

Wonderwall to Be Here. *Wonderwall*

World of Stone. *Extra Texture (Read All About It)*

Wreck of the Hesperus. *Cloud Nine*

Writing's on the Wall. *Somewhere in England*

You. *Extra Texture (Read All About It)*

You Took My Breath Away (The Traveling Wilburys). *The Traveling Wilburys Volume Three*

Your Love Is Forever. *George Harrison*

Zig Zag (George Harrison/Jeff Lynne). B-side to "When We Was Fab"

Printed in
June 2004
at Gauvin Press Ltd., Gatineau, Québec